SPI
EGE
L&G
RAU

Who Am I?

And If So, How Many?

Who Am I?

And If So, How Many?

A Philosophical Journey

RICHARD DAVID PRECHT

Translated by Shelley Frisch

SPIEGEL & GRAU   NEW YORK   2011

Published in the United States by Spiegel & Grau, an imprint of
The Random House Publishing Group, a division of Random House, Inc., New York.

SPIEGEL & GRAU and design is a registered trademark of Random House, Inc.

Who Am I?—And If So, How Many? by Richard David Precht was first published in 2007 in Germany
under the title *Wer bin ich, und wenn ja, wie viele?* by Wilhelm Goldmann Verlag, a division of
Verlagsgruppe Random House GmbH, Munich, Germany, copyright © 2007 by Wilhelm Goldmann
Verlag, a division of Verlagsgruppe Random House GmbH, Munich, Germany.

The translation of this work was supported by a grant from the Goethe-
Institut, which is funded by the German Ministry of Foreign Affairs.

Library of Congress Cataloging-in-Publication Data

Precht, Richard David.
[Wer bin ich—und wenn ja, wie viele? English]
Who am I?—and if so, how many? : a philosophical journey /
Richard David Precht; translated by Shelley Frisch.
p. cm.
ISBN 978-0-385-53118-4
eBook ISBN 978-0-385-53117-7
1. Philosophy—Introductions. I. Title.
BD13.P7413 2011
190—dc2   2010035304

Printed in the United States of America

www.spiegelandgrau.com

2 4 6 8 9 7 5 3 1

First U.S. Edition

For Oskar and Juliette, David and Matthieu

Contents

What Can I Hope For?   183

Introduction

The Greek island of Naxos is the largest of the Aegean Cyclades islands. Mount Zas rises more than three thousand feet in the middle of the island. Goats and sheep graze on the fragrant fields; grapes and vegetables flourish. Back in the 1980s, Naxos still had a legendary beach at Agia Anna, with miles of sand dunes where a few tourists had put up bamboo huts and spent their time snoozing in the shade. One day in the summer of 1985, two young men who had just turned twenty were lying under a rock ledge. Jürgen, from Düsseldorf, was one; I was the other. We had just met at the beach a few days earlier, and we were discussing a book I had plucked from my father's library to take along on vacation: a dog-eared paperback, its pages yellowed from the sun, with a Greek temple and two men in Greek clothing on the cover: *The Four Socratic Dialogues of Plato*.

The atmosphere in which we passionately exchanged our modest ideas left as deep an impression on me as the sun did on my skin. That evening, while our group enjoyed cheese, wine, and melon, Jürgen and I continued our discussion. We were especially taken with the Apologia, the speech Plato tells us Socrates gave before being sentenced to death for corrupting youth.

It eased—for a while, at least—my fear of death, a subject I found deeply unsettling. Jürgen was not as convinced.

I can't remember what Jürgen looked like. I never ran into him again, and I'm sure I wouldn't recognize him if I passed him on the street today. And I've heard from a reliable source that Agia Anna beach, to which I have never returned, is now a resort town with hotels, beach umbrellas, and lounge chairs you have to pay to lie in. But entire passages from Socrates' apologia have stuck in my mind and will surely follow me right to the old age home. It remains to be seen whether they will retain the power to soothe me.

I never lost my passionate interest in philosophy, which has lived on since my days in Agia Anna. When I came home from Naxos, I signed up for a stultifying community service job in lieu of joining the military. My job as a parish worker did not exactly spark bold ideas; once I'd seen the Lutheran Church from the inside, I warmed up to Catholicism. But I did retain my interest in seeking the meaning of a life well lived, and in finding convincing answers to the great questions in life. I decided to study philosophy.

My course work in Cologne got off to an inauspicious start. I had pictured philosophers as fascinating people living lives as exhilarating and uncompromising as their ideas: people like Theodor W. Adorno, Ernst Bloch, or Jean-Paul Sartre. But my vision of bold ideas and a bold life evaporated the instant I caught sight of my new teachers: boring middle-aged gentlemen in pedestrian brown or navy suits. I thought of the writer Robert Musil's surprise that the modern and progressive engineers in the Wilhelminian era who were conquering new worlds on land, in water, and in the skies still sported old-fashioned handlebar mustaches, vests, and pocket watches. It struck me that the philosophers in Cologne were similarly failing to apply their inner freedom of mind to their outer lives. Still, one of them ultimately taught me how to think by training me to probe for the "why" behind every question and not to settle for easy answers. He impressed upon me the need to keep my lines of thought and argumentation unbroken, and to be careful to build each individual step on the one before it.

My student days were wonderful. My memory has merged them into one long succession of stimulating readings, spontaneous cooking, leisurely talks over noodle dinners, cheap red wine, heated classroom debates, and endless rounds of coffee in the cafeteria, where we'd put our philosophical education to the test, arguing about the limits of knowledge and what it means to lead a good life. We also analyzed soccer games and wondered why men and women had so much trouble getting along. The great part about philosophy is that there is never an end to it. It is also wonderfully interdisciplinary. The obvious career choice for me would have been to stay at the university. But the lives my professors were leading seemed drearily uninviting. I was also bothered by how ineffectual academic philosophy was. Essays and books were read with an eye to picking them apart. The symposia and conferences I attended as a doctoral student stripped away any illusions I might have had about the participants' interest in fostering communication.

Still, the questions and the books stayed with me as time went on, and a year ago I realized that there are very few satisfying introductions to philosophy. Of course there are plenty of witty books full of quips and brainteasers, but they were not the ones I had in mind, nor were the handy guides to the lives and works of selected philosophers or introductions to their writings. What I couldn't seem to find was a systematic discussion of the major overarching questions. A good deal of what passes for an introduction to philosophy is merely a parade of currents of thought and isms. These kinds of books are typically too historically oriented for my liking, or they are unwieldy and insipid.

The reason for this unappetizing state of the literature is obvious: Universities rarely foster innovation. Even today, academia privileges the regurgitation of secondary texts over intellectual creativity. What I find especially problematic is the designation of philosophy as a field separate from other disciplines. While my professors were explaining human consciousness on the basis of Kant's and Hegel's theories, their colleagues in the medical school just down the street were conducting highly enlightening experiments with brain-damaged patients. But "just down the street" is quite a long distance at a university. Professors in different disciplines might as well live on different planets.

How do philosophical, psychological, and neurobiological findings about the nature of consciousness intertwine? Do they clash or complement one another? Is there a "self"? What are feelings? What is memory? The most intriguing questions did not even make it into the philosophical curriculum when I was a student, and, as far as I can tell, far too little has changed today.

Philosophy is not the study of history. Of course we need to preserve our heritage and to keep inspecting and refurbishing the historic structures of our intellectual life, but the academy spends far too much time and effort looking backward, especially when you consider that philosophy is not nearly as etched in the stone of its past as many believe. The history of philosophy is to a great extent a history of intellectual climates and trends, of knowledge that was forgotten or suppressed, and of numerous apparently new beginnings that seem so new only because much of what had been thought before was neglected. Ideas rarely appear out of thin air. Most philosophers have constructed their ideas on the ruins of their forebears', but not, as they have often thought, on the ruins of the history of philosophy as a whole. Many clever insights and approaches fall by the wayside, while quirky and improbable ideas continue to be reconsidered and revived. And many philosophers themselves waver between new insights and old prejudices. Back in the eighteenth century, David Hume was in many respects an exceptionally modern thinker, but his attitude toward certain nations, especially in Africa, was chauvinistic and racist. In the century that followed, Friedrich Nietzsche became one of the most incisive critics in the field of philosophy, but his own ideals for man were kitschy, presumptuous, and downright preposterous.

Moreover, the influence of a thinker does not necessarily depend on whether his or her insights were actually correct. Friedrich Nietzsche had a huge impact on philosophy even though most of what he said was not nearly as new and original as it sounded. Sigmund Freud was rightly considered one of the greatest innovators who ever lived, the many flawed details of his psychoanalysis notwithstanding. And the enormous philosophical and political significance of Georg Wilhelm Friedrich Hegel is disproportionate to the many incongruities in his speculations.

The history of Western philosophy also reveals that most skirmishes play out within well-defined binary oppositions, in feuds between materialists and idealists, or empiricists and rationalists. These approaches appear and reappear in every conceivable shade and combination, and in ever-new guises. Materialism—the belief that there is nothing, neither God nor ideals, outside of what we apprehend with our senses—first came into vogue in the eighteenth century during the French Enlightenment, and it resurfaced in the second half of the nineteenth century in reaction to advances in the field of biology and to Darwin's theory of evolution. Today materialism is enjoying its third heyday in connection with modern findings in neuroscience. Between those points, however, there were phases in which an array of idealist thinking predominated. In contrast to materialists, idealists put very little stock in knowledge gained by the senses, relying instead on the largely independent power of reason and the ideas it generates. Of course these two labels have encompassed a great variety of motives and models over the course of the history of philosophy. Plato's idealism differed sharply from Kant's. And this is why no "true" history of philosophy can be written as a chronological succession of the great philosophers or as a history of philosophical currents, which would require glossing over a great deal of vital information.

This introduction to philosophical questions of human existence and mankind is therefore not arranged along historical lines. It is not a history of philosophy. Immanuel Kant divided the great issues facing mankind into a series of questions: What can I know? What should I do? What can I hope for? What is man? These questions lend themselves well to the organization of this book, apart from the last, which is addressed in detail by the first three, so I have not devoted a separate section to it.

The classic epistemological question of what we can know about ourselves has extended far beyond the bounds of philosophy and is now centered in neuroscience, which explores the foundations of our cognitive faculties and capacity for knowledge. Philosophy functions somewhat like an adviser to help neuroscience clarify its undertaking. In this book I present a highly personal selection of stimulating insights that philosophy still has to offer in examining these fundamental questions, through the lens of a generation that was marked by tremendous upheaval and helped usher in modernity. The physicist Ernst Mach was born in 1838, the philosopher Friedrich Nietzsche in 1844, the pioneer in neuroscience Santiago Ramón y Cajal in 1852, and the psychoanalyst Sigmund Freud in 1856. A mere sixteen years separate the birth dates of these four pioneers of modern thought, whose lasting impact can hardly be overstated.

The second part of the book turns to an ethical and moral question: What should I do? It begins by exploring basic issues pertaining to why people act morally and the extent to which good or evil behavior accords with human nature. Here, too, philosophy is no longer the only one standing at the lectern; neuroscience, psychology, and behavioral science now have something of substance to contribute. Once man is defined as an animal capable of moral judgment, and we recognize that stimuli in the brain reward moral actions, natural science retreats to the background, because the many practical questions that our society is tackling today require philosophical responses. To tackle issues such as abortion and euthanasia, genetic engineering and reproductive medicine, or environmental and animal ethics, science isn't enough; this is the ideal playing field for philosophical discussions and considerations.

In the third part, "What Can I Hope For?" I consider several central questions that most people ponder in their lives—questions about happiness, freedom, love, God, and the meaning of life. Such questions are not easy to answer, but they merit serious thought.

The theories and views that are often thrown together quite casually in this book are actually from disciplines that rarely intersect in scholarly studies. Even so, I think it makes sense to combine them in this manner, although I am fully aware that specialists in each field would pick apart many of the specifics. The various topics also take us on a little trip around the globe to the scenes of the events—to Ulm, where Descartes founded modern philosophy in a farmhouse, to Königsberg, where Immanuel Kant lived, to Vanuatu, home of the world's happiest people according to an international survey, and so forth. I have had the privilege of meeting in person some of the brain researchers introduced in this book—Eric Kandel, Robert White, and the late Benjamin Libet—and two of the philosophers, Peter Singer and the late John Rawls. I learned a great deal by listening to and debating with them and came to realize that the merit of one or another theory does not necessarily emerge in an abstract comparison of theories, but in the benefits that can be reaped from them.

We should never stop asking questions, because a combination of learning and enjoyment is the key to a fulfilled life. Learning without enjoyment wears you down, and enjoyment without learning is mindnumbing. This book aims to awaken and enhance the reader's pleasure in thinking, and it will have succeeded if the reader learns to live a more mindful life based on progressive self-awareness and takes the reins of his or her own life, perhaps like Friedrich Nietzsche, who sought to become the "poet" of his own life (not that it worked for him). Nietzsche commented in a fragment: "It is a good ability to be able to observe one's condition with an artistic eye and even in pain and suffering, awkwardness, and matters of that sort to have the Gorgon gaze that instantaneously petrifies everything into a work of art."

And while we are on the subject of artistry, this introduction would not be complete without a word about the book's title. It is a remark by a great philosopher, and my good friend, the writer Guy Helminger. One night, when we'd had too much to drink, I was worried about him—though he can certainly hold his liquor better than I can. When he started holding forth loudly on the street, I asked him if he was okay. "Who am I? And if so, how many?" he answered hoarsely, with a wide-eyed stare, tossing his head histrionically, which made me realize that if he could carry on like this, he was quite capable of finding his own way home. But his question stuck in my head. It could serve as a slogan for modern philosophy and neuro-science in an age of deep-seated doubt about the self and the continuity of experience. I owe Guy a huge debt of gratitude—above and beyond this pro-nouncement. It was through Guy that I met the woman who is now my wife. Without her, my life would not be the happy life that it is.

Richard David Precht
Ville de Luxembourg
March 2007

What Can I Know?

Clever Animals in the Universe
What Is Truth?

Once upon a time, in a faraway corner of the universe, poured out and glistening in infinite solar systems, there was a constellation in which clever animals invented knowledge. It was the most arrogant and devious minute of "world history": but still only a minute. After just a few breaths that nature took, the constellation froze, and the animals had to die.

Someone could invent a fable of that sort and still not illustrate adequately how wretched, how shadowy and volatile, how purposeless and random human intellect appears within nature. There have been eternities when it was not there; when it is done for again, nothing will have happened. For this intellect has no further mission that would lead beyond human life. Rather, it is human, and only its owner and creator gives it such dramatic importance, as if the world pivoted around it. But if we could communicate with the mosquito, we would learn that it floats through the air with the same self-importance, feeling within it the flying center of the world.

––––

Man is a clever animal with an overinflated sense of self, and a mind focused not on the great truths, but only on life's minutiae. Rarely has any text in the history of philosophy held a mirror to man that was so poetic, yet so harsh. These lines, possibly the most beautiful opening lines of any philo-

sophical work, were written in 1873 and published posthumously as the be-
ginning of an essay called "On Truth and Falsehood in an Extramoral
Sense." The author wrote it as a young professor of classical philology at the
University of Basel at the age of twenty-nine.

But Friedrich Nietzsche never published his text about the clever and
haughty animals that humans are. When he wrote it, he had just sustained
deep wounds after publishing a book about the foundations of Greek culture, which his critics attacked as unscientific, speculative nonsense—and
they were essentially correct. At the time, Nietzsche was spurned as a
prodigy who had failed to live up to his promise, and his reputation as a
classical philologist lay in ruins.

His life had gotten off to a promising start. Little Fritz, who was born in
the Saxon village of Röcken in 1844 and grew up in Naumburg an der Saale,
was considered a highly gifted and devoted student. His father was a
Lutheran pastor, and his mother was also devout. When he was four years
old, his father died, and shortly thereafter his younger brother died as
well. His family then moved to Naumburg, and Nietzsche grew up in a
household of women. Even in elementary school, Nietzsche's talents were
startlingly evident. Nietzsche attended Schulpforta, an elite boarding
school, and in 1864, he enrolled at the University of Bonn to study classical philology. He gave up his second major field of study, theology, after
one semester. He would have been happy to do his mother the favor of becoming a pastor, but he lacked religious conviction. Eventually, the "little
pastor," as his schoolmates had mockingly called him, fell away from the
faith. But while he tried to free himself from the prison of his mother's expectations, the parsonage, and faith, he remained racked with guilt for the
rest of his life. After a year, Nietzsche followed his professor to Leipzig.
His professor, who was a surrogate father to him, thought so highly of
Nietzsche that he endorsed him for a faculty appointment at the University
of Basel. In 1869, the twenty-four-year-old became an associate professor, and the university granted him his missing diplomas and doctoral and
postdoctoral credentials. In Switzerland, Nietzsche got to know the scholars and artists of his time, most notably Richard Wagner and his wife,
Cosima, whom he had already met briefly in Leipzig. Nietzsche's enthusiasm for Wagner's grandiose music was so great that it inspired him to write
an equally grandiose book in 1872: *The Birth of Tragedy from the Spirit of
Music.*

Nietzsche's book was brushed aside by his contemporaries. The distinction that Nietzsche drew between the alleged "Dionysian" spirit of music and "Apollonian" nature of the fine arts was hardly new—it had been in common use since the early Romantic period—and by the standards of historical truth it seemed wildly speculative. Also, at that time, European scholars were coming to terms with the birth of a far more significant tragedy. One year earlier, the British theologian and renowned botanist Charles Darwin had published *The Descent of Man*. Although the notion that man could have evolved from earlier primitive forms of life had been under discussion for at least twelve years—Darwin had claimed that his *Origin of Species* would "throw some light" on the origin of man—the book caused a sensation. In the 1860s, numerous naturalists had drawn the same conclusions and classified man as a close relative of the recently discovered gorilla. The Church, particularly in Germany, fought Darwin and his followers all the way up to World War I, although it was clear from the start that there could be no going back to the earlier view of the world. The notion of God as a personal creator and guide of man had been laid to rest. The natural sciences celebrated their triumphant progress with a new down-to-earth image of man. People were more interested in apes than in God, and the lofty image of man as a godlike creature was replaced by the simple truth of man as an intelligent animal.

Nietzsche was keenly interested in this new view of life. "All we need," he later wrote, "is a *chemistry* of moral, religious, aesthetic ideas and feelings, a chemistry of all those impulses that we ourselves experience in the great and small interactions of culture and society, indeed even in solitude." In the last third of the nineteenth century, numerous scientists and philosophers were hard at work on this "chemistry," a biological theory of existence without God. But the questions on Nietzsche's mind were altogether different: What does the sober scientific view mean for man's self-image? Does it render man larger or smaller? Does man stand to lose everything, or is something to be gained from seeing things more clearly? These questions formed the backdrop for his transcendent essay "On Truth and Falsehood."

Nietzsche's outlook on whether man had become smaller or larger varied according to his mood. If he was despondent—as was often the case—he grew subdued and contrite and preached what Thomas Carlyle called the "gospel of dirt" (a contemptuous reference to Darwin's explanation of

man's common ancestry with the apes), but when in high spirits, Nietzsche
was seized by a proud pathos and dreamed of the *Übermensch*.

Nietzsche's ambitious fantasies and the thundering self-assurance in
his books were in stark contrast to his short and pudgy physical appearance. A defiant toothbrush mustache was intended to liven up and give a
manlier look to his soft features, but the many illnesses he had endured
since childhood made him look and feel weak. He was quite nearsighted
and suffered from stomach ailments and severe migraine attacks. By the
age of thirty-five, feeling like a physical wreck, he stopped teaching in
Basel. A syphilis infection may have been what eventually finished him
off.

In the summer of 1881, two years after leaving the university, Nietzsche
happened upon his very own paradise, the small town of Sils Maria in the
Upper Engadine in Switzerland. He was stirred and inspired by its mar-
velous landscape. In the years that followed, he traveled there again and
again, taking long solitary walks and hatching grandiose new ideas, many of
which he committed to paper during the winter in Rapallo and on the
Mediterranean coast, in Genoa and in Nice. Most of these writings display
Nietzsche's fiery intelligence and literary bent. He was a merciless critic
who poked his fingers into the wounds of Western philosophy. As far as his
own suggestions for a new epistemology and morality were concerned, he
endorsed a half-baked social Darwinism and often wallowed in impres-
sionistic kitsch. The more his texts swaggered, the more they missed the
mark. He made a point of noting that "God is dead," but most of his contemporaries already knew that from Darwin and others.

In 1887, the penultimate year that Nietzsche gazed out onto the snow-
capped peaks of Sils Maria, he rediscovered the theme of the limitations of
human knowledge, which he had written about in his essay about the clever
animals. His polemic *On the Genealogy of Morals* opened with these words:
"We are unknown to ourselves, we men of knowledge—and with good reason. We have never sought ourselves—how could it happen that we should
ever *find* ourselves?" Here, as elsewhere in his writings, he spoke of himself in the plural, as though discussing an extraordinary, newly discovered
animal species: "*Our* treasure is where the beehives of our knowledge are.
We are constantly making for them, being by nature winged creatures and
honey-gatherers of the spirit; there is one thing alone we really care about
from the heart—'bringing something home.'" He did not have much time

left to do so. Two years later, Nietzsche suffered a breakdown in Turin. His mother came to get her forty-four-year-old son and brought him to a clinic in Jena. Later he lived with her, but he no longer wrote. When Nietzsche's mother died eight years later, her mentally deranged son was moved to the apartment of his sister Elisabeth, with whom he had a strained relationship. On August 25, 1900, Nietzsche died in Weimar at the age of fifty-five.

Nietzsche's self-confidence soared as he wrote: "I know my destiny. Someday my name will be associated with the memory of something tremendous." But what was so tremendous about Nietzsche that he would become arguably the most influential philosopher of the coming century?

Nietzsche's great achievement lay in his unsparing yet spirited pronouncements. More passionately than any other philosopher before him, he showed how arrogantly and ignorantly man passes judgment on the world by employing the logic and truth of the human species. The "clever animals" think they have an exclusive status, but Nietzsche insisted that man is just an animal whose thinking is determined by all that being an animal implies: drives and instincts, primitive will, and a limited intellect. Most philosophers in the West were wrong, he contended, to regard man as something special, as a kind of supercomputer of self-knowledge. Can man really know himself and objective reality? Philosophers had rarely questioned this, and had simply equated universal thought with human thought. It had always been assumed that man was not just some clever animal, but a being on an altogether different plane. The leading philosophers had systematically denied their animal nature even though it stared them in the face every morning when they shaved their beards and every evening when they crawled into bed seeking sexual gratification. They had built a barrier between man and animal, insisting that man's reason and intellect and ability to think and form opinions privileged man over animals. Man's physical existence was deemed of lesser importance.

For their lofty self-image to be correct, philosophers had to assume that God had provided man with outstanding cognitive faculties to read the truth about the world in the Book of Nature. But if God was dead, these faculties would not be faultless but flawed, like every other product of nature. Nietzsche had read this idea in Arthur Schopenhauer: "We are simply temporal, finite, transient, dreamlike, fleeting beings like shadows. What could such beings do with an intellect that grasped the infinite, eternal, and absolute relations of things?" The intellect, as Schopenhauer and Nietz-

sche presciently observed, was directly dependent on the demands of evolutionary adaptation. Man is able to grasp only what the cognitive powers he
was handed down in the course of evolution enable him to grasp. Just like
any other animal, man models the world on what his senses and consciousness enable him to understand. One thing is clear: Our knowledge derives
first and foremost from our senses. We cannot register what we cannot
hear, see, feel, taste, and touch; hence it does not enter into our world.
Even the most abstract things have to be read or seen in the form of signs to
enable us to imagine them. For a completely objective view of the world,
man would need a truly superhuman sensorium that taps the full potential
of sensory perceptions: the sharp vision of the eagle, the keen sense of
smell of the bear, the lateral line system of the fish, the seismographic abilities of the snake. But because humans have none of these features, they
cannot gain an objective outlook. Our world is never the world "in itself"
any more than the world envisioned by a dog or a cat, a bird or a beetle is.
"The world, my son," says the father fish in the aquarium to his son, "is a
big tank full of water!"

Nietzsche's brutally frank assessment of philosophy and religion had
revealed the hyperbolic nature of most self-definitions of man. (The fact
that he himself created new hyperboles and tensions is another matter.)
Human consciousness was shaped not by a burning desire for truth but by
an attempt to survive and move ahead. Anything immaterial to that attempt
would fall by the wayside in human evolution. Nietzsche held out a vague
hope that this very self-discovery could make man cleverer, could perhaps
create an *Übermensch* who truly expands the parameters of his knowledge.
But here, too, caution is surely the better path than pathos. Any insight into
human consciousness and its "chemistry," which, as we will see, has made
enormous strides since Nietzsche, and even the most ingenious measuring
devices and keenest observations do nothing to change the fact that man
can never attain purely objective knowledge.

But is that really so terrible? Might it not be far worse if man knew
everything about himself? Do we really need a truth that hovers over our
heads? Sometimes traveling down the path of knowledge is pleasant in and
of itself, particularly when such a thrilling and labyrinthine road ends up
leading us to ourselves. "We have never sought ourselves—how could it
happen that we should ever *find* ourselves?" Nietzsche had written in the

Genealogy of Morals. So let us embark on a journey to find ourselves as best we can. What path should we take? What method should we use? And what might we find at the end? If all our knowledge depends on and takes place within our vertebrate brains, it is probably best to start there. So our first question is: Where does our brain come from, and why is it constructed the way it is?

Lucy in the Sky
Where Do We Come From?

This is the story of three stories. The first goes like this: On February 28, 1967, the United States was bombarding North Vietnam with napalm and Agent Orange; students were protesting in Berlin; Kommune 1, the first politically motivated commune in West Germany, had just formed a few weeks earlier; and Che Guevara was beginning his guerrilla war in the central Bolivian highlands. Paul McCartney, John Lennon, George Harrison, and Ringo Starr had been holed up in the Abbey Road Studios in London for the past couple of months, recording *Sgt. Pepper's Lonely Hearts Club Band*. One of the songs on the album was "Lucy in the Sky with Diamonds." The title and surreal text convinced many Beatles fans that John Lennon had written the song during an LSD trip and that the whole colorful dreamscape paid homage to the hallucinatory drug. Some still believe this account, but the truth is somewhat simpler and sweeter. Lucy was a classmate of Lennon's son Julian, who had drawn a picture of her and shown it to his father, titling it *Lucy in the Sky with Diamonds*.

Now on to the second story. Donald Carl Johanson was in his twenties when he arrived in the dusty and dry highlands of Ethiopia near the town of Hadar in 1973 with an international team of paleoanthropologists. Johanson was considered an expert on chimpanzee teeth, a reputation that rattled him. He had spent three years writing a dissertation on the teeth of chimpanzees, combing through all the museums of Europe and searching for hominid skulls, and his interest in chimpanzee teeth had run dry. But a man with his knowledge was worth his weight in gold to some of his more renowned French and American colleagues. An expert on teeth is invaluable when investigating human fossils, because teeth are often the best preserved element in the fossil record, and human teeth bear a strong resemblance to chimpanzee teeth. Johanson was delighted to join the expedition. As a son of Swedish immigrants who grew up in Hartford, Connecticut, he had not exactly been destined for a career in science. His father had died when Don was just two years old, and Johanson had spent his childhood in poverty. An anthropologist in the neighborhood took little Don under his wing, gave him advice, and awakened his interest in prehistory and ancient history. Johanson went on to study anthropology in college and graduate school, and followed in the footsteps of his mentor, whose achievements he wound up surpassing. But back when the dark-haired, gangly young man with the long sideburns was down on the ground in the scorching desertlike region of the so-called Afar Triangle in the camp near the Awash River hunting for remains of prehistoric creatures among stones, dust, and earth, he did not anticipate the future that lay before him. After a short time there, he stumbled upon a couple of strange bones: the upper part of a shinbone and the lower part of a thigh. The two fit together perfectly. Johanson determined that the bones were the knee of a small bipedal primate, about 90 centimeters tall, that must have lived more than 3 million years ago. What a find! No one had known, or had even suspected, that humanlike creatures had walked upright 3 million years ago. Who would ever believe *him*, a young, unknown chimpanzee tooth expert? There was only one thing for him to do: He had to find a complete skeleton. Johanson soon returned home, but a year later he traveled back to the Afar Triangle, and on November 24, 1974, he and an American student named Tom Gray headed to the site of the discovery. On the way, Johanson made a little detour and found an arm bone in the debris. Everywhere he looked, he found more bones: pieces of a hand, vertebrae, ribs, skull fragments. They were parts of an ancient skeleton.

And this is the connection to the third story—the story of a small female who lived in an area that is now part of Ethiopia. She walked upright, and although her hand was quite a bit smaller than an adult's hand today, it was amazingly similar. The little lady was small in stature, but her male relatives may have been up to four and a half feet tall. For her size, she was very strong. She had stable bones, and her arms were relatively long. Her head resembled that of a hominid, not a human. Her upper jaw jutted out, and she had a flat braincase. Presumably she had dark hair, like other African hominids, but we cannot establish this with any certainty. It is also difficult to determine how intelligent she was. Her brain was almost exactly the size of a chimpanzee's, but who can say what went on inside it? She died at the age of twenty, of unknown causes; 3.18 million years later, "AL 288-1" is by far the oldest reasonably complete skeleton of a humanlike individual that has been found to date. The young lady was a member of the species *Australopithecus afarensis. Australopithecus* means "southern ape," and *afarensis* designates the site in the Afar Triangle where Johanson and Gray discovered her.

The two researchers raced back to the camp in their off-road vehicle. "We've got it," Gray was shouting. "Oh, Jesus, we've got it. We've got The Whole Thing!" The mood was euphoric. "That first night we never went to bed at all. We talked and talked. We drank beer after beer," Johanson recalled. They laughed and danced. And this is where the first story links up with the second and third: The tape recorder was blaring "Lucy in the Sky with Diamonds" at full volume over and over again under the Ethiopian sky. At some point everyone began to refer to the 40 percent complete skeleton as "Lucy," and the name stuck. Lucy O'Donnell, Julian Lennon's classmate, could take pleasure in being the namesake for what may be the most famous discovery of all of prehistory.

Don Johanson's Lucy proved what had already seemed highly likely: that human civilization emerged in Africa. But more problematically, Johanson's discovery also raises hope for identifying the boundary between animal and man, not only locating precisely where humankind first came into existence but also pinpointing the time when man emerged from the great geological Gregory Rift in East Africa and gradually developed into a *Homo erectus*, a hand-ax-wielding big game hunter capable of speech. But was Lucy really the same species as human beings today? And was she really a member of the first and only primate species to choose to walk upright, use tools, and hunt game?

Fossils of the first *Hominoidea* superfamily of primates are estimated to be 30 million years old. The only thing we know about them is that we really know nothing at all. All that scientists have to go on are a couple of incomplete, damaged lower jaw halves and two or three skulls. In classifying later hominids, paleoanthropologists also have little concrete evidence dating from before the era when the forests cleared and there was open grassland. Powerful forces lifted the earth's crust in the eastern part of Africa almost 15 million years ago and raised it more than 9,000 feet above sea level. The continental rock stretched to form a geological gash that ran more than 3,000 miles and created conditions for a wholly transformed vegetation. The renowned paleoanthropologist Richard Leakey describes the formation of the Gregory Rift and the Great Rift Valley as crucial for the evolution of new kinds of primates, and thus of man: "A geological episode of unimaginable proportions, the formation of the rift played a vital role in the evolution of our species. It is possible that had the Gregory Rift not formed when and where it did, the human species might not have evolved at all—ever."

In the western region of the Great Rift, primeval forests with ample food offered climbing apes an ideal habitat. Four or five million years ago, in the new, varied habitats in the east, by contrast, where deforestation resulted in semideserts, savannas, small riverside woods, and swampy fluvial topographies, some hominids—such as the australopithecines—began to walk upright. Some of them died out eventually, while others continued to evolve. Approximately 3 million years ago, the australopithecines split off into several somewhat better known species, including one species, *Australopithecus robustus*, that was probably vegetarian, with a large skull and strong cheekbones, traces of which were lost about 1.2 million years ago, and another, *Australopithecus africanus*, with a thinner skull and smaller teeth. The latter is now considered the base form of *Homo habilis*, the first hominids, which consisted of at least two species that may or may not have been closely related.

The brains of the australopithecines were typical of apes. As in the case of all primates, apes' eyes are at the front of their skulls, which means that they can look in only one direction. To expand their range of vision, they have to turn their heads, with the apparent consequence that primates can have only one state of consciousness at a time. Since they are unable to make out several things simultaneously, things enter into their consciousness only in succession. An angle of view this limited is uncommon among mammals, not to mention in other animal classes, some of which—notably flies and octopuses—have an extremely wide range of vision. The visual acuity of all apes is neither as sharp as that of birds of prey nor as weak as

that of horses or rhinoceroses. Like most vertebrates, primates have a right
and a left side of perception. The notion of "right" and "left" informs primate thinking and experience of the world. By contrast, the perception of
jellyfish, starfish, and sea urchins is not bifurcated but circular. Primates
are also unable to detect changes in electricity the way sharks and other animals can. Primates' sense of smell is quite poor; dogs and bears, as well as
many insects, are far superior to us in this regard. Primates have reasonably sharp hearing, but dogs and bears outshine us in that regard as well.

The spectacular process that began with a few primates about 3 million
years ago continues to puzzle scientists. In a relatively brief period of time,
the size of the australopithecine brain tripled. The brain of the australopithecines originally weighed between 400 and 550 grams, but *Homo habilis,* about a million years later, had a brain that weighed between 500 and
700 grams. Only 200,000 years after that, *Homo heidelbergensis* and *Homo
erectus* brains weighed between 800 and 1,000 grams. The brain of modern
man, *Homo sapiens,* who first appeared about 400,000 years ago, weighs
between 1,100 and 1,800 grams.

In the past, scientists tended to explain this major increase in brain
mass with reference to the new demands that were placed on man's ancestors. The savanna of the Rift Valley offered living conditions that differed
from those of the rain forest, and the australopithecines and early forms of
humans adapted, possibly causing the brain to increase in size. But this
kind of rapid increase in brain size in response to a change in environment
deviates substantially from the norm. While it is not unusual for animal
species to adapt to their environment, sometimes by changing in size, their
brains never increase in size in such a dramatic fashion. But in the early
stages of humans, there was a highly unusual development: Their brains
grew faster than their bodies—a process that has evidently occurred in only
two species: humans and dolphins.

In the 1920s, the Frenchman Émile Devaux and the Dutchman Louis
Bolk found the mechanism responsible for the human brain's remarkable
development. Independently, each discovered that man, in contrast to
other primates, is not fully developed at birth. Man remains in the fetal
stage far longer than other mammals do, and thus remains highly receptive
to learning. Neuroscience can now confirm this hypothesis. While the
brain of every other mammal grows more slowly than the body after birth,

in man it continues to develop for quite a while at almost the same pace as in the womb. In this way, the human brain grows to a size that substantially surpasses that of other primates. The cerebellum and the cerebral cortex in particular profit from this continued growth. And within the cerebral cortex, it is above all the regions that are important for orientation in space, musicality, and powers of concentration that continue to develop.

Although Devaux's and Bolk's findings explain *what* began happening in the human brain about 3 million years ago, we have yet to figure out *why*. A change this momentous cannot be explained by adaptations to the environment, even if we think—and this is by no means certain—that life on the savanna required major shifts and adaptations. It is certainly true that walking upright altered the flight response, and most likely the savanna gave rise to a different way of life from that in the rain forest. That man developed different forms of sustenance is certainly logical, too. But none of these facts accounts for a tripling of the volume of the brain. The human brain is far too complex for a transformation of this magnitude to arise as a response to the environment. "Man," writes Gerhard Roth, a neuroscientist in Bremen, Germany, "does not have this large a frontal or prefrontal cortex because of some pressing need for one. It was more like an added 'bonus.'"

The human brain is not merely a reaction to environmental demands. In the first chapter we discussed the fact that the vertebrate brain is an outgrowth of evolutionary adaptation, but the precise connections are still hazy. Scientists have not yet been able to figure out why an "optimization" occurred. Our earliest forefathers evidently made very little use of the high-performance machines that were evolving in their heads. The brain's increase in size at a colossal pace in the development of *Australopithecus* to *Homo habilis* and *Homo erectus* clearly took some time to yield cultural achievements such as a sophisticated use of tools. Even after the brain had essentially reached its ultimate size, about a million years ago, hominids' high-powered brains took hundreds of thousands of years to produce little more than a measly hand ax. The tools of the Neanderthals, who died out about 40,000 years ago, were still relatively simple and unsophisticated, even though the volume of their brains actually surpassed that of man today.

There is little doubt that the size and structure of the human brain was the determining factor in the development and incomparable cultural achievements of modern man. But why did man wait so long to put the human brain's capacity for technical innovation to use? Evidently the brain needed to fulfill very different functions back then. Today's great apes, whose use of tools is just as primitive as that of the australopithecines, are clearly more intelligent than a simple use of rocks and branches would require. Great apes use the far greater part of their intelligence for their complex social interaction, and even for humans the greatest daily challenge is dealing with members of our own species. (See "The Sword of the Dragon Slayer," p. 84.) Still, we use only a fraction of our brain capacity, because intelligence comes into play only when we reach an impasse. Even if primatologists had trained their binoculars on Albert Einstein the way they now observe apes, they would have seen little out of the ordinary. Einstein did not make much use of his genius in his normal daily routines—sleeping, dressing, eating, and so forth—because brilliant ideas and inspiration are simply unnecessary for those activities.

The human brain is impressive, but most of the time it runs on a low level, just as our forefathers' brains did. Like apes, humans have instincts for war and aggression and possess a sense of family and community. The more we learn about the lives of animals, the more clearly we recognize ourselves, and the more we see the echo from 250 million years of mammalian development in the convolutions of our brains.

Nietzsche's clever animals are thus truly animals, but their unparalleled intellect still remains an enigma. Some philosophers in the early-nineteenth-century Romantic era insisted on regarding man as nature's crowning achievement—as the creature created to understand the world and to make nature aware of itself. In reality, of course, there is no reason to believe that man and his actions are the goal of evolution, and indeed even the concept of a "goal" itself is dubious. Goals represent a very human approach to thinking (do salamanders have goals?) and are associated with typically human notions of time, as are the terms "progress" and "meaning." But nature is physical, chemical, and biological, and the term "meaning" is on an entirely different plane from, say, the term "protein."

The cleverer among Nietzsche's clever animals—namely, those who have grasped this—do not focus on the big picture of "objective" reality, but instead ask themselves: What am I capable of knowing? And how does this ability to know *function*? Philosophers like to speak of a "cognitive turn" to the foundations of our self-awareness and our understanding of the world. To probe this idea, I would like to take you along on a journey to the foundations of our knowledge. Let us fly with Lucy into a cosmos more exhilarating than just about anything philosophers in earlier eras could visit; let us explore the center of feeling and thinking, and voyage inside our brains.

The Cosmos of the Mind
How Does My Brain Function?

What is the most complex thing in the world? That is a difficult question, but for science, the answer is clear: It is the human brain. Granted, there is nothing particularly spectacular about it on the outside. At barely three pounds, it is shaped like a giant walnut and has the consistency of a soft-boiled egg. But hidden within it is likely the most complex mechanism in the universe, with 100,000,000,000 (one hundred billion) neurons firing and up to 500,000,000,000,000 (half a quintillion) connections between them. A common analogy holds that there are about as many leaves on the trees in the Amazon rain forest as there are neuron connections in a human brain.

Until about 120 years ago, we knew next to nothing about what goes on inside the brain. Anyone who was writing or speculating about the brain before that time was merely skimming the surface, which makes it all the more astonishing that the first scientist to interpret the overall operations of the brain and decipher its basic mechanisms is today virtually unknown. His name—Santiago Ramón y Cajal—ought to appear on any objective list of the most important researchers and thinkers of the twentieth century, yet relatively little has been written about him.

Ramón y Cajal was born in 1852 in Navarra, Spain, in the town of Petilla de Aragón. He was eight years younger than Nietzsche, and at the time of the Spaniard's birth and early childhood, Darwin was in Downe, a few miles

south of London, working on his magnum opus, *On the Origin of Species.*
Ramón y Cajal did not originally intend to study biology; he had always
dreamed of becoming a painter. When he was a young man, he and his father dug up bones at a former cemetery to study the human body. Ramón y
Cajal's father was on the faculty of the anatomy department at the hospital
in Zaragoza, where he practiced surgery. Working with these bones eventually drew Ramón y Cajal away from painting to anatomy. In stark contrast to
the great Darwin, who had broken off his study of medicine because he was
revolted by the need to dissect cadavers, Ramón y Cajal's examinations of
corpses fired up his enthusiasm, and he became a doctor at the age of
twenty-one. His fascination with corpses and skeletons also led him to join
the army. From 1874 to 1875, he took part in an expedition to Cuba, where
he contracted malaria and tuberculosis. Upon his return, he became an in-
tern at the University of Zaragoza medical school. In 1877, the Complutense
University of Madrid awarded him a doctorate. As a professor of descriptive
and general anatomy at the University of Valencia, he began to discover the
magic of the brain. Why had no one ever made a thorough study of the
human brain, beyond its basic anatomical structures? Ramón y Cajal came
up with an ambitious plan: He would find out what he could about the
processes in the brain and establish a new science he would call "rational
psychology." Piece by piece, he examined the cellular tissue of the human
brain under the microscope and sketched what he saw. In 1887, he was appointed professor of histology and pathology at the University of Barcelona,
and in 1892, he joined the faculty of the Complutense University of Madrid,
the largest and most renowned university in Spain. In 1900, he also became
the director of the National Institute of Hygiene and of the Investigaciones
Biológicas.

A photograph shows a bristly-bearded Ramón y Cajal in his book-filled
study in Madrid, his head resting on his right hand and his deep-set dark
eyes gazing at a human skeleton. Another picture captures him in a similar
pose in his laboratory wearing an Eastern-looking lab coat and a Maghrib
cap, looking more like a painter than a scientist. As he grew older, his face
took on a sinister aspect, suggesting a shifty Hollywood character or a mad
scientist in league with the devil. In fact, Ramón y Cajal was anything but
sinister. His contemporaries liked and respected him greatly. He was modest, generous, and easygoing, and he had a good sense of humor.

Ramón y Cajal examined the dead brains of humans and animals. Un-

fortunately for him, the time was not yet ripe for research on living brains.
How could people find out how the brain functioned if its processes could
not be observed in action? Still, Ramón y Cajal's accomplishments were
nothing short of amazing. The only thing about him that might be called de-
monic was his remarkable ability to bring dead neurons to life. He fancied
himself a friendly Frankenstein, describing the brain cell sequences he
observed under the microscope as though he were actually watching them
at work. His essays and books provide spirited descriptions of dynamic
activity, with neurons feeling, acting, and anticipating, emergent fibers
groping to find others. Ramón y Cajal's description of this microstructure
laid the foundation for the modern study of the brain's nervous system, and
during his long years as a researcher, he wrote 270 scientific essays and 18
books, which made him perhaps the most important neuroscientist of all
time. In 1906, he was awarded the Nobel Prize in the category of Physiology
or Medicine.

Ramón y Cajal's research was so noteworthy because neurons in the
brain did not resemble normal somatic cells, and their odd, irregular shapes
and many fine extensions had baffled scientists before him. Ramón y Cajal
drew highly detailed sketches of these cells with their strange cobweb patterns that looked like bits of algae strung together. Although he did not actually coin any of the key terms that are still used today, he described the
elements of the nervous system in the brain more precisely than anyone before him had. He drew and explained the neurons and the axons, which are
the long fibers on both sides of the neurons. He described in detail the
branched projections, known as dendrites, for the first time. He adopted the
word "synapses" from his British friend and colleague Charles Scott Sherrington to describe the neural communication points at the ends of the dendrites. Ramón y Cajal's meticulous studies yielded a veritable alphabet of
neurons in the brain, but he had to use his imagination to generate the corresponding mental grammar, and even more to envisage the spoken language of his neurons in what he called "neuronal circuits."

Much of what Ramón y Cajal assumed later proved to be correct. His key
assumptions were that nerve impulses were conducted in only one direction on their path through the brain and the spinal cord, and that the
synapses of one neuron communicated with the synapses of another. He
correctly hypothesized that nerve tracts are one-way streets—an information flow is never reversible. Of course Ramón y Cajal was working with

dead brains, which gave no indication of electrical or chemical activity, so he was unable to demonstrate how the synapses communicated. Still, even if he was not able to see these signal transmissions in action, he knew that they occurred, because the German physiologist Otto Loewi had shown in 1921 that nerve impulses are transmitted chemically, not electronically.

Ramón y Cajal died in 1934 at the age of eighty-two. Over the following three decades, some scientists in Europe, the United States, and Australia investigated the basic mechanisms of electrochemical signal transmission in the brain, while others aimed to provide a more precise interpretation of the individual areas in the brain. What was responsible for what, and why? Attention focused on Paul MacLean's clear-cut model of a triune brain, which MacLean developed in the 1940s. Since man had developed from the lower animals, MacLean postulated that the different regions of the human brain corresponded to the different stages of human development. In his model, the brain is actually made up of three distinct brains. The first is a primitive reptilian brain, which consists primarily of the brain stem and the cerebellum and constitutes the "lowest" form of the brain, where innate instincts are located. According to MacLean, the primitive reptilian brain is nearly incapable of learning and has no role in social interaction. He called the second brain the "paleomammalian brain" and argued that it corresponded to the *limbic system*—the locus not only of instinctual drives and emotions but also of nature's early attempt to develop a consciousness and a memory. The third brain, the "neomammalian brain," corresponds to the *neocortex* as the seat of reason, understanding, and logic. In MacLean's schema, the neomammalian brain works irrespective of the regions of the brain that preceded it in our evolutionary heritage. MacLean argued that there are few connections between the brain's three component parts. Feelings and intellect, he claimed, are controlled by two different brains, which helped explain why our intellect has so much trouble exercising control over our feelings.

MacLean's neat little divisions were easy to grasp, and they quickly caught on. He subdivided the brain into three parts to mirror the distinctions philosophers had been drawing for two millennia among animal instincts, higher feelings, and clever human reason. The only problem was that MacLean's theory, which can still be found in many textbooks today, is wrong. The human brain is not made up of three essentially independent brains. And the simple idea that the three brains originated sequentially in the development from reptile to man is incorrect. Reptiles also have a limbic system that is quite similar to that of man, as well as an endbrain, a simpler variant of the neocortex in mammals. But the crucial point is that the connections among the brain stem, cerebellum, and cerebrum are actually very close; they are not simply stacked on top of one another, as MacLean had suggested. Their tight and complex connection is extremely important and is our key to understanding the way instincts, sensations, volition, and cognition really function.

Much of what brain researchers have surmised about our brains over the past hundred years has been subject to ongoing revision. In the 1820s, the French physiologist Jean Pierre Marie Flourens (who later became a sworn enemy of Darwin) had established that many brain functions are interrelated. He had removed various parts of the brain, one by one, from various laboratory animals, especially rabbits and pigeons, to see which functions subsequently ceased. To his astonishment, he found no reduction in individual capabilities; many became worse in clusters, somewhat like the computer HAL in Stanley Kubrick's *2001: A Space Odyssey*, which became slower and more sluggish as a whole as each memory module was removed from service. Flourens realized that the old model of brain regions that governed discrete abilities such as addition and subtraction, speech, thought, and memory was incorrect, but he went too far the other way in claiming that everything in the brain was responsible for everything else. The generation between Flourens and Ramón y Cajal focused on tracking down and sorting out the areas and centers of the brain according to basic functions. Every self-respecting researcher drew an atlas of the brain. The most spectacular discoveries in this field were made by the French anatomist Paul Broca and the German neurologist Carl Wernicke, when the two of them, independently of each other, identified two distinct speech centers in the human brain: *Broca's area* for speech production, in 1861, and *Wernicke's area* for speech comprehension, in 1874.

Today the brain is divided up into the brain stem, the diencephalon, the cerebellum, and the cerebrum. The *brain stem*, located in the middle of the head, constitutes the lowest segment of the brain and consists of the midbrain, the pons, and the medulla oblongata. The brain stem communicates sense impressions and coordinates our involuntary movements, such as heartbeat, breathing, and metabolism, and our reflexes, including blinking, swallowing, and coughing.

The *diencephalon* is a relatively small area above the brain stem, consisting of the upper part of the thalamus, the hypothalamus, the subthalamus, and the epithalamus. Its role is essentially that of an agent and emotional evaluator. It registers sense impressions and conveys them to the cerebrum. As a sensitive system of nerves and hormones, the diencephalon controls our sleeping and waking, our sensations of pain, the regulation of our body temperature, and our drives and instincts, such as our sex drive.

The *cerebellum* has a major influence on our motility and our motor learning. In other vertebrates it is much more prominent than in man, especially in fish, whose movements somehow seem more sophisticated than those of humans. In our species, the cerebellum also governs unconscious tasks involving cognitive acts, speech, social conduct, and memory.

The *cerebrum* is located above the three other regions; in man it is more than three times as large as the other parts of the brain put together. It can be divided into numerous regions, which can in turn be subdivided into the "simpler" sensory areas and the "higher" associative areas. All complex human mental functions depend heavily, though not exclusively, on the activity of the associative cortex.

Our cognitive performance is dependent on what we experience, as Immanuel Kant pointed out in the opening sentences of his magnum opus, the *Critique of Pure Reason:*

> There can be no doubt that all our knowledge begins with experience. For how should our faculty of knowledge be awakened into action did no objects affecting our senses partly of themselves produce representations, partly arouse the activity of our understanding to compare these representations, and, by combining or separating them, work up the raw material of the sensible impressions into that knowledge of objects which is entitled experience?

Our attentiveness determines our feelings and thoughts, just as our feelings and thoughts determine our attentiveness. People can focus on only one thing at a time; so-called multitasking does not mean that we are able to concentrate on several things at once, but only that we switch back and forth very quickly. The range of our attention is often compromised in the process, not only by our biologically determined perceptive capabilities but also by our limited capacity to engage the full range of our neurons in the brain. We use only a fraction of our brain capacity, and it is difficult to expand this range. Our attentiveness comes up against limits, and when we focus on one thing, other things recede into the background. My four-year-old son, Oskar, is fascinated by animals and can tell me the names of many different kinds of dinosaurs and distinguish between eared sea lions and earless seals, yet he still has trouble putting on a T-shirt by himself. It is not the sum of our neurons but our attention span that limits our learning ability.

At least we have a rough idea today of how attentiveness takes shape and what happens neurochemically when we learn something. Technical progress in measuring devices has enabled neuroscientists to learn about these and other basic processes in the brain and clearly define the function of individual areas. Near the end of Ramón y Cajal's life, in 1924, the German psychiatrist Hans Berger invented electroencephalography (EEG), which finally made it possible to measure electrical activity in the brain. In the 1950s, the introduction of sensitive microelectrodes refined the measuring field to enable researchers to observe the activity of individual neurons. The next step was the study of magnetic fields. Like all electrical currents, brain currents form magnetic fields. Since the 1960s, sensitive magnetic field sensors have been measuring these fields and computing the power sources in the brain, and magnetoencephalography (MEG) shows where the brain is particularly active. In the 1970s and '80s, new methods made it possible to measure the recently discovered neurochemical processes in the brain. Since the 1990s, brain research has been able to work with beautiful color pictures of the brain. Today, imaging procedures such as Roentgen computer tomography and magnetic resonance imaging (MRI) provide fantastic insights into the workings of our brains. Previously only electrical or chemical processes could be shown, but the new devices can now measure the blood flow in the brain and furnish high-resolution images. For the first time, it is becoming possible to begin deciphering the limbic system, the seat of our emotions and feelings.

Many brain researchers are so enthusiastic about the new opportunities available to them that they believe their research will sooner or later put philosophy (and maybe even psychology) out of business. Neuroscientist William H. Calvin at the University of Washington calls consciousness "the Janitor's Dream." To him, consciousness is a janitor who is uncomfortable being held down in "the dark basement of chemistry or the subbasement of physics" and hopes against hope to emerge from this basement into its rightful place in a brightly lit penthouse. In a similar vein, neuroscientists often aim to leap up from the cells and proteins in the brain into the lofty realm of philosophy. But the jump from proteins to meaning is enormous. Even if brain research is well on its way to making sense of the centers and functions of the brain, the mechanism that produces mind, meaning, and intellect is still quite a mystery. Indeed, we know more about what we do not know than about what we do know. The more we learn about the brain, the more complex it appears.

The very personal elements of consciousness—our highly subjective experiences—remain a big mystery. Why something feels a certain way to us is hard to fathom. Personal feelings and passions cannot be explained by general neurochemical findings. Neither measuring devices nor psychological conversations convey the quality of an experience. Louis Armstrong was once asked what jazz is, and his response was spot-on: "If you have to ask what jazz is, you'll never know." Similarly, subjective perceptions of our experiences remain inaccessible to brain research. When jazz music is played, the MRI scanner indicates an increased blood supply to certain emotional centers of the brain, but it does not reveal how or why it feels the way it does.

Even so, neuroscience is today considered the discipline that can best reveal the foundations of our knowledge of ourselves and the world around us. The reasons are clear: Many more intriguing approaches now come from neuroscience than from philosophy. The question, though, is whether we can sort these out without the help of philosophy. Exploring the brain is a very peculiar and precarious undertaking, since it entails human brains attempting to discover something about human brains; that is, a system trying to understand itself, with the brain as both the subject and the object of the investigation. Aren't neuroscientists doing exactly the same thing as philosophers, who have spent the past two thousand years thinking in order to understand their own thinking, only with a different method? Examining oneself with the tools of thinking and observing the process of thinking while doing so, to whatever extent possible, was long the predominant method of exploring the human mind. Its modern culmination occurred about four hundred years ago, one memorable winter's eve . . .

A Winter's Eve in the Thirty Years' War
How Do I Know Who I Am?

The setting is cozy: a big, elaborate tiled stove and a twenty-three-year-old man clad in the heavy overcoat of an imperial soldier. We know his face quite well from a painting by the great Dutch portrait painter Frans Hals: the big dark eyes, the wide thin-lipped mouth with the merest hint of a smile, the trace of stubble, and the shoulder-length dark hair, a face as impish as it is melancholy, intelligent and lost in reverie. It was a winter's eve in 1619, in a farmhouse near Ulm. Let us hear from the man himself:

> At this time I was in Germany, where I had been called by the wars that are not yet ended there. While I was returning to the army for the coronation of the Emperor, the onset of winter detained me in quarters where, finding no conversation to divert me and fortunately having no cares or passions to trouble me, I stayed all day shut up alone in a stove-heated room, where I was completely free to converse with myself about my own thoughts.

Conversing with himself about his thoughts had a very ambitious aim. While the Thirty Years' War was heating up—a war that would lay waste to all of central Europe—this man was seeking peace, order, clarity, and absolute, ultimate certainty about himself and the world. First, he established a rule that he would not consider anything true that could not be recognized clearly and distinctly. And he cast doubt on everything that could be open to doubt. He would not trust his eyes, nor any of his other senses; it was too easy to be led astray. He groped his way forward skeptically. Even thinking could not be relied on. Maybe an evil demon was distorting his thoughts. But wait—isn't there something that lies beyond any doubt? If I cast doubt on everything, he thought, I cannot doubt that I am doubting, and that I am the one doing the doubting. And if I know that while doubting it is *I* who am doubting, I must be *thinking* that I doubt. There is thus an undoubtable certainty, a first principle that precedes all others: *Cogito ergo sum*—I think, therefore I am! By the time the fire died down, this sentence had been conceived and expressed, and the world of philosophy would never be the same.

This man, who revolutionized philosophy one winter's eve at the start of the Thirty Years' War, was René Descartes. He came from a noble family. Descartes' father was a magistrate who served in the parliament of Brittany in Rennes. His mother died in 1597, a year after his birth, and Descartes spent his childhood with his grandmother. At the age of eight, he enrolled in a Jesuit school—a grueling experience, but he graduated at sixteen with a splendid classical and mathematical education. The gifted student studied law in Poitiers, then enrolled at an academy for young noblemen in Paris to catch up on all he had missed out on in life. He learned fencing, dancing, riding, etiquette, and other indispensable skills, although he did not have the foggiest notion what he would do with them. (Two decades later, he would have an opportunity to put one of these skills to good use in a duel.) When he was twenty-two, eager for adventure, he entered the service of the Dutch general Maurice of Nassau, which taught him a great deal about the natural sciences, but Descartes did not think much of life in the army. He traveled aimlessly through Denmark and Germany, then joined the army once again, this time under Duke Maximilian of Bavaria. He took part in the conquest of Prague, where he also viewed the workplace of the astronomer Johannes Kepler, which made him realize that he wanted to become an enlightener who would introduce clarity into the dark mysteries of the sciences. Brimming with self-confidence, he dreamed of a clear, logical, and "universal method to discover the truth"—and he, Descartes, would be the one to find it.

In April 1620, while he was still in Ulm, the twenty-four-year-old met the mathematician Johannes Faulhaber and solved a highly complex mathematical puzzle. Descartes delighted in pointing out that the puzzle had confounded the smartest minds of the era. The time was ripe for him to start finding simple and elegant solutions to an array of problems. One year after his meditation in the farmhouse, he gave up life as a soldier, which he disliked, and headed to Loretta, after which he traveled through Germany, Holland, Switzerland, and Italy. In 1623, Descartes moved to Paris and established contact with the intellectual circles there. He was a frequent guest at dinner parties, but he was not particularly sociable. After several years, he left Paris and moved to the Netherlands, which boasted the greatest intellectual and religious freedom on the Continent, where he hoped to write the magnum opus he had been planning for quite some time. He had little contact with the outside world, apart from a lively correspondence, particularly with women. He funneled all his energy into his "Treatise on the World"—but the work was never published. In 1633, he learned that his Italian colleague Galileo Galilei had been forced to recant his new scientific ideas about the cosmos and the world before the Inquisition. The Catholic Church was a dangerous adversary, even for a man like Descartes, who believed in God, but a relatively abstract God that he sought to prove as the highest principle. Although the Netherlands was more tolerant than Italy or France, Descartes was on his guard, continually changing his residence. He wrote studies of geometry, algebra, and physics and gained an excellent reputation as a mathematician. He waited until 1637 to publish the book that grew out of his musings some eighteen years earlier, in which he had reduced the world to a stove-heated room and a now famous line: "I think, therefore I am." He called this slender volume *Discourse on the Method of Rightly Conducting the Reason, and Seeking Truth in the Sciences*. Descartes took the precaution of publishing the book anonymously, but his identity soon got out. Fame was now his, but his arrogance and his deep-seated distrust made him bristle at criticism. His following books, which employed very similar arguments, provoked vehement opposition in Leiden and Utrecht, causing Descartes's unease to escalate into paranoia. He had recurrent fantasies of moving to England, and he made a series of quick trips to France. In 1649, Descartes accepted an invitation from Queen Christina of Sweden, with whom he had been corresponding. But his stay in wintry Stockholm cost him his life. The queen insisted on early-morning philosophy lessons in an unheated room, and in February 1650, the fifty-three-year-old succumbed to pneumonia.

What had Descartes achieved? First of all, he had introduced a method: to accept as correct only what is proved by an unassailable case built up step by step. And he had made the "I" the center of philosophy. Philosophers before him had attempted to find out how the world is "in itself," but Descartes chose a very different approach: I can find out about the world "in itself" only by fathoming how it becomes manifest to my thinking. Everything I know about the world I know not by any objective bird's-eye view, but solely by way of the thinking in my head. Friedrich Nietzsche later called Descartes "the grandfather of the Revolution, who granted authority to reason alone."

Descartes had provided an answer to the question of how I know who I am: It is by virtue of my thinking. This answer was far superior to any previous one, notwithstanding the fact that Saint Augustine had framed it in similar terms back in the fourth century. Over time, however, the shortcomings in his line of reasoning began to emerge. The statement is not as devoid of preconditions as Descartes had thought. To formulate my doubts about everything in this world, I require adequately functioning language. But Descartes did not open language to doubt, and he was unconcerned that words, sentences, and grammar can also mislead us. Some philosophers criticized Descartes' failure to distinguish between logic and reason. Is something logical necessarily rational? Aren't the two meanings being conflated? A third point of criticism is that Descartes went to great lengths to explore *thinking*, but he did not have much to say on the subject of *being*.

This last objection is precisely the point we need to probe. Descartes was an enormously influential philosopher, one of the most influential of all time. Although he was greeted with hostility at first, he came to represent many new ideas about the body, the brain, and the mind. But as skilled as he was in exploring thinking, we now recognize that his weak spot was in conceptualizing the human body. The body, he argued, is really just a useless appendage attached to the head. He got a kick out of informing his readers that bodies are a mere assemblage of limbs that add up to a mechanical device. The organs of the body, in his view, function like seventeenth-century water gardens: Nerves correspond to water pipes, brain cavities to storage containers, muscles to mechanical springs, and breathing to the ticking of a clock, all controlled by a little man in the brain, namely the pineal gland. Explaining the human body as a physical mechanism was all the rage in the natural sciences, and Descartes was quite adept at it. Virtually overnight he became the chief ideologist of a new attitude toward the body, and when confronting his mostly religious critics he came across as rational, modern, and progressive. If Descartes were alive today, he would surely have become a pioneer in the field of artificial intelligence—or a prominent neuroscientist.

It is intriguing to imagine how Descartes would have perceived the relationship between the mind and the body if he had lived during the twenty-first century. What would he reply to his four-hundred-years-ago self if he were now to go on a meditation retreat and undertake a clear and level-headed quest for the ultimate certainties about man and the world? Let us imagine what would happen:

Spring 2007. A white wooden bungalow with a large front yard and lovely green lawn on the outskirts of Boston. This is the home of neuroscientist René Descartes, Jr. He is sitting in his living room near the fireplace. His attire is casual: corduroy pants, checked shirt, sweater. He leans back on his sofa and tells his story:

"I am in the United States, where my career has taken me after France and the Netherlands. I've just returned from an NIH conference in Washington. The new semester hasn't started yet, and I'm not distracted with lectures and exams, so I have the leisure time to indulge in my own thoughts. And since I have decided to cast doubt on everything that is not clear and unequivocal and not subject to full determination and representation, which is the only path to the truth, I feel compelled to start by doubting the false unsubstantiated 'certainties' that philosophy has introduced. Let's start with the disastrous separation between mind and body that my alter ego may not have invented, but did establish quite radically in philosophy. The fact is that mind and body cannot be separated, and attempting to do so gets you nowhere. The brain is not hardware that comes equipped with mind software; rather, both interact in an inseparable and highly complex manner. The proposition 'I think, therefore I am' may be famous, but it has an unfortunate connotation. Not only does it say that I know about myself and my existence only by means of thinking, but it also suggests that thinking and the awareness of thinking are the actual foundations of existence. And since this thinking is supposed to take place in strict separation from the body, the proposition underscores the radical division between the spiritual mind and the biological body. No neuroscientist today would subscribe to what my alter ego wrote back then:

I knew I was a substance whose whole essence or nature is simply to
think, and which does not require any place, or depend on any material thing, in order to exist. Accordingly this 'I'—that is, the soul by
which I am what I am—is entirely distinct from the body, and indeed
is easier to know than the body, and would not fail to be whatever it
is even if the body did not exist.

If this were true, the mind would be a spirit within a machine, but it is not,
because there is no separate and distinct place called 'mind' in the brain.
That would be about as absurd as, for example, imagining a place called 'university' separate and distinct from buildings, streets, lawns, and people.

"Neuroscience has now established that neither feelings nor complex
mental functions can be separated from the structure and activities of the
biological organism. If they could, neuroscientists attempting to understand the workings of the mind would have no need to examine regions of
the brain, mark electrical connections, or identify chemical substances. Of
course one cannot claim to have identified the mind simply by pinpointing
a brain region and listing a couple of substances. Human consciousness is
the product of the body's interaction with its environment. To understand
our mind, we have not only to situate it in the brain instead of in a disem-
bodied space, but also to find a way of understanding it as part of the organism as a whole. Our senses, our nerves, and our neurons all act in concert
with the outside world, with what we see, hear, smell, taste, and touch. The
question of how I know who I am can thus be answered along these lines: I
know who I am because my senses relay signals to neurons in the brain,
where they extend along complex circuits, so complex that something wonderfully complicated and abstract results: insight into my own thinking and
a notion of my existence."

That is how the modern neuroscientist in Boston sees the matter, but
his worn-out predecessor from the Thirty Years' War has one final ace up
his sleeve: Did the neuroscientist really answer the question of how I know
who I am? To fathom how my brain functions, and to describe how my
senses and my neurons convey a picture of myself to me, I have to think
these thoughts. All these things, no matter how concrete, thus originate as
thoughts and ideas in my head. From that point of view, there really is
something to the statement "I think, therefore I am," but not because
thinking constitutes my being or that the only thing that counts is thinking,

which is incorrect. But it *is* correct to say that my thinking is the only window into my existence.

So the road to self-discovery has two separate paths. I can start with my thinking and figure out where my certainties come from. This is the path that Descartes, and hence modern philosophy, has chosen. This path of self-observation led to a highly reflective way of looking at things that brought claims about the world to their subjective origins and examined them. As scientific epistemology, however, this path has come up against its limits, and there is little new ground left to be broken. The second path explores man as though the observer and highly personal perceptions and ideas are not the crux of the matter. This is the path of the modern natural sciences. While less reflective, it is now producing exciting new results. The kinds of insights these two paths yield could hardly be more divergent.

Many neuroscientists claim that their route of access to the mind is the only valid one. Neurobiology seeks to assume the place philosophy once held. If man wants to know who he is, the logic goes, he has to understand his brain, and brain research replaces speculations about human emotions, thoughts, and actions with rational scientific research. But many neuroscientists tend not to notice that they are not on the path to an absolute truth either. Any science is itself a product of the human mind that it seeks to investigate with its own means, and the cognitive faculties of the human mind depend directly on the requirements posed by evolutionary adaptation. Our brains are the way they are only because they have apparently prevailed in the evolutionary contest. Their task in the rain forest and savanna was never to obtain completely objective knowledge of the world, so it is no wonder that they are not optimally tailored to this task.

Assuming that human consciousness was not developed according to the criterion of absolute objectivity, man can grasp only what the cognitive apparatus that arose in the evolutionary contest enables him to grasp. Our understanding of science is subject to our cognitive constraints. If it were not, there would be no need for progress, opposition, or revisions in the sciences. The prerequisites for research, such as freedom to contest existing views, repeatability, and validity, are not autonomous criteria; they reflect the human cognitive faculty at a given time in a specific situation in which knowledge is presented. Information that scientists considered indisputable a century ago is now dismissed out of hand, and this pattern is likely to carry into the next century.

For philosophers, it still makes sense to proceed from the thinking "I," which deciphers the world one step at a time. In this regard, Descartes remains just as modern as he was nearly four hundred years ago. But of course, philosophers should realize that they are not thinking independently of and unaided by the brain. The brain thinks, and it also produces the self, which thinks that it thinks. Was Descartes right to have used the word "I"? Shouldn't he have said: If it is indisputable that doubting requires thinking, thinking must occur? Instead of "I think, therefore I am," shouldn't it have been "There are thoughts"? How did this "I" get slipped in?

Mach's Momentous Experience
Who Is "I"?

Once-in-a-lifetime experiences sometimes get buried in footnotes, as was literally the case back in 1855, when Ernst Mach, then a seventeen-year-old student of physics, went for a stroll on the outskirts of Vienna and had an epiphany:

> On a bright summer day under the open heaven, the world with my ego suddenly appeared to me as *one* coherent mass of sensations, only more strongly coherent in the ego. Although the actual working out of this thought did not occur until a later period, yet this moment was decisive for my whole view.

The student was unaware of it at the time, but this moment was tantamount to the insight of the century. Fifty years after the fact, it was relegated to a footnote in his *Analysis of the Sensations*.

Ernst Mach was born in 1838 (six years before Nietzsche) in Chrlice, which was then part of Austria-Hungary and is now in the Czech Republic. His family was in the German-speaking minority. Mach's father was a farmer and tutor who educated his son at home. At the same time, the young Mach completed an apprenticeship in carpentry. At the age of fifteen, this highly gifted teenager finally enrolled in high school, and then breezed through his college entrance examinations. He studied mathematics and science in Vienna and wrote his dissertation on electricity. A year later he became a professor and moved from Graz to Prague, and later to Vienna. His interests were wide-ranging; indeed, he was interested in just about everything. He taught physics and mathematics, philosophy and psychology. As a physicist he calculated the speed of sound, which was later named after him; supersonic aircraft fly at "Mach 2" speed.

Mach enjoyed great renown in Prague and Vienna. He experimented with rocket projectiles and explored the dynamics of gases. His criticisms of Newtonian physics became Einstein's inspiration for the theory of relativity. Einstein liked to refer to himself as Mach's student, although Mach had never been his instructor. Politically Mach was a liberal who was increasingly drawn to the Social Democratic Party, which was then considered radical. He was also an agnostic who liked to take on the Church. Physicists and philosophers grappled with Mach's theories, and Mach's philosophy was much in vogue among Russian intellectuals; the young Lenin wrote a thick book about it. Sense physiology arose as a new discipline, and American behaviorism was inspired by Mach. But no matter how many sciences Mach had helped shape, his fame faded quickly after his death in 1916. World War I shook Europe to its very foundations, and physics now pursued a different path. In 1970, NASA commemorated the nearly forgotten pioneer in rocketry by naming a lunar crater after him.

Mach's philosophical ideas were radical. He considered valid only what could be verified in experience or in calculations. In examining everything to ascertain its physical correctness, Mach dismissed nearly the entire history of philosophy. He found particular fault with Descartes' dualism, because Mach was convinced that sensations in the body and ideas in the mind are one and the same. As a young man on that summer's day, everything had seemed to join together, and in that same spirit he merged the dualism of "I" and "world" into a monism in which everything in the world consists of the same elements. If they appear in the brain, we call them "sensations," but that does not mean they are demarcated from the world outside the mind.

The focal point of Mach's theory of sensations was the death of the "I." For more than two millennia, philosophers, like most other people, had used the word "I" to refer to themselves. But Mach deemed this usage problematic. What might this "I" be? "The ego," he asserted, "is not a definite, unalterable, sharply bounded unity." There is no "I" in the human brain, only a jumble of sensations in the animated exchange with the elements of the outside world. Mach quipped that a sensation could go "a-roaming by itself in the world." His most famous statement on the self is this: "The ego is unsavable. It is partly the knowledge of this fact, partly the fear of it, that has given rise to the many extravagances of pessimism and optimism, and to numerous religious and philosophical absurdities."

Mach was not the first to come up with the idea of eliminating the self or at least diminishing its significance. He had proudly believed that it took a physicist to arrive at his conclusions, but an unsuccessful lawyer and pensive merchant had done so long before him. The Scottish philosopher David Hume was twenty-eight years old when he published his *Treatise of Human Nature* in 1739. Hume's quest for the self led nowhere, because soul and self were not tangible objects. Man does not need a self to perceive sensations, grasp concepts, and experience feelings; that happens all by itself. The self was nothing more than one idea among many. The only thing Hume could think of to rescue this self was to call it a "succession of perceptions"—an illusion, though perhaps a necessary one, that gives man the pleasant (and indispensable?) feeling of having a supervisor in the brain.

Is that true? Is the self an illusion, nothing but mental hocus-pocus, even though we all think we have a self? Were Western philosophers fooling themselves for two thousand years when they confidently based their ideas on a self that grapples with the important questions in the world? Isn't our self the little attic room where all our intellectual, emotional, and intentional acts go in and out, the bastion that endures through all the vicissitudes of life, the uncut movie that guarantees I will regard myself as one and the same person throughout the decades of my life? Who in Mach's and Hume's name is talking to you right now, if not my self? And who is reading this book, if not you, who also address yourself as "I"?

So let us start by liberating the self once again from the stranglehold of oddball physicists and unsuccessful lawyers and ask the experts, such as psychologists, what the self really is. The psychologists nod their heads, knit their brows, and exchange meaningful glances and a few words, then knit their brows still more tightly. "Well, you know," says one, "we are not likely to do away with the self. But my colleagues and I disagree about what the self might be. We cannot regard the self as a certainty, because psychology, as you probably know, is a science, and scientists define as existing only what they can see, hear, or measure. And that is not true of the self. If there is a self, it derives from something; Mr. Hume is correct on that score. The question is only: From what? Do we derive the self from sensations—is there a *sense* of self?—or from thoughts—an *idea* of self? We're not quite sure about this. The self acts like a switchboard for our will and judgment. We like to draw a distinction between self-concept and self-esteem. The self-concept tells us how we perceive ourselves. In order to do so, we have to reintroduce the 'I,' but just as a minor construct to function as a contrast to 'me.' The two share a task: The 'I' acts, and the 'me' judges the action. And self-esteem is the very subjective evidence that documents the 'me' to the 'I.' We have observed and described hundreds of thousands of people having this soliloquy. But on behalf of William James, who came up with these ideas, we ask that you refrain from asking for proof. That is just the way it is. God—or Darwin, or whoever—knows why."

That is as far as psychology gets us. Of course this depiction is greatly abridged, and psychology is a vast arena with many different theories and schools. But it is also apparent that psychology cannot provide a clear and simple reply to the question of the self. The remaining option is to consult the neuroscientists, who have often weighed in vociferously in recent years. More than everyone else, it would appear, they feel that they are now best suited to answer the question. The answer of many (or even all) neuroscientists to the question of whether there is a self is "No! There is no self. No one has ever been or possessed a self! There is no actual core of the self. David Hume and Ernst Mach were absolutely right: The self is an illusion!"

To understand their answer, one must of course ask what kind of evidence it would take to persuade a neuroscientist that the self has been located. Would it be enough to find a region, an area, or a center in the brain that controls or generates the self? Most likely not, because then the scientist would examine the control mechanisms and ascertain that this center, like all centers in the brain, does not function independently but is connected to others. And he or she would examine the neurons, the transmission of electrical impulses, and the chemical reactions, and conclude that the self is nothing but a complex electrochemical mechanism, somewhat like the way a child might cut open a talking doll and find nothing but a mechanical device inside.

Now common sense wins out, and, fortunately, no such center of the self can be pinpointed. That is very good news, and certainly not disappointing, as many a neuroscientist enjoys pointing out. The famous

anatomist Rudolf Virchow gleefully disabused philosophers of the existence of the self back in the nineteenth century with this statement: "I have
opened up thousands of corpses, but I never managed to see a soul." Even
those of us who are not religious would surely greet that finding with a cry of
"Thank God!" Not finding a soul or a self is of course far better than finding
a self that could be picked apart and demystified.

So there we have it: There is no center of the self. That is hardly surprising, because who—aside from René Descartes with his pineal gland—
believed so anyway? No noted philosopher in the past two hundred years has
claimed that the self is a material substance in the brain. Most skirted the
question entirely. Immanuel Kant, for example, used vague language in describing the self as an "object of inner sense" as opposed to the "object of the
outer senses," the body. This hazy statement keeps the issue up in the air.

Philosophy thus leaves the question of the self largely unresolved. The
basic idea is that you don't talk about the self, you *have* it. It is not surprising that neuroscience cannot seem to find the self; the way neuroscientists
examine the brain would not reveal it. In their world there is no self that
could be pinpointed somewhere on a map of the brain, and hence the self
does not exist.

But don't we continually experience our selves anyway? Could it really
be that these experiences are misleading us? Isn't it indisputable, then,
that there is a sense of self, albeit a nebulous one? Might the self extend
over the entire brain—perhaps even throughout the entire nervous system—or at least through many key parts of it? Couldn't a melody arise from
the concert of neurons in the brain, a melody of the self, so to speak, which
may not be ascertainable biologically, but indisputably exists on a psychological level even so? Just as the description of each individual instrument
in a concert hall does not yield a symphony, one simply cannot get at the
self with the methods of brain anatomy. Couldn't we see it that way?

Perhaps. But neuroscience has a second way of getting to the root of the
question: by examining people who deviate from the norm, patients with
disorders that shut down, debilitate, or distort their sense of self. The famous British neurologist and psychologist Oliver Sacks spent forty years
with patients in these situations. Sacks himself is a very colorful and high-
profile personality, and his book *The Man Who Mistook His Wife for a Hat* describes the lives and worlds of people with identity disorders; Sacks calls
them "travelers to unimaginable lands—lands of which otherwise we

should have no idea or conception." One is a musician who suffers a tiny injury to the left hemisphere of the brain and begins to experience profound visual agnosia, an inability to recognize objects. If he means to grab his hat, he reaches for his wife's face instead. Another is a professor of music who pats the heads of parking meters, thinking they are children; and yet another patient, an elderly woman suffering from neurosyphilis ("Cupid's disease"), develops an insatiable appetite for younger men.

The phenomena that Sacks was able only to sketch more than twenty years ago have since been explored from many angles. Many neuroscientists tend to the view that there is not a *single* self, but rather many different *states* of the self. My corporal self makes me aware that the body in which I am living is really my own body; my locational self tells me where I am at a given time; my perspectivist self tells me that I am the center of the world experienced by me; my "I" as experiential subject tells me that my sensory impressions and feelings are really my own and not those of others; my authorship and supervisory self makes it clear to me that I am the person who has to accept responsibility for my thoughts and actions; my autobiographical self makes sure I do not step out of my own role and that I experience myself throughout as one and the same person; my self-reflexive self enables me to think about myself and to play the psychological game of "I" and "me"; and my moral self works as conscience to tell me what is good and what is bad.

There are disorders in which one or another self does not function correctly, as in Oliver Sacks's stories. If these patients are examined using imaging procedures (see "The Cosmos of the Mind," p. 18), the areas of the brain that are apparently not working normally can be identified. The corporal self and the locational self, for example, are associated with the work of the parietal lobe, and the perspectivist self with the right inferior temporal lobe. The self as an object of experience is also linked to the right inferior temporal lobe, to the amygdala, and to other centers of the limbic system.

In this scheme of things, there are several selves, but there are other ways of sizing up the self. After all, the taste of individual ingredients tells us nothing about the meal as a whole. No matter how neatly these states of the self are distinguished here, they blend within the brain; sometimes we notice one ingredient, sometimes another, and they mingle within our consciousness so as to become virtually indistinguishable. Some hover at the brink of our consciousness, while others remain front and center. And they seem to originate in very different ways; some are only felt, while others are simply known. I have little say about my perspectivist self, which is normally a fixed entity. The same applies to the corporal self. But my autobiographical self is clearly something that I create for myself, by speaking. I talk about myself, and in doing so I tell myself and others about my self, embellishing it in the process. The same is true of my self-reflexive self and perhaps of my moral self as well (if that really exists; we will come back to this issue in detail later).

The various facets of the self as seen by neuroscience are useful classifications, but these kinds of constructs cannot always be cleanly divided, nor do they necessarily add up to an overall state of mind that can be called a stream of consciousness, as some neuroscientists argue. So why not just call it the "self," pure and simple?

One of the oddities in the field of brain research is that many neuroscientists dispute the existence of the self, all the while examining its origins. The self is frequently the bête noire in the laboratory that has to be postulated in order to be combated, so that brain researchers can provide a detailed picture of how a personality—and hence the self—is formed. The limbic system arises in the early embryonic stage. After birth, the brain establishes contact with the outside world and is revolutionized all over again. The brain structures adapt, reducing the number of neurons and coating the paths. At the age of eighteen to twenty-four months, a sense of self develops, and toddlers are able to recognize themselves in photographs. Only later does a "person" in the social and legal sense of a responsible member of society take shape. Some of these abilities and characteristics do not develop in the brain until puberty and beyond. All these descriptions explain the growth of the personality and are at the same time inextricably linked to the sense of self, because people say "I" when referring to themselves. Approximately one-half of this personality development, it is generally assumed, is closely linked to innate abilities. About 30 to 40 percent depends on impressions and experiences before the age of five. And only 20 to 30 percent of this development is significantly affected by later influences in the home, at school, and so forth.

Demystifying the self is a problematic undertaking. When Copernicus demonstrated that the Earth revolved around the sun, he discovered a hitherto unknown fact, and the old notion of the Earth as the center of the universe was refuted once and for all. When Darwin showed that all living creatures developed from primitive ancestors and that man was no exception, he was quite obviously describing a fact, and the assumption that man is God's unique creation was clearly false. But if neuroscientists today seek to do away with the self, they are not necessarily establishing a new fact. The old notion that man is held together mentally by a supervisor named Self is not refuted. This self is a complex matter; even if it can be broken down into various selves, it is still a perceived reality that science cannot simply dispense with. Isn't the fact that we feel we have a self enough to establish that there is one? "Man is an individual," Niklas Luhmann wrote, "simply because man claims to be one. And that is sufficient." The same could be said of the self.

"The ego is not a definite, unalterable, sharply bounded unity." Ernst Mach was correct on that score, unless we should find evidence of what some neuroscientists like to refer to as a "frame." But it is rather unlikely that our sensation goes "a-roaming by itself in the world." The self is like a reasonably attentive schoolchild—on the ball, caring, and alert. People do not have a core, a "true self" that can be pinned down in some specific spot. But even if we were to find one, it would not mean much, because the true demystification would have been to find a mechanism of the self, slap it down in front of it the philosophers, and declare: *This is it!* Instead, we have an inscrutable, multilayered, and multiperspectivist self. Brain research does not prove that there is no self, but rather that the self we recognize represents an incredibly complex and amazing process in the brain. Neuroscience is still miles—or rather, decades—away from solving the mystery of the nature of our selves, assuming it ever gets there. If the observation of simple emotions was the moon landing of neuroscience, the journey to the self is a manned voyage to Jupiter at the very least. As of now, we can only imagine what we will find. . . .

Mr. Spock in Love
What Are Feelings?

The year is 2267, stardate 3417.3. The starship *Enterprise* is off on a new mission. The planet Omicron Ceti III is in deep trouble, having been bombarded by berthold rays, which have wiped out all animal life on the planet, and the *Enterprise* is being sent to ascertain the whereabouts of the surviving colonists, although there is little cause for hope. Omicron Ceti III has been showered with rays for three years, seemingly too long to allow for any survivors, yet when Captain Kirk beams down onto the planet with a landing party, he is astonished to find the colonists alive and well. It turns out that the spores of a mysterious plant have protected them from the berthold rays. But the effects of these spores extend well beyond their protective function; they also transform the colonists' entire outlook on life. Anyone who breathes in the spores is suddenly infused with a great sense of peace, coupled with a desire never to leave the planet again. In this galactic Shangri-La, even Spock, the Vulcan who is otherwise impervious to human emotions, undergoes a transformation. Feelings take over his brain, which had been capable only of rational thought. Spock falls in love with a young colonist, and the confirmed rationalist turns into a hopeless romantic. The entire *Enterprise* crew eventually give in to their feelings, and Captain Kirk wages a solitary battle against the emotional pull of the planet. Duty calls, but the crew members refuse to return to their posts. Kirk figures out that he can neutralize the effect of the spores by raising the crew's adrenaline

levels. On some pretext he lures Spock back into the *Enterprise*, then taunts
the Vulcan until he flies into a rage. As his adrenaline rises, Spock regains
his foothold on reality. Kirk and Spock come up with a method to combat
the effect of the spores. They send a subsonic frequency down to the planet
that will spark quarrels among the remaining happy-go-lucky crew members of the *Enterprise*. The therapy does the trick, and everyone returns to
the business of flying through the galaxy.

"This Side of Paradise," filmed in 1967, is an episode from the first season of *Star Trek*. Philosophy is front and center in the episode. Spock would
seem to be a veritable ideal toward which all apostles of reason since
Descartes have been striving. Baruch Spinoza, Gottfried Wilhelm Leibniz,
George Berkeley, Immanuel Kant, Johann Gottlieb Fichte, and many other
philosophers would have encouraged man to attain the emotional sobriety
of the Vulcan. The story of the expulsion from the Neverland serves as a
nice little lesson, too: Don't give in to feelings and dopy notions of peace,
love, and happiness; they are just delusions. In real life, everyone has to
fulfill his mission and carry out his duties.

But as we take a closer look at the episode, doubts creep in. How believ-
able is the figure of Mr. Spock? In contrast to earthlings, Vulcans neither
express nor fall victim to feelings, but they must have at least some *potential*
for feelings. If Spock is capable of love under the influence of spores, he
must have what it takes to feel love, otherwise his feelings could not have
been activated. In fact, Spock continually reveals feelings in other *Star Trek*
episodes. His predominant disposition is a strong *feeling* of duty and responsibility. He is loyal and cooperative, and in order to size up conflicts,
he needs to know what is more "valuable." He has to weigh human lives
against risks, orders against destinies. All these considerations occur on
the basis of values. And moral values are never emotionally neutral (we will
return to this point later). In other words, despite Spock's rather odd facial
expressions and body language, he is a person like you and me. And he is
living proof of what he was evidently invented to disprove: that a human or
humanlike creature without feelings is inconceivable.

The reason is simple: Feelings and reason are not opposites. In everything we do, these partners of the mind work in concert. Their interaction
is smooth at times and quite bumpy at others, but they cannot function independently of each other. Feelings can sometimes get by without too much
involvement of reason, but without feelings, reason gets stranded, because

feelings orient thought. Without an emotional impetus, one's thought process cannot get moving. Without a feeling of duty, Mr. Spock would not be able to think strategically.

Feelings are the glue that binds us together and are therefore anything but superfluous. Nor are they harmful, bothersome, or primitive per se, and they do not stand in the way of what really matters, as many philosophers would have us believe. Of course, feelings can sometimes get in the way and have the potential to muddy clear thinking. During heated confrontations, I often find that I can't manage to come up with good arguments until later, when I've calmed down. When I was head over heels in love with my high school girlfriend, I couldn't think about anything else, and Latin class was a total waste of time. But even though we may often wish feelings away, a life without them would be catastrophic. It is better to have been beside yourself with joy, overwhelmed with fury, or rattled with jealousy at some points in your life than not to have known these vexing elixirs of our existence at all. Life without emotions would be pitiful; we would be absolutely incapable of action and have no idea what to think. Our neurons would no longer have anything to fire them up. Even a resolution to be totally rational and disregard feelings is emotionally based. Our thoughts, be they joyous, unsettling, devastating, dismaying, romantic, or somber, are invariably colored by our feelings.

But what are feelings? Where do they come from, where do they go, and what do they do in the interim? Philosophers have been pondering these questions since antiquity—although it must be admitted that feelings aren't exactly philosophers' favorite subject. It is very difficult to get at the root of feelings by means of contemplation. And many philosophers gloss over, dismiss, or disparage anything that doesn't fit neatly into their scheme.

Nevertheless, even the ancient Greeks and Romans tackled the subject of feelings. Their vocabulary of feelings centered on *pathos* and *passio*, words that originally connoted suffering. The English *emotion* sounds somewhat more neutral, but it comes from the Latin word *movere*—move— thus indicating that feelings are something that "move" a person. And the French distinguish between *sentiment* (for complex feelings) and *sensation* (for simple stimuli).

So feelings begin as physical stimuli—and very useful ones at that. Some feelings—for example, fear—can prove essential to survival. Flight reflexes are indispensable in the lives of primates, and they have endured. The same applies to most emotions: They contribute to survival and adaptation to the environment and to others of their species. Anyone lacking one of the basic feelings, such as fear, is not likely to live long. A person who is unable to experience disgust might wind up poisoned or gravely ill. Those who do not feel affection for others are isolated in the community, and a lack of sympathy arouses suspicion and dismay in others.

Passions, drives, instincts, and emotions serve a vital biological function. They promote individual survival and group solidarity. Whether the issue is hunger, the need for sleep and warmth, the impulse to attack or flee, or the desire for sex, basic feelings—whether in response to external events or arising from within—invariably boil down to one of two things: *pursuing* or *avoiding* something. On the one hand, emotions help us to react appropriately to an external stimulus, and on the other, they regulate our state of mind. When my emotional pendulum swings wildly in one direction, there is almost always a counterswing to restore my emotional equilibrium. It is nearly impossible to remain furious, or sexually aroused, for an entire week, from morning to night, and even the most profound period of mourning or melancholy is bound to let up over time.

Many of us are frustrated by how hard it is to turn feelings on and off. People who are pigeonholed as impassive wish they could be more spontaneous and impulsive, and quick-tempered people often wish they could be mellower and more serene. It is not easy to control our feelings, although they certainly control us. Actually, they do more than that. In the same way that we don't just *use* our brains to think but rather *are* our brains, so, too, when it comes to our feelings: We *are* our feelings, in a sense. But in which sense?

This is no easy question for philosophers, and it is no wonder that in recent years neuroscience has taken it up instead. Since magnetic resonance imaging and computer monitors have made it possible for us to see and observe manifestations of arousal in the brain, the study of emotions has become *the* hot topic among neurobiologists. They have gotten into the habit of differentiating between emotions and feelings, like the French when they speak of *sentiment* and *sensation*. Neuroscientists define emotions as the complex interaction of chemical and neuronal reactions. They construct patterns that often look quite similar in humans and in animals. Emotions are rather stereotypical and automatic processes. Feelings, on the other hand, are a far more complicated matter, involving a major dose of consciousness. Feelings can be hidden, and people can try not to let them show. That is difficult with emotions, because we have no control or influence over them. Feelings are a special mixture of emotions and ideas. They have a personal quality to them and unfold as if within a private spot inside of us. Lizards, magpies, and bats feel hunger and have flight reflexes, like humans, but they do not experience the human emotions of a broken heart, nostalgia, or melancholy.

In the second half of the nineteenth century, long before the dawn of neuroscience, the new field of psychology explored the nature of feelings, which had been neglected by philosophers, and began to conduct systematic research. And it did what psychologists love to do: generate lists! The crucial question was: How many different emotions are there? The idea was to distinguish a fixed set, a basic repertoire common to all cultures of the world. They knew there would be few basic emotions, because it was assumed that it would be highly unlikely for a new one to be developed or invented.

Even so, psychologists could not agree on what they were. At about the turn of the century, Wilhelm Wundt identified three central contrastive pairs: pleasure-displeasure, arousal-serenity, and tension-relaxation. But isn't there significant overlap among the pairs? Can we always differentiate between pleasure and arousal? Later psychologists favored lists with pairs of "basic emotions," and in the 1920s, a list of twelve was developed: happiness, grief, anger, fear, disgust, gratitude, shame, love, pride, sympathy, contempt, and fright. More recently, Paul Ekman, an anthropologist and psychologist at the University of California, San Francisco, proposed a list of fifteen: amusement, anger, contempt, contentment, disgust, embarrassment, excitement, fear, guilt, pride in achievement, relief, sadness/distress, satisfaction, sensory pleasure, and shame. One can continue this game in various ways, but perhaps one ought not to attach too much significance to it, because all these emotions get distorted when expressed in linguistic terms. Every language has a different mode of expression, and someone in China or Kenya might well compile different lists even if their basic emotions are identical to those of Paul Ekman.

Neuroscientists also encounter these translation problems when they interpret and describe emotions and feelings. It is easier and more fruitful to track down the chemical substances that trigger our emotions and to study the neurotransmitters that relay information from one neuron to another. The transmitters of emotions—acetylcholine, dopamine, serotonin, noradrenaline, and others—act as stimuli.

Neurotransmitters have astonishing capabilities, some of which have yet to be fully analyzed. Acetylcholine might be thought of as the athlete and coach among the transmitters, conveying stimuli between nerves and muscles and activating the sweat glands. But it can do much more. It is clearly involved in learning, and it has a direct connection to Alzheimer's disease, which is characterized by a severe depletion of acetylcholine. Dopamine prods and motivates; it has a major role in blood flow and regulating the hormone balance. Very low blood pressure can be raised with dopamine. In its effect on the hormones, this neurotransmitter is also closely associated with psychoses and other disorders; it is assumed that an excessively high level of dopamine is responsible for schizophrenia. Serotonin is a diplomat and mediator that promotes blood flow and regulates blood pressure. In the lungs and kidneys, serotonin is vasoconstrictive, but in the skeletal muscles it is vasodilatory. This neurotransmitter also regulates circadian rhythms and evens out stress. If the serotonin level gets off track, there are pleasant and less pleasant consequences. People in love appear to experience a rise in the level of serotonin, which conveys a sense of well-being and contentment. Low serotonin levels can cause migraines and other maladies. Noradrenaline is a race car driver and accelerator, primarily in the arteries. Like dopamine, it raises blood pressure. In emergency rooms it is used to treat shock and to accelerate blood flow when poisoning results in paralysis.

All four neurotransmitters are found throughout the limbic system and are also used elsewhere in the body. The three major components of the system, the periaqueductal gray (PAG, also called the "central gray"), the hypothalamus, and the amygdala, are centers of innate affective states and behavior patterns. The periaqueductal gray controls aspects of our sexual behavior, aggression, and defense as well as feelings of hunger and modulation of pain. The hypothalamus is also involved in the intake of food and fluids as well as in sexual behavior and in aggression and defense. Additionally, it helps regulate circadian rhythms and circulation. Noteworthy for our sexuality is the fact that a nucleus of the hypothalamus, the nucleus praeopticus medialis, is more highly developed in men than in women, making it one of the few striking anatomical gender differences in the brain. It has a major role in both aggressive behavior and in sexuality, which are closely linked here. As small as the amygdala is, it is hard to over-state its role in regulating our emotional stability. Neurologists have been showering attention on it, yet the amygdala remains elusive. It contains substantial quantities of noradrenaline and serotonin, and the concentra-tion of acetylcholine is particularly high. The amygdala is the fear center of the brain, and it also has a role in learning new facets of our emotions. Emotions can indeed be learned; something that throws us the first time we experience it may no longer do so by the tenth time.

Our feelings, thoughts, and actions are prompted by chemical signal substances; the quality of all feelings and stimuli is neurochemically deter-mined and neurochemically controlled. It is actually quite plausible for Mr. Spock's rude awakening from his endorphin and serotonin high on Omi-cron Ceti III to have been triggered by a release of adrenaline, but that would suggest that he has the same basic neurochemical apparatus as any normal human being, and if he does, it has to be linked to his higher brain func-tions, that is, his thinking—unless Vulcans have some kind of dopamine and noradrenaline block, which is unlikely, because it would make them lethar-gic, sluggish, and aimless.

But is that all we need in order to explain emotions and feelings? Hardly. Only a naïve neuroscientist would lean back at this point and say: *There you have it!* So far we have explored only the grammar of feelings, but not the timbre and range of meaning of the spoken language. As indispens-able as invigorating dopamine molecules, soothing serotonin molecules (the Spock molecule), and stimulating noradrenaline molecules are, they are not activated on their own. They are messengers that have to be sent out from one neuron to the next and from one brain center to another. When they arrive at their destination, they trigger specific reactions—slowing down, speeding up, motivating, or blocking. In short, transmitters relay and trigger meanings when they arrive, but they do not themselves initiate the thought process.

A full-blown feeling entails complex interactions among specific re-gions or centers in the brain, including the sending and receiving features of the neurons, the transmitters, a complex connective pattern with other brain structures, and of course the environmental stimuli that the senses introduce into the system. Why do some people feel uplifted by a certain kind of music while others can't stand the racket? Why do some people love the taste of oysters while others can't stomach them? And how can we feel flashes of hatred for those we think we love? Feelings are quite simple to explain on a chemical level, but figuring out how they come about, and how they appear and disappear, is no easy matter. Many neuroscientists must entertain fantasies of how much easier things would be if we were more Vulcan—the way Dr. McCoy does on the *Enterprise*. When Spock, whose otherwise matter-of-fact thinking is muddled by the spores, sends the crew an emotionally charged lyrical message, McCoy is taken aback:

McCoy: That didn't sound at all like Spock, Jim.

Kirk: No, it . . . I thought you said you might like him if he mellowed a little.

McCoy: I didn't say that!

If feelings, rather than Vulcan rationality, are indeed the glue that binds us together, then do feelings hold the ultimate sway? Are we ruled by our subconscious rather than by conscious thought? And what is the subconscious, anyway?

Ruling the Roost
What Is My Subconscious?

He was a difficult man. He used cocaine, neglected his children, had a terrible attitude toward women, and did not tolerate any opposition from his followers, and his scientific studies later proved to be anything but scientific. Yet he was a key figure of his day and one of the most influential thinkers of all time.

Sigïsmund Schlomo Freud was born in 1856 in Příbor, Moravia, then part of the Austrian Empire and now in the Czech Republic. His father was a Jewish wool merchant who went bankrupt shortly after the birth of his son. One of eight children, Sigismund grew up poor. The family moved to Leipzig, and soon after to Vienna. As the eldest son, he was the apple of his mother's eye, and he proved an excellent pupil. He passed his final secondary school examinations with distinction, and in the fall of 1873 enrolled in the medical school of the University of Vienna. Freud made a study of freshwater eel testicles and switched to the Physiological Institute at the University of Vienna, where he was awarded a doctorate in medicine in 1881 with a dissertation titled "The Spinal Cord of Lower Fish Species." But financial constraints made it impossible for him to remain at the university. With a heavy heart, he joined the staff at the Vienna General Hospital, where he remained for three years. As a medical resident under the supervision of the renowned neuropathologist Theodor Meynert, he continued to examine fish brains, primarily of the lamprey. At the time, he was also experimenting with cocaine, which he thought could be used to treat hysterical nervous diseases. The ambitious young scientist wanted to make a name for himself, but even though he published five studies about cocaine, he failed to achieve the breakthrough he was after. His attempt to cure his friend of a morphine addiction with cocaine had also failed, a detail Freud (who had shortened his first name to Sigmund by this point) opted not to disclose in his writings. In 1885, he left for a study trip to Paris brimming with self-assurance, writing in a letter: "Oh, how wonderful it will be! I will come back to Vienna with a huge, enormous halo . . . and I will cure all the incurable nervous cases." In Paris, Freud met Jean-Martin Charcot, known as the "Napoleon of the neuroses," who was the leading expert in the field of nervous diseases. He opened Freud's eyes to the nonphysiological, psychological causes of many mental disorders and introduced him to the art of hypnosis and suggestion. After his return to Vienna, Freud set up a neurology practice on Rathausgasse. At the same time, he headed the neurology department in the First Public Children's Hospital. He married Martha Bernays, from a respected family of rabbis and scholars, and they had six children. But Freud was not a warmhearted, loving father; for the most part, he remained aloof from his children. In the early 1890s, the thirty-five-year-old, who was still researching the anatomy of the brain, wrote an essay about speech impediments that resulted from brain diseases, and he realized what a colossal future brain research would have in solving many problems of the mind. But his "Project for a Scientific Psychology" (1895), an attempt to explain the "psychic apparatus" using Ramón y Cajal's new neuron doctrine, was never completed.

Neurology had a long way to go before it could be used to cure nervous diseases and, as Freud was hoping, to alleviate psychic disorders. Ramón y Cajal's insights into the function and interaction of neurons in the brain were too abstract and too general to be useful. Ramón y Cajal studied the brains of cadavers laid out on a dissection table in Madrid as a basis for his "rational psychology," while Freud analyzed the brains of living subjects as they lay on a couch in Vienna. The latter practice resulted in the new science of psychoanalysis. In 1889, Freud had gone to Nancy to visit Hippolyte Bernheim, who was conducting experiments using posthypnotic suggestion, and Freud concluded that there had to be an unconscious mind that was responsible for many human actions.

The term "unconscious" was not new. In 1869, the young philosopher

Eduard von Hartmann had written *Philosophy of the Unconscious,* a rather
simplistic study that was heavily influenced by Schopenhauer (see "The
Libet Experiment," p. 95). The book, which became a bestseller, brought
together many of the issues to which materialist philosophers in the mid-
nineteenth century took exception in the reason-based philosophies of
Kant, Fichte, and Hegel. Nietzsche, who criticized the same philosophers
from a similar position, was terribly upset, primarily because the less as-
tute Hartmann enjoyed far greater success than he. But Hartmann did not
coin the term "unconscious" either. That distinction went to the doctor and
naturalist Carl Gustav Carus, a friend of Goethe, who described the "unconscious" and "unconsciousness" as the essential basis of the psyche in
his 1846 book, *Psyche: On the History of the Development of the Soul.*

Freud's earnest attempt to explore this unconscious systematically set
him apart from his predecessors. He had a rough idea of where it was located; he assumed it was in the subcortical centers of the endbrain and the
brain stem, as his teacher Meynert had established. But the brain research
tools available in the 1890s were inadequate to investigate the unconscious.
In 1891, Freud moved to Berggasse 19 in Vienna, where he lived and worked
for the next forty-seven years. He used the term "psychoanalysis" for the
first time in 1896, adopting it from an "intricate exploratory procedure"
used by his friend and colleague Dr. Josef Breuer, who had motivated his
traumatized patient Bertha Pappenheim to open up and talk about her
emotional pain. Freud went on to investigate sexual abuses his patients—
primarily women—had endured by getting them to talk about their experiences. In his male patients, he diagnosed an early childhood sexual
attachment to the mother, a condition he called the Oedipus complex. Later
he used this and other ideas to construct a highly controversial theory of
drives and instincts, which he went on to modify quite often, but its sweeping statements were eventually refuted. Between 1899 and 1905, Freud
wrote four books about the power of the unconscious, and these books en-
sured his lasting fame. Their topics were dreams, the psychopathology of
everyday life, including slips of the tongue ("Freudian slips"), jokes, and
sexuality. In 1902, Freud was appointed associate professor at the University of Vienna, and he founded the Psychological Wednesday Society, which
later came to be called the Vienna Psychoanalytical Society.

In light of the controversy surrounding his publications and his tepid
reception in the scientific community, Freud's self-confidence was aston-

ishing. In 1917, he placed his discoveries about the unconscious on a par with the theories of Copernicus and Darwin. All three of them, he declared, had rocked mankind. Copernicus had shifted the earth from the center of the world to the margins; Darwin had replaced the divine nature of man with that of monkeys; Freud had shown that man's conscious mind did not rule the roost, because the unconscious was far more dominant. Freud contended that about 90 percent of human decisions are unconsciously motivated.

In 1923, Freud developed the idea of a tripartite psyche to explain how the unconscious controls consciousness. In this scheme of things, three components determine our emotional life: the id, the ego, and the superego. Freud claimed this triadic division as his own achievement, although Nietzsche had used all three concepts in much the same way. The *id* corresponds to the unconscious, instinctual element of the human psyche and is controlled by hunger, the libido, envy, hate, trust, and other involuntary feelings. Its adversary is the *superego*, which embodies the norms, ideals, roles, models, and views of the world we acquire from the time of our childhood. Between these two lies the *ego*, a rather pathetic intermediary worn down by overpowering opponents. As the servant of three masters—the id, the superego, and the social environment—the ego tries to resolve and reconcile conflicts that arise from these opposing forces, but it is relatively weak. As a rule, the id wins out, which eludes consciousness and thus escapes control by the ego. Unconscious drives and early childhood formative experiences are not manifest and are therefore difficult to classify.

Freud developed this model relatively late in life, and he certainly did not base all his later writings on it, but he did stick to the view that the primary motivation underlying human behavior arises from the unconscious conflict between instinctual impulses and reason, which is often overburdened in the process. He applied this idea not only to individuals but also to the dynamics of drives and instincts in human society as a whole.

He suffered terrible physical distress while writing his next books, which were critical of contemporary culture. By the 1920s, Freud enjoyed international renown, but cancer of the soft palate took a heavy toll on him and greatly limited his mobility. After the National Socialist accession to power, Freud's writings were banned and burned. When German troops marched into Austria in March 1938, he was forced to emigrate to London. Four of his five sisters remained in Vienna and were taken into custody and murdered by the Nazis in concentration camps. On September 23, 1939, a critically ill Freud took his life in London with a fatal dose of morphine.

What is Freud's legacy? First of all, it is to his great credit to have made feelings, psychic conflicts, and the unconscious the center of the study of man. The form of therapy Freud adopted from Breuer and honed continues to be used throughout the world, even though psychoanalysis has been fragmented into numerous schools that have distanced themselves from Freud to one degree or another. As far as Freud's scientific contribution to the exploration of the human psyche is concerned, he had fine instincts, but that is as far as it went. He journeyed through the psyche of his patients like a cartographer who has no ships to survey the continent he is drawing and has to make do with knowledge passed on by others. Freud's smug attitude came from his realization that no one else had come as far with his methods as he had. The unconscious was a new continent, and he was the leader of the expedition. But Freud understood that his days at the forefront were numbered. Brain research, which he had once abandoned because it was not useful to his work, was beginning to come into its own, and it would eventually surpass his achievements; the question was only how many of the coastlines, rivers, mountains, and islands he had sketched onto the map would remain. His book about the pleasure principle sounded uncharacteristically self-critical in concluding that it would be up to biology to unravel the mysteries of the mind with surprising new revelations, and these might "be such as to overthrow the whole artificial structure of hypotheses."

Psychoanalysis is not a science but a method, and its assumptions cannot be verified scientifically. Thirty years after Freud's death, neuroscience and psychoanalysis seemed irreconcilable. Psychoanalysis was then in its heyday, and neuroscience, at the height of its electrophysiological phase—when every emotion was rendered in micrometers and millivolts—seemed just as far-fetched to Freud's followers and disciples as psychoanalysis did to neurobiologists, who regarded it as an unscientific and naïve pursuit no better than reading tea leaves. Now that neurobiology has gained widespread acceptance, some brain researchers are beginning once again to pay tribute to Freud's achievements.

Matters that remained speculative to Freud are plainly evident to neuroscientists, who can look at the brain and identify regions in the associative cortex that are responsible for consciousness. And there are regions that create and store unconscious processes, namely the brain stem, the cerebellum, the thalamus, and the subcortical centers of the endbrain. As Freud had assumed, there is a clear anatomical distinction between the conscious and the unconscious. Even so, neuroscience steered clear of exploring the unconscious for quite some time, and neurobiologists found the unconscious difficult to grasp and describe. Unconscious processes often unfold quite rapidly, and they are—as Freud knew—not communicable in language, precisely because the person is not aware of them. So the psychotherapist has no choice but to read between the lines and try to decipher the unconscious—or to send a patient into a CAT scanner and observe what reactions to specific test questions activate the regions of the brain responsible for the unconscious.

Although it is easy enough to name these regions, its composition can be quite varied. Our field of perception is full of impressions of which we are entirely unaware, and of events that are experienced subliminally. Our attention can focus on only a fraction of what we actually see, hear, and feel. The rest ends up in our subconscious mind. Some of that is stored deep down, but we have no control over what winds up where. We focus selectively on what suits our task at hand or our goal or needs. A person who is hungry is more likely to notice everything pertaining to food or restaurants, and a tourist views a city differently from someone who is looking for a job. The more you train your attention on one thing, the less you notice everything else, as is evident, for example, in the aftermath of car accidents, when drivers claim not to have seen the other vehicle.

When our attention is focused on one thing, our brain often fails to register other elements in our surroundings, even bizarre ones that ought to leap to our attention. One well-known example is the gorilla suit experiment conducted by psychologists Daniel Simons of the University of Illinois at Urbana-Champaign and Christopher Chabris of Harvard. Two teams of basketball players face each other, one dressed in white and the other in black. The players pass the ball to others on their own team while a group of test subjects observe the action on video. Their job is to count how many times the ball is passed among the members of the white team. Most of the test subjects have no problem completing the assignment and supplying the correct number. The scientist conducting the experiment, however, is looking for a different piece of information. He wants to know whether the viewers picked up on anything out of the ordinary. More than half the test subjects do not. Only when they see the video for a second time, without concentrating on the counting, do they become aware, to their amazement, that a woman in a gorilla suit strode straight across the court, stood still in the middle, and thumped her chest. Most of the viewers were so busy counting during the first round that they failed to notice the gorilla at all. When psychologists conducting the same experiment ask the test subjects to count how many times the ball was passed by the team dressed in black, only a third of them fail to spot the gorilla. The woman in the gorilla suit catches the eye of the viewers of the black team because her costume is also black. The film is a very striking example of how our attention screens what we perceive even though we are largely unaware of it. Our attention is a spotlight that illuminates only a portion of the total picture, and the dark remainder ends up in our unconscious.

A large part of our unconscious draws on these kinds of dimly discerned perceptions. Another substantial portion is culled from our experiences in the womb and over the first three years of life. During this time, we register a great deal quite intensively, but our associative cortex is not mature enough to store these events as conscious experiences. About two-thirds of our personality evolves in this manner, but we cannot recall or reflect on those experiences later.

There are still more elements to the unconscious beyond our everyday unconscious perceptions and the early childhood unconscious impressions buried deep within us. One example is when we're on "autopilot." I have often been surprised by how well I'm able to make my way home in a state of complete intoxication and arrive safely, even though the next day I can't recall a moment of the walk home. And as I sit here typing this sentence, how do my fingers find the keys on the keyboard in a mere tenth of a second? If someone were to ask me to draw a keyboard that is covered up, I imagine I'd have trouble labeling any keys correctly. Evidently my fingers know more than I do! And so many things that I have experienced and then forget will occur to me all of a sudden when something triggers them, even though they were not on the surface of my consciousness in the interim. The standard example is aromas that have the power to conjure up a whole chain of long-lost images in our heads.

Keeping all the above in mind, we have to admit that Freud was substantially correct. Most of what goes on in our brains occurs on an unconscious level, and this unconscious activity affects us powerfully. We might even say that unconscious perceptions are the norm, and the conscious ones—which are of course especially important to us—are the exception. Our awareness depends on the involvement of the associative cortex, which, it should be noted, is clearly dependent on the unconscious. As we saw in the previous chapter, feelings are the glue that binds. Without unconscious impulses from the limbic system, the associative cortex would have nothing to obtain, consider, assess, and express. It would be a high-performance machine devoid of electricity. The unconscious thus controls our consciousness far more strongly than the other way around. In our personal development it originated before consciousness, and it shaped us long before our consciousness began to awaken. The sum of our unconscious experiences and abilities—subconsciousness—is a powerful force over which we have little control. The most common route to our subconscious mind is by way of psychotherapy administered by others.

Brain researchers today dream of a psychoanalysis informed by neuroscience. A 1979 essay ("Psychotherapy and the Single Synapse") by Eric Kandel, the world-famous researcher on memory, laid out his ambitious vision of fusing the two disciplines. But to psychoanalysts, Kandel's suggestions for a new scientific accuracy read like an ascetic diet, devoid of speculations or bold claims or fantasies about curing mental and physical ailments with psychoanalysis. Instead, he proposes the use of empirical research, statistics, strict outcomes assessments, and the use of brain scans and magnetic resonance imaging to verify the progress of therapy in individual regions of the brain.

The use of the experimental methods of neuroscience to explore the unconscious is just getting under way. The unconscious, a stepchild of philosophy that first began to be taken seriously in the second half of the nineteenth century, may well be today's key area of research on the path to a scientific self-awareness. Epistemology informed by biology thus sees humankind doubly bound: first by our senses, with the typical abilities and the typical limits of the primate brain, and second by the boundary between consciousness and subconsciousness. The access into the unconscious that constitutes the great majority of our experiences and our personality is largely blocked to us. Before we move on to questions of our behavior in the second part of this book, we need to have a closer look at one more aspect that has been tacitly understood up to this point: memory. What is memory, and how does it function?

Now What Was That?
What Is Memory?

Eric Kandel has certainly earned the right to rest on his laurels, but basking in all his past accomplishments is not in his nature. Sporting wide suspenders, a flashy red bow tie with blue polka dots, and a gray pinstripe suit, he stands straight as an arrow in his study, looking like one of the Broadway greats from the 1950s. But Kandel is not an entertainer. He is the world's foremost memory researcher.

His twelfth-floor office is simply furnished but inviting. The scholarly tomes on the bookshelf are dog-eared, among them a thick, well-worn copy of *Principles of Neural Science*, the standard neuroscience textbook, which made Kandel famous. On the windowsill are photos of his family and colleagues. Through the tinted glass you can see Upper Manhattan; down below, the traffic on Riverside Drive crawls through this desolate area of dark high-rises, housing projects, and barbed wire. Ten years have passed since Kandel was awarded the Nobel Prize in Physiology or Medicine for a lifetime of memory research full of sparkling ideas and astounding discoveries. He has spent the second half of his long career up here on this floor. The crowded laboratories down the corridor from his office look the way they do everywhere in the world, but the unremarkable interior is deceptive. The Howard Hughes Medical Institute at Columbia University is one of the world's leading institutions in the field of neuroscience. And the lively octogenarian behind it all has no intention of relaxing into retirement.

Kandel still holds sway over a large number of eager colleagues, and is still in the prime of his research.

Sometimes it is hard to tell whether the world is made up of atoms or of stories. Eric Richard Kandel's story begins with Hitler's invasion of Austria. On November 7, 1938, little Erich was given a blue battery-operated remote control model car for his ninth birthday. His parents, a Jewish couple in Vienna, owned a toy store, and the car was Erich's pride and joy. Two days later, late in the evening, the family was startled by loud banging on the apartment door. It was *Kristallnacht* (Night of the Shattered Glass), and anti-Semitism descended on Vienna more brutally than anywhere else in the Greater German Reich. Erich, his mother, and his brother had to leave the apartment. His father was taken into custody, interrogated, and humiliated, and did not return to his family for ten days. For an entire year, the Kandels endured increasing persecution by the Nazi regime; they were robbed of their belongings, forced out of their home, and stripped of their rights. Erich's father was unemployed, and Erich lost all his friends. The Jewish community organization in Vienna helped keep the family afloat. In April 1939, the sons were able to leave for the United States, and their parents followed later. The surviving Jews' pledge to "never forget" always stayed with Erich. His parents had trouble adapting to life in New York, but Erich, who now went by Eric, settled in quickly. He attended the Yeshivah of Flatbush, a well-known Hebrew day school, then Erasmus Hall High School on Flatbush Avenue. He was one of two Erasmus graduates (in a class of more than 1,150) to be accepted to Harvard; both were awarded scholarships. There he met Anna Kris, who came from a family of psychoanalysts. He fell in love with Anna, but even more with psychoanalysis, calling it "the most fascinating science there is—imaginative, comprehensive, and empirical all at the same time." Kandel immersed himself in the writings of Sigmund Freud and discovered "the only promising approach to understanding the mind." To become a psychoanalyst, though, he would have to study medicine, which he considered to be "an indescribably boring subject." In the fall of 1955, he sat in the office of Harry Grundfest at Columbia University and laid out his research interests to the astonished neurophysiologist: "I want to find out where Freud's 'ego,' 'id,' and 'superego' are located in the human brain."

Thinking back to that time sends him into gales of laughter—a series of sharply inhaled breaths that sound like the mating call of a hornbill. In his

engaging narrative style, a blend of Viennese charm, Jewish humor, and
American nonchalance, he tells about his evolution from dreamer to serious
scientist. Grundfest advised him to look at one brain cell at a time, and to use
a simple animal for his experiments. After all, Freud had also begun as a
neurobiologist and tried to develop his theory of the "psychic apparatus" on
the basis of neural science. Kandel wanted to venture into territory beyond
what the limited knowledge in Freud's time had offered. Over the next two
decades, he would spend more time with *Aplysia*, a giant marine snail, than
with his wife. His first experiments with microelectrodes attached to crayfish neurons sent the budding neuroscientist into raptures. You can feel his
euphoria even today when he stretches his arms and his crescendoing voice
declares: "I listened to the deep, hidden thoughts of my crayfish!" But
Aplysia proved still more spectacular. "It was large, proud, attractive, and
intelligent." *Aplysia* is an uncomplicated animal, with a mere 20,000 brain
neurons, as opposed to 100 billion in humans. Some of these cells are fifty
times as large as in mammals, and they can be seen with the naked eye. Kandel threw himself into his work with boundless enthusiasm.

Kandel paints a glowing picture of the excitement of those early days, a
world in which there is nothing more thrilling than brain research, exploring an unknown continent, akin to seventeenth-century astronomy and the
Renaissance voyages of discovery. In the 1950s and '60s, the brain was
largely uncharted territory. And the path from *Aplysia* neurons to the explanation of human feelings, thinking, and behavior could hardly be
longer. But Kandel was optimistic. The biochemical building blocks of the
cells of marine snails and man were largely the same. He guessed that the
cell mechanisms that underlie learning and memory might have remained
intact during evolution and might function in at least a similar manner in
all living creatures. He administered mild electroshocks at the tip of the tail
of the *Aplysia* to stimulate gill withdrawal reflexes, observed the reaction in
selected neurons, and found that they were altered. He soon realized that
"learning," in the short-term memory of the *Aplysia*, increased the plasticity of the synapses and strengthened synaptic connections. His first essays
about marine snail "learning" amazed his colleagues, and he reveled in the
knowledge that his magic tricks had worked. "The mammal chauvinists
didn't know what to think," he told me. "They had believed that experiments of this kind would work only with mammals."

The terrain onto which Kandel had ventured—memory research—could not have been more mystifying. The term "memory" is hard to pin down. After all, doesn't memory go to the very heart of our identity? Without it, we would have neither biography nor life—certainly not a conscious life. Understanding requires relating information to something else we know, and we can know only what we have stored. To understand the sentence you have just read, you have to recognize the individual words and at the same time get the gist of the sentence as a whole—its *meaning*. And it is helpful to recall the sentences you read before, not word for word, but at least their essential *meaning*. I put the word "meaning" in italics because it tells us something significant: As a rule, we don't store words and sentences in our brains, but something along the lines of personal essences, the *meanings* that these things have for us. This applies not only to words but to everything. Very few of us could draw from memory faces that are familiar to us—even talented artists have trouble doing so. If I think about my grandfather, whom I loved very much as a child, I see images and selected scenes that form small emotional snippets, more like film clips than full-fledged films. And when I picture my own apartment, I never see all the rooms before me at the same time, but only individual rooms, or parts of them.

How can we explain these blurry film clips? How does information evolve into meaning? And who determines the selection? Why do I still know the name of the dog who lived downstairs when I was in elementary school, but forget to call my wife on the anniversary of the day we met, even though I know the date full well, and the dog means nothing to me, while my wife means so much? When I was trying to think of an example, why did I light on that dog, after not having thought about him for a good thirty-two years? Memory, it would appear, is for the most part elusive. It flashes through your mind and appears before your eyes unawares. You have little control over it; in fact, you cannot even opt to forget what you remember! What is this unspecified power of memory that plucks certain images from a shadowy oblivion and sends them back to my consciousness? How much of my memory is conscious and how much unconscious? Who or what controls the transfer of conscious knowledge into the storage chest of the forgotten and now and then pulls out one thing or another? Not too long ago, when I visited Berlin after a twelve-year hiatus, I happily inhaled that well-remembered and unmistakable odor wafting up from the subway, yet I hadn't realized that I had ever noticed it before—or that I evidently had pleasant associations with it. Am I the one doing the remembering, or does memory have an intangible life of its own? Am I really the subject of the process of recollection, or more like the object?

The fact that our brains store meanings rather than data makes memory research quite a challenging endeavor. Someday, neuroscience will find a way to *describe* all the processes—genetically, chemically, and electrophysiologically—but will it *understand* them? What do our insights into molecular interaction really tell us about human memory? Memory research appears to represent a far headier task for philosophers and psychologists than research on feelings or subconsciousness.

When we engage our memories, we think of thoughts and feelings that have left traces in the brain. We think and feel them again, somewhat the way we did the first time around. A small group of so-called savants, people who are capable of astonishing feats of memory, are a notable exception. In the film *Rain Man*, Dustin Hoffman played an autistic savant based on the story of Kim Peek. Peek, who lived in Salt Lake City until his death in December 2009 at the age of fifty-eight, knew some twelve thousand books by heart, word for word, and could tell you off the cuff what day of the week was associated with any calendar date you could name. But he paid a high price. Peek, who lived with his father, was unable to dress himself, scramble eggs, or make a sandwich. Some memory researchers see savants as a unique window into the human brain, but unfortunately the information they provide is perplexing. Because some specific brain functions are absent or diminished in the majority of savants, they compensate for these deficits by switching to different circuits that sometimes produce astonishingly high-level achievements. But science has yet to figure out why a savant like Stephen Wiltshire can take a forty-five-minute flight over Rome, a city he has never seen before, then draw each individual house from memory, right down to the correct number of windows, or why he fails to pick up on meanings but instead amasses chunks of information.

There is, of course, a plus side to the fact that we nonsavants forget so much of what we experience. Memories embellish our lives, but forgetting is what makes them bearable. But how do recalling and forgetting take place? Brain researchers now divide memory into declarative (explicit) and nondeclarative (tacit) memory, a distinction that parallels consciousness and subconsciousness. Declarative memory retrieves what is consciously experienced or deliberated, and is subject to "declarative" expression; hence the name. Nondeclarative memory applies to what we store unwittingly, as in the case of my subway smells in Berlin. Both types of memory can in turn be subdivided, somewhat like the various facets of the self and the unconscious. Declarative memory has three distinct components: episodic memory, factual memory, and familiarity memory. Episodic memory accompanies us on a conscious level throughout our everyday lives. Noteworthy things that happen to me today, things that grab my attention and matter to me, enter into this episodic memory. Of all the types of memory, this is the one that most strongly shapes my self-image and my identity. This is where we "invent," in the words of the novelist Max Frisch, "the biography we come to regard as our life."

The things that do not mesh with the movie of my life, in which I play the lead and others who are important to me have supporting roles, are consigned to factual memory. The words I am now writing about memory come from this factual memory and may now also enter into yours. Recipes and bank account numbers, timetables for trains I take on a regular basis, all my knowledge about the world is stored here. But this memory requires a particular set of conditions to function. In order for me to recognize the things in my life, I have to know that I know them. The familiarity memory sees to that, telling me whether something seems familiar to me. Normally it does not take long to figure that out. This memory seems to work fairly effortlessly and automatically: I know whether I know something or not, and the number of uncertain exceptions is very limited. The automatic nature of familiarity memory functions much like nondeclarative memory; it is intuitive memory in which consciousness plays little or no role. The previous chapter mentioned "knowing" fingers on the computer keyboard and "knowing" feet heading home. Clearly they remember the correct keys and the correct route astonishingly well without requiring much input from a slower-operating (or alcohol-impaired) consciousness. An experienced driver shifts gears "automatically" and analyzes traffic situations "intuitively." A good soccer forward makes a split-second decision where to shoot, and a goalie raises his arms "reflexively." In all these processes, the nondeclarative memory of our subconscious is at work.

Among the biggest mysteries involving memory is a second decision memory makes, once it has distinguished the familiar from the unfamiliar: It sorts out the important from the unimportant. We can scarcely take note of every object in a room, but as soon as there is something out of the ordinary, we usually pick up on it right away. Evidently the new and unexpected are particularly important to us, and we store deliberately only what we deem sufficiently important. But who determines what is important? Clearly the sense of importance can have both a conscious and an unconscious origin, which means that declarative and nondeclarative memory cannot be divided as cleanly as we have been suggesting. Although neuroscientists all use these terms, this construct is quite hypothetical. A closer look reveals that these handy distinctions are vague and speculative. Strictly speaking, they originate not in brain research but in psychology, and they are no more valid than Freud's id, ego, and superego. These are practical and reasonably plausible categories, but they cannot be hard-and-fast, for the obvious reason that there is no particular spot with a hard disk called "memory" in the brain that one could describe and in which individual repositories assume specific functions. There is neither a region "short-term memory" nor a site "long-term memory," and even declarative and nondeclarative memory have no visible location. On a physiological level, neuroscientists have pitifully little to go on.

But if there is no site of memory, how was Eric Kandel able to examine the "short-term memory" of *Aplysia* and observe the synapses of this marine snail strengthen as they learn? The answer is that the biochemical mechanism Kandel was examining appears at quite a few different neurons. In order to conduct the pertinent experiments, all you have to figure out is which neurons are responsible for which bodily functions. Kandel's crucial achievement was showing that experience leaves a trace in the brain, that it causes modifications of the synapses. The plasticity of the synapses enables us to store experiences for the short term, and the synapses of all animals are continually modified depending on their experiences, within the framework of defined possibilities. Neurons cannot, of course, learn everything; there are limitations to their flexibility. Kandel became a candidate for the Nobel Prize when he succeeded in showing that experiments similar to those with *Aplysia* could also be conducted using rats. In the 1980s, he identified the protein CREB (cAMP response element binding). When CREB is released in a neuron in the brain, the synaptic connections are strengthened, and, as Kandel discovered, the synapses become more efficient in short-term memory. Long-term memory, by contrast, does not originate in qualitative improvement within the synapses, but because the *number* of synaptic connections increases in response to CREB. This discovery brought Kandel the crucial breakthrough—and the first noteworthy theory of how long-term memory originates. He was awarded the Nobel Prize in 2000, along with Arvid Carlsson of Sweden and Paul Greengard of the United States. Carlsson had laid important foundations for understanding and managing Parkinson's disease. Greengard discovered how neurotransmitters act on the cell and perform changes in cell reactions in the brain, which is an important foundation for Kandel's work on long-term memory as well.

Kandel knows that he has only scratched the surface of long-term memory. He was the first to do so, but certainly not the last. There are still quite a few unanswered questions. His experiments had concentrated on the hippocampus of rats, which is responsible for spatial orientation. While rats learned how to find their way through a labyrinth, CREB was released in the hippocampus. Of course, you find the same biochemical activity in other regions of the brain that have no known connection with learning and memory. The process that takes place in the neurons triggered by CREB is a necessary but clearly not sufficient explanation for the formation of long-term memories. If we compare the memory with the system of higher mathematics, we might say that neuroscientists are just at the point of figuring out what a number is.

The manner in which our brain stores impressions and sorts the important from the unimportant—and why it does so—remains a puzzle, but it is clearly the case that for me to remember something deliberately and to pull it out of the recesses of memory on my own, I have to have reflected on and captured the experience in language. Evidently, the human brain is incapable of reflection in the complete absence of language. But if everything we know—or think we know—is linked to language, we have to analyze language itself. Does language assure us a privileged access to reality? Does it impart an objective knowledge of the world?

The Fly in the Bottle
What Is Language?

In the fall of 1914, a young aeronautics engineer sat in a patrol ship on the Vistula River. Since July, Austria-Hungary had been in a war that would go down in history as World War I. But the twenty-five-year-old engineer at the eastern front was not interested in the war, even though he had enlisted in the army. He had discovered a mesmerizing magazine article about a courtroom in Paris and a lawsuit concerning an automobile accident that had occurred a year earlier. Complicated traffic accidents involving automobiles were still a rarity in the metropolises of Europe. To reconstruct the exact course of events, the court reenacted the accident by means of a miniature model. Miniature houses, a miniature truck, miniature people, and a miniature baby carriage were put into position and moved about. The engineer was riveted. How was it that a model could stand in for reality? First, by making the figures correspond as closely as possible to the real objects, and second, by ensuring that the relation of the figures to one another was exactly analogous to the actual relations among the real objects. If reality can be represented by figures, he thought, can't it also be represented in the same manner by the figures of thinking, namely, by words? "In the proposition," he noted in his diary, "a world is as it were put together experimentally." In other words, linguistic statements constitute a world.

Just as Descartes had launched philosophy in a new direction at the onset of the Thirty Years' War, this aeronautical engineer altered the course of philosophy at the beginning of World War I. More radically than anyone before him, he made the logic of *language* the center of philosophical thought. And this paradigm shift made him one of the most influential philosophers of the twentieth century. His name was Ludwig Wittgenstein.

Wittgenstein was born in 1889 in Vienna, the city of Sigmund Freud, Ernst Mach, Gustav Mahler, and Robert Musil. He was the youngest of nine children of Karl Wittgenstein, one of the most powerful steel magnates of his era. Wittgenstein's mother was a pianist. The combination of old money and a love of music in the Wittgenstein family bears a striking resemblance to the eponymous family in Thomas Mann's novel *Buddenbrooks*. Compared to the nine Wittgenstein children, of course, the fictional characters of Thomas, Christian, and Toni Buddenbrook are almost normal. One of the Wittgenstein sons became a famous pianist, but three of the other children later committed suicide. Ludwig was also extremely high-strung and insecure, depressive at times and arrogant and domineering at others. Like all of his siblings, Ludwig was homeschooled. When he was fourteen, he finally went to school, but he was not a good student. He passed his college entrance examinations by the skin of his teeth and enrolled at the university as a student of engineering. Wittgenstein had a passionate interest in technology and machinery, which was not unusual at a time when engineers were revolutionizing life with automobiles, airplanes, elevators, skyscrapers, and telephones.

In 1906, he matriculated at the renowned Technical University in Berlin-Charlottenburg and in 1908 transferred to Manchester, where he worked with varying degrees of success on airplane motors and propellers, but he was drawn to logic and mathematics. In Jena, he visited the mathematician Gottlob Frege, whose attempts to fathom the general laws of logic in mathematics and other disciplines went relatively unnoticed. Frege recognized Wittgenstein's talent and drew his attention to the leading philosophical authorities of the day, Alfred North Whitehead and Bertrand Russell at the University of Cambridge, whereupon Wittgenstein enrolled at Trinity College in Cambridge to study philosophy. Russell initially dismissed the eccentric young engineer: "My ferocious German . . . came and argued at me after my lecture. . . . It is really rather a waste of time talking with him." But within a few weeks, Russell came to consider Wittgenstein a genius, ranking the brilliance of his ideas above his own. He encouraged

Wittgenstein to criticize and improve on his *Principles of Mathematics*, and he hoped to learn a great deal from the Austrian, who was seventeen years his junior. Wittgenstein threw himself into the project, interrupted only by extensive travels, primarily to Norway, where he had a hut built at a fjord and could enjoy a homosexual relationship with a friend from Cambridge. But he aimed much higher than merely building upon Russell's logic, and he set about creating his own "definitive" work, the *Tractatus Logico-Philosophicus*. During the war, he continued his studies, and his aspirations soared: "My work has extended from the foundations of logic to the nature of the world." He finished the project in the summer of 1918, before the war ended, but it did not appear in print until 1921, when it was published in a journal, and in the following year, as a bilingual book edition in German and English. This slender volume was less than a hundred pages in length, and its consecutive numerical system grouped sections and paragraphs in the quotable manner of biblical chapters and verses. The book enjoyed an enthusiastic reception in Cambridge and in philosophical circles throughout western Europe.

What was it that made this formerly poor student the star of the philosophical world? What was the nature of his universally hailed "genius"? As the story with the model of the Paris traffic accident shows, Wittgenstein's innovation was to shift language to the center of philosophical inquiry. As astonishing as it may sound, language had been a neglected area in philosophy until then. Although philosophers were, of course, well aware that they expressed their thoughts in words and sentences, the dependence of their thoughts and conclusions on language was rarely addressed. Even Kant, who had shifted the rules governing our experience and thinking to the center of his philosophy, had barely looked into the complexities and necessities of language. Wittgenstein noted the same omission in Whitehead and Russell. How could one make sense of the logic of the human experience and human knowledge of the world while ignoring the language in which this logic is formulated? "All philosophy," Wittgenstein contended, "is a 'critique of language.' "

Wittgenstein thought about the traffic accident model and the way the figures and their relation to one another provided a picture of reality, and he realized that the same thing occurs in a proposition: Its words and syntax convey a picture of reality. The nouns ("names") correspond to the "things" of the world, and their juxtaposition imbues them with meaning.

If the names and syntax agree with the things and their alignment, a proposition is *true*—in principle, anyway, because for a mirror of this kind truly to mirror reality, all constructional flaws in everyday usage have to be remedied and language must be streamlined by eliminating all senseless and nonsensical propositions. Senseless propositions are those that require no reality to ascertain their truth value; for example, "Green is green." And the truth of nonsensical propositions, such as "The proposition I am now uttering is false," cannot be verified at all, because they have no basis in reality. Wittgenstein was even determined to banish all moral statements from language, because "good" and "bad" do not represent things that exist in reality. Morality, he contended, can be expressed only in signs, gestures, or facial expressions, because "what we cannot speak about we must pass over in silence."

Wittgenstein dreamed of a precise language that would enable people to grasp and describe reality objectively in all spheres of life. The Ernst Mach Society, a group of positivist-minded scientists and philosophers in Vienna who in 1922 formed the Vienna Circle, devoted fourteen years to developing the ideas in Wittgenstein's *Tractatus*. The project was ultimately an utter failure, which was probably just as well; after all, what good could have come of an authoritarian language forced down society's throat? How much would be lost if schoolteachers made their pupils stop crafting sentences that featured ambiguity, irony, and metaphor? And even if Wittgenstein's reform had been limited purely to philosophical language, it still would have been exceptionally dry and devoid of nuance.

Precise language failed not because of any shortcomings on the part of the Vienna Circle but because a precise language represents a profound misconception of human evolution and the basic function of language. The motor driving the development of language was quite clearly not the desire for truth and self-knowledge, but rather the social need to communicate. Nonetheless, Wittgenstein regarded language as an exclusive instrument of knowledge. He viewed it with the eyes of a technician and engineer, and he evaluated its usefulness solely according to logic. He shared this inflated view of language with Whitehead and Russell, who regarded logic as tantamount to the world formula of thinking—which it is not. It is one means of thinking among others, and it is only one element of language. Judging everything according to the laws of logic leads to absurd conclusions in the real world.

In order to understand how highly intelligent people like Russell and Wittgenstein came to explain the world exclusively by the rules of logic, we need to picture the charged atmosphere in Cambridge at that time. The pioneer spirit in technology and engineering had extended to philosophy, which had been rather lackluster for several decades but was now flourishing in Cambridge. Russell and Wittgenstein could not tell whether they would be leading philosophy to new heights or signaling its eventual end. But they were so taken with their ideas that they believed they could do without many of life's key components. Their attitude toward the other disciplines that studied the human condition was dreadfully arrogant. Wittgenstein had read Freud, but since Wittgenstein's only yardstick was a text's usefulness for logic, he found psychoanalysis just as unproductive as psychology. As might be expected, he was unaware of recent developments in brain research; Ramón y Cajal and Sherrington were completely unknown to most thinkers in his day.

The range of Wittgenstein's philosophical knowledge was clearly demarcated, in sharp distinction to Russell's. Wittgenstein did not dwell on the question of whether man can attain an adequate grasp of objective reality—a question that had been pondered in philosophy at least since Kant—nor did he inquire into the psychology of perception, which was a major issue for many of his contemporaries. And his *Tractatus* made no attempt to address the social context of language and speech. This is the only way to explain why Wittgenstein's vision of an ideal language bore some resemblance to the language used by Joseph, an eleven-year-old boy discussed in Oliver Sacks's *Seeing Voices*:

> Joseph saw, distinguished, categorized, used; he had no problems with *perceptual* categorization or generalization, but he could not, it seemed, go much beyond this. . . . He seemed completely literal—unable to juggle images or hypotheses or possibilities, unable to enter an imaginative or figurative realm. . . . He seemed, like an animal, or an infant, to be stuck in the present, to be confined to literal and immediate perception, though made aware of this by a consciousness that no infant could have.

It is important to note that Sacks's Joseph was not a pupil who had Wittgenstein's precise language thrust upon him, but rather a deaf boy who grew up without sign language for the first ten years of his life. Joseph's experience of language is devoid of the nuances that arise through usage because he was never exposed to spoken language or signing during his earliest childhood. Even so, Joseph came out with a good grasp of words and syntax, and an understanding of language that is logical, in a rudimentary sense, but not social.

In the 1960s, Noam Chomsky provided a credible explanation for how we learn language: People are born with an innate sense of language and grammar, and toddlers learn their first language virtually automatically. It grows within them in a manner resembling the growth of their arms and legs. It is, of course, crucial to this process that toddlers imitate the language they hear. Like chimpanzees in the wild, people use only about three dozen different sounds to construct complex sentences. In chimpanzees, it would seem, each sound has a specific meaning. In human development, by contrast, sounds like "ba" or "do" gradually lost their meaning and became mere syllables. Humans combine meaningless sounds to form meaningful words.

Why this process occurred in man and not in other primates is a matter of controversy. One reason may be that the larynx lowered during the development of man, which greatly expanded the linguistic capabilities of human speech. But no one has found a good explanation for that either, though we do know that the region of the brain associated with grammar and the ability to form meanings from a sequence of sounds is Broca's area, which is located just above the left ear. Until about the age of three, children develop their language skills primarily there. If Chomsky is right and there is an innate sense of grammar of the language we learn first, it would have to be located in Broca's area, because second language acquisition evidently occurs with the help of adjacent areas in the brain. Broca's area is associated with speech production, articulation, pronunciation, and the formation of abstract words. Understanding and perhaps also imitation of language are ascribed to another region, Wernicke's area. This bipartite division, discovered in the nineteenth century, is still valid today, although speech processing is clearly a highly complex process, and neuroscientists have recently begun to include additional areas of the brain in describing it.

At least our native language is learned unconsciously at first, then "aped" in social situations. Its most important function is to understand and be understood. Both grammar and context determine whether something is comprehensible. The sentence "It's black out there" can mean that I am describing what I see in front of me, but it could just as well mean that I am feeling pessimistic. Wittgenstein loathed sentences of this kind, but language is full of ambiguities. The simple truth is that the meaning of a sentence is formed by the *use* of words, which condemns any idea of a precise language to failure.

Wittgenstein initially refused to acknowledge any criticism of the *Tractatus*. In his inimitable way, he claimed that the book had provided the definitive answers, so it would make no sense for him to continue in philosophy, where he had made such a momentous mark. He distributed his enormous fortune among his siblings and donated considerable sums of money to young writers, painters, and architects. The next stage was an excursion into practical pedagogy. This philosopher, who had enjoyed great renown, at least in England, attended a pedagogical institute in Vienna and spent several years quasi-incognito, working as an elementary school teacher in a rural area in Austria. His teaching stint was spectacularly unsuccessful, and the children appear to have loathed him. By 1926, he had had enough of teaching, and he resigned. Wittgenstein spent the next few months as a gardener's assistant in a monastery, until he found a new project to throw himself into. Working with an architect, he designed and built his sister Margarete a Cubist villa in Vienna; he focused primarily on the interior design. The house became a gathering point for the Viennese intelligentsia, and the Vienna Circle often met there. In 1929, Wittgenstein returned to Cambridge after an absence of fifteen years. He was finally awarded his doctorate for the *Tractatus*, but his subsequent work in many ways belied the claims in his earlier writings. He wrote and worked around the clock, but he did not consider any of the results suitable for publication. He cobbled together a paltry living from lecturing and stipends, but at the age of fifty he finally became a professor after all. During all that time he was a "hermit, ascetic, guru, and *Führer*," as one of his students later recalled—a character in a novel who fell from riches to rags and was a legend unto himself even in his lifetime.

It eventually dawned on Wittgenstein that his theory of language as a picture of reality was incorrect. A colleague in Cambridge, the Italian economist Piero Sraffa, dealt his theory the final blow. When Wittgenstein emphasized that language mirrored the logical structure of reality, Sraffa brushed the underside of his chin with an outward sweep of his fingertips and asked: "What is the logical form of *that*?" Wittgenstein gave up his picture theory. He dedicated his final work, the *Philosophical Investigations*, which he began in earnest in 1936 after numerous false starts, to Sraffa. The book, which did not appear in print until 1953, two years after Wittgenstein's death, relinquished not only the picture theory but also the idea that language can be grasped solely by means of logic. The most picturesque sentence in this book, which would later delight the writer Ingeborg Bachmann, reads: "Our language can be seen as an ancient city: a maze of little streets and squares, of old and new houses, and of houses with additions from various periods; and this surrounded by a multitude of new boroughs with straight regular streets and uniform houses." Wittgenstein realized that "the meaning of a word is its use in the language." Instead of pinning down meanings and sentence structure by means of logic, philosophers would have to endeavor to clarify the rules of language use, the various "language games." He now discovered the significance of psychology, which he had dismissed before. Since language games exist not in a vacuum but in human communities, they ought to be explained not logically but *psycho*logically. The world needs psychologists not to analyze our emotions, but to explain language games in their social context, because "a main source of our failure to understand is that we do not *command a clear view* of the use of our words." Later in the text, he gave this idea a nice metaphorical twist: "What is your aim in philosophy?—To show the fly the way out of the fly-bottle."

Wittgenstein enlisted in the army for World War II, as he had for World War I, although this time he was on the British side. As a medical orderly, he put his experience in building airplanes to good use by developing laboratory equipment to measure pulse, blood pressure, respiratory rate, and respiratory volume. He spent another four years in Cambridge teaching until taking early retirement at the age of fifty-eight. He spent his final years in Ireland and in Oxford, dying of cancer in 1951. His last known words were a greeting to his friends: "Tell them I've had a wonderful life."

Wittgenstein's *Tractatus* may have been a dead end, but the *Philosophical Investigations* gave a tremendous impetus to both philosophy and the emerging field of linguistics. The new discipline of analytical philosophy, inspired by Wittgenstein, was quite possibly the most significant philosophical approach of the second half of the twentieth century. Philosophical problems, he argued, always need to be understood and analyzed as problems of linguistic expression, because the manner in which people experience the world is always influenced by their language. There are no "pure" sensory perceptions uncolored by thinking (in language), nor is meaning ever unequivocal, because language is plurivalent. Analytical philosophy carves its paths through this intertwined jungle of sensory perception and language.

The field of linguistics took up Wittgenstein's theory of "language games" and explored the meaning of speech in its broader context. In the 1950s and '60s, John Langshaw Austin in England and John Rogers Searle in the United States developed a theory of "speech acts." Austin realized that "by saying something, we *do* something." And the crucial question in understanding statements is not whether something is true or false, but rather whether the communication is successful or unsuccessful in the intended sense. A theory establishing the truth value of language had evolved into a theory of social communication.

Human language is an outstanding means of communication, but Wittgenstein showed that language does not provide our exclusive access to the truth. It is only when we recognize that thinking and language, the organizational tools of the mind, do not organize reality per se, but act as models to explain the world in accordance with their own rules, that we gain a better understanding of man. As we notice different things, our experience takes a different path, which shapes our thinking and makes us employ a different mode of expression. The fact that our differing perceptions result in different ways of thinking and speaking is what truly distinguishes man from the other animals. The boundaries of our sensory apparatus and our language are the boundaries of our world, because the words we choose to clothe our thinking in come from a neatly organized closet of the human species. We might say that the tacit mandate of language is to "fool" us about the realistic nature of its statements. It was made to "construct" reality and the world according to the needs of human species. If the serpent had needed a language for orientation—which it did not, because it connected sense perceptions without the aid of language—it would have been a "serpent language," altogether unsuitable for man, just as "human language" would serve no purpose for a serpent. "If a lion could talk," Wittgenstein noted astutely in the *Philosophical Investigations*, "we would not understand him."

Our philosophical, psychological, and biological journey to the capabilities and the limits of our cognition now comes to a temporary conclusion. We have learned about the origin and function of the brain. We have seen its potential and its limitations, and we have noted that feelings and intellect are often inseparably bound up in our brains. In doing so, we have touched on the question of how a sense of self develops. We have seen how conscious and unconscious intermingle, and that we still know very little about how the brain stores and forgets meanings. We have learned that the brain is a highly complex and ingenious organ of self-understanding, albeit one that was not constructed for the purpose of an objective knowledge of the world. We have seen what purpose our language serves, and the difficulties it has in being "objective." Contemplating ourselves and the world is like crossing a river by car, or the Sahara by tricycle. It can be done, but it is quite a laborious process. Still, we now know several important pieces of the puzzle, and we are gaining some insight into what makes us tick.

Now our journey inside ourselves will venture in another direction and explore the question of how we assess our actions. Neuroscience, which has come in handy along the way, will now step back for a bit and cede center stage to philosophy. We will continue to return to it on occasion, even when considering the question of good and evil. But whatever biology has to tell us, questions of morality are first and foremost philosophical, and at times psychological as well: Where do our criteria for right and wrong originate? What do we use to gauge our behavior, and why do we do so?

What Should I Do?

Rousseau's Error
Do We Need Other People?

The receptionist at the broadcasting company where I sometimes work is a haggard middle-aged woman whose grouchiness is legendary. Her abrasive manner annoys everyone who comes in expecting to receive a friendly greeting. But whenever she sees my son Oskar, she becomes a different person. Her eyes sparkle, her face lights up, and she showers Oskar with affection. It doesn't seem to matter to her that my son doesn't reciprocate her enthusiasm. When we leave, she hovers in the doorway with a look of bliss on her face.

I know nothing about this woman's personal life, but I can't imagine that she has many close friends. I assume that even with the social interaction required by her job, she is deeply lonely. Her plight seems downright depressing to me—yet the philosopher Jean-Jacques Rousseau might well have disagreed.

Rousseau was a true eccentric. Born in 1712 in Geneva, he was apprenticed to an engraver, but he left after a short time and took to the road. He dreamed of becoming a musician, but he did not play an instrument. The only thing that came of his dream was a strange new system of musical notation that did not interest anyone. For most of his adult life, he wandered about aimlessly, living off women who found his dark hair and big brown eyes handsome and supported him despite his nuttiness. Rousseau never stayed in one place for very long. In Paris he met the leaders of the Enlightenment, but they did not take well to him.

One day in October 1749, when Rousseau was thirty-seven, his life changed so drastically that he later referred to that day as a true "illumination." The vagrant music critic was heading southeast on a country road from Paris to the castle of Vincennes, which was then a state prison that housed several famous inmates, most notably Count Mirabeau, the Marquis de Sade, and the Enlightenment philosopher Denis Diderot. Rousseau was on his way to visit the latter because he was writing brief entries for inclusion in Diderot's famous comprehensive encyclopedia, the *Encyclopédie*. Somewhere along the way to Vincennes, Rousseau came across a copy of the *Mercure de France*, the most influential newspaper in Paris at the time, and read an announcement for a prize being offered by the Academy of Dijon for the best essay answering the question of whether advances in science and art had led to moral progress. In a histrionic letter to his friend Malesherbes, Rousseau conveyed the sense of epiphany and mission he felt when he saw the essay question. As is evident from his letter, modesty and restraint were not his strong suits:

> I fell across the question of the Academy of Dijon which gave rise to my first writing. If anything has ever resembled a sudden inspiration, it is the motion that was caused in me by that reading; suddenly I felt my mind dazzled by a thousand lights; crowds of lively ideas presented themselves at the same time with a strength and a confusion that threw me into an inexpressible perturbation; I feel my head seized by a dizziness similar to drunkenness. A violent palpitation oppresses me, makes me sick to my stomach; not being able to breathe anymore while walking, I let myself fall under one of the trees of the avenue, and I pass a half-hour there in such an agitation that when I got up again I noticed the whole front of my coat soaked with my tears without having felt that I shed them. Oh Sir, if I had ever been able to write a quarter of what I saw and felt under that tree, how clearly I would have made all the contradictions of the social system seen, with what strength I would have exposed all the abuses of our institutions, with what simplicity I would have demonstrated that man is naturally good and that it is from these institutions alone that men become wicked. Everything that I was able to

retain of these crowds of great truths which illuminated me under that tree in a quarter of an hour has been weakly scattered about in my three principal writings, namely that first discourse, the one on inequality, and the treatise on education, which three works are inseparable and together form the same whole. . . . That is how when I was thinking about it least, I became an author almost in spite of myself.

Rousseau's submission—*A Discourse on the Arts and Sciences*—earned him first prize and made him famous overnight, but more famous still was his astonishing submission to another essay competition a few years later, which came to be known as *A Discourse on Inequality*. This second essay, which put Rousseau's quarrelsome temperament on full display, was not what the judges were expecting, and he did not win the prize. In the essay, Rousseau declared in no uncertain terms that culture and society made man not better, but worse: "Men are wicked; a sad and constant experience makes proof unnecessary; yet man is naturally good, I believe I have proved it. . . . Let human Society be ever so much admired, it remains none the less true that it necessarily moves men to hate one another in proportion as their interests clash."

In Rousseau's view, people were good by nature, but all the lying and killing in the world were evidence that something had prompted the rise of evil. Rousseau regarded man as inherently unsocial. Like other animals, he argued, human beings by nature try to avoid confrontation and conflict. Aside from caring for his own well-being, the only pronounced feeling that comes naturally to man is empathy with others. Unfortunately, however, man does not have the luxury of remaining in solitude. Natural catastrophes and other external circumstances force people to join forces, but living together in a community also pits them against one another. They grow distrustful and malevolent; in comparing themselves to others, their own sense of self twists into narcissism, and their "innate goodness" breaks down.

Rousseau's essay was criticized harshly, although most Enlightenment philosophers shared his critical stance regarding western European feudal society. In the mid-eighteenth century, both the nobility and the peasants lived off the fields, with the nobility getting the wheat and the peasants the chaff. But few could accept Rousseau's proposition that society and culture themselves turned man bad. The intellectuals at that time cherished the arts and the social sphere, and they hailed and supported scientific progress. Science in particular seemed to be the key to liberating the bourgeoisie from the dominance of the nobility. In place of the omnipresent feudal society, many dreamed of a society that valued vigorous discussion and knowledge over social hierarchies.

Rousseau was furious at the reception of his essay, and he defended his position stridently. He was a talented writer, and several of his books had become quite popular; indeed, he was the most widely discussed philosopher among the European intellectuals of his day. But he could not tolerate criticism, and he became increasingly abrasive. Wherever he turned up on his travels through western Europe, he was sure to spark controversy. As a father he was a total failure; his five children wound up in a foundling hospital, where they apparently died soon after. By the final years of his life, Rousseau had become so antisocial that he seemed to be making himself a test case for the ruinous nature of civilization. He sought solitude at the castle of Ermenonville, outside Paris, and devoted his days to gathering and identifying plants.

Which of Rousseau's claims proved correct? Is man good by nature? And does man really not need other people in order to be happy? The question of whether people are happier in society or in solitude is more of a psychological question than a philosophical one, and one that was overlooked for quite some time after Rousseau. In the early 1970s, a discipline known as "loneliness research" was established. Its founder was Robert Weiss, now professor emeritus at the University of Massachusetts. He contended that loneliness was one of the chief problems in society, particularly in urban areas. Were people happier in solitude because they did not have to contend with anyone else?

Weiss was certain that Rousseau was mistaken. Lonely people suffer when few or no people take an interest in their well-being, and their suffering is most intense when no one connects emotionally with them. This fact was already common knowledge and is relatively intuitive. But Weiss discovered something far more exciting: More frustrating than the lack of outreach from others is the lack of outreach we ourselves extend. Not being loved is difficult, but, Weiss discovered, having no one to love is even worse. Weiss's contention explains why a dog or a cat can be so important to lonely senior citizens who have lost a spouse, even though these pets are clearly not adequate substitutes for their deceased loved one.

Weiss's discovery brings us back to the receptionist who was happy to see my son even though he paid no attention to her, let alone loved her. Simple interactions with him—touching and complimenting him—were all she needed to brighten her day. Loving someone or showering attention on another person is a very nice way of doing yourself some good in the process, which goes against Rousseau's theory that people can be truly happy only in solitude.

People, like all other primates, are social by nature. Among the more than two hundred species of apes, not a single one lives in complete isolation. Some people are naturally more social than others, but people who do not engage with others at all invariably suffer from a clear behavioral disorder. Frustration and disappointment may have embittered them and driven them to behave in an abnormal manner. Normal people seek out other people because they are interested in them (in some more than others, of course), and because their interest in other people does them good. People trapped within their own narrowly defined confines have stunted psyches and typically become claustrophobic, rigid, inflexible, and less able to cope with outside pressures. Because they lack the opportunity to compare their perceptions to those of other people, they misjudge many things about others and themselves.

A willingness to interact with and care for others is a way of reaching beyond one's own boundaries. Doing unto others gives your own psyche a boost. If you pick out a nice present for someone and witness the recipient's pleasure, you have given yourself a gift. This pleasure in giving and in doing good deeds goes back to the roots of mankind. But where does the pleasure in caring for and helping others and the joy in doing good deeds come from? Does this mean that man is "good," as Rousseau thought? Was he right in at least that regard?

The Sword of the Dragon Slayer
Why Do We Help Others?

The situation was dire. Three adults lunged at a small and vulnerable girl named Fawn, while her mother and sisters stood rooted to the spot with fear. The three assailants, who far surpassed Fawn in strength, bit Fawn on all sides in a brutal attack, regularly turning to glare at Fawn's mother and sisters so as to keep them away. Fawn was beside herself. Eventually, another bystander interceded, and the assailants dispersed, leaving Fawn on the ground. She lay there for quite a while, screaming. In time, she assumed a seated position, but she remained hunched over, looking wretched and exhausted. Her older sister came over and put an arm around her. Fawn was too dazed to react, and her sister gently prodded her, as though attempting to wake her up, then embraced her again, and the two sisters cuddled together.

This dramatic scene is a true story that took place in the 1980s in Madison, Wisconsin, but the police did not intervene, and no newspaper carried the story. Frans de Waal, the interceding bystander, was the only witness able to provide an account of the events surrounding the attack. The reason is simple. De Waal is an ethologist, and the attack on Fawn took place in the Wisconsin National Primate Research Center. Fawn, her family, and her assailants were rhesus monkeys.

De Waal has been working with monkeys for the past thirty years. His early studies of chimpanzees in the Arnhem Zoo in Holland, when very little was known about their patterns of behavior, revealed the astonishing extent to which they are social animals who require life in a community. He learned that chimpanzees cheat, lie, and deceive one another, but that they are also tender and affectionate and establish complex social relationships. De Waal chose the revealing title *Chimpanzee Politics* for his book about the chimpanzees of Arnhem.

Chimpanzees are not the only apes capable of feeling sympathy and affection. Fawn's sister—a rhesus monkey—embraced her and cuddled with her when she evidently felt her sister's pain and wanted to ease her plight. Although the genetic difference between rhesus monkeys and humans amounts to approximately 3 percent, rhesus monkeys display signs of empathy and "moral" behavior. But where do these feelings come from, and why do they exist?

The question is more difficult than it first appears. Charles Darwin's mid-nineteenth-century proof that people are close relatives of primates, and hence animals, provided a persuasive explanation for the origins of human "evilness": Man can be evil because he descended from animals. Darwin used the phrases "struggle for existence" and "survival of the fittest" to describe evolution. Although he had not invented these concepts himself, he was the first to apply them to the way all living creatures, from a blade of grass to an ant to a man, compete with one another and among themselves. In simple terms, survival of the fittest means that there are billions upon billions of organisms whizzing through the world with a single mission: to assert their genetic makeup against all others, to the detriment, suffering, or even death of others. And every human being is part of this evil and immoral game.

But Darwin was a very cautious individual. He acknowledged that the principle he had come upon was somewhat questionable, and he stopped short of drawing conclusions about human interaction from his insights into biology. Others, however, have not been as cautious, claiming that only the best and strongest should survive and that the sickly and weak should simply be killed. Darwin's evidence that man is essentially an animal was greeted with alarm by philosophers. It forces us to question what human nature really is. When Rousseau spoke about "nature," he had in mind nature as an ideal state of unalloyed happiness. But was nature actually good? Wasn't it also barbaric, ruthless, and cruel?

In 1893, the auditorium in Oxford was packed when Thomas Henry

Huxley, a close friend of Darwin, gave a lecture with the grand title "Evolution and Ethics." The crowd hung on the great biologist's every word. Nature, Huxley proclaimed, is not good but cruel, perfidious, and utterly indifferent to man. Man is undeniably an animal that owes its existence to chance and to a succession of apelike animal species, not to a "master plan" guided by clever reason. If there was only chaos and no master plan, Huxley concluded, the will to be good or to act rationally cannot be a characteristic of nature.

In Huxley's view, Rousseau's "innate goodness" was utter nonsense. Animals and humans were not good by nature, but amoral. But even so, Huxley could not deny that humans were capable of moral behavior. In England, where he lived, there were laws against murder and theft. Law and order enforced by the state meant that people could go out into the street without always having to fear for their lives.

But where did this order come from? Huxley concluded that civilization and culture were meant to harness man's primal, animalistic drives, which was the exact opposite of Rousseau's view that man was innately good and civilization bad. For Huxley, man was bad, but civilization kept man in check. Morality, Huxley stated, is not a natural characteristic of man: "The ethical progress of society depends not on imitating the cosmic process, still less in running away from it, but in combating it." Frans de Waal has added lyrical punch to Huxley's argument by calling society a "sword forged by *Homo sapiens* to slay the dragon of its animal past."

Anyone who, like Rousseau, was convinced that man was good by nature found it necessary to explain the rise of evil. Huxley faced the opposite question. If man was bad by nature, where does "the ethical progress of society" come from? Since Huxley was not religious, he did not find its origins in God. If there is nothing good in man by nature, how was it possible for the interaction of all those bestial people to have led to a reasonably well regulated society? Where does morality come from—if not from human nature? And if man is not moral by nature, why does he have the capacity to act morally?

The question is thus whether there is something within man that impels him to behave well toward others. If Darwin and Huxley had known as much about apes and primates as Frans de Waal, they would have had an easier time coming up with an explanation, and terrible misunderstandings might have been avoided. Primatology has shown that there is no contradiction between morality and evolution. Morality, which strikes some people as a stupid error on the part of nature, which otherwise recognizes only the right of the stronger, is actually a biologically ingenious adaptation. Thirty years of observing apes have convinced de Waal that being good-natured and helping others are behaviors that can bring great rewards to both the individual and the group as a whole. The more that apes help and care for one another, the better the whole community fares. The manner of social support varies tremendously. Even the four major great apes (orangutans, chimpanzees, bonobos, and gorillas) are quite different in this respect. While sex for chimpanzees nearly always entails power, dominance, and subjugation, bonobos use their very frequent sexual intercourse to dispel tension quickly. Bonobos indulge in sex virtually all day long, especially in the so-called missionary position, with the partners face to face. (Strictly speaking, it ought to be called the "bonobo position," because bonobos used it long before missionaries.)

The "struggle for existence" does not occur among isolated animals—Darwin and Huxley were wrong on that score. With rare exceptions, humans are not merciless lone warriors; most of us are also members of a family and of larger social groups, in which we seek not merely to supplant others but also to care for those within the group. The ability to think and act on behalf of another person is known as altruism. Great apes also exhibit many facets of altruistic behavior. De Waal distinguishes an altruism *aimed at inclusive fitness*, such as the instinctive love a mother has for her offspring, from *reciprocal* altruism, which may have been the origin of human morality: One ape helps another in order to be helped when in need, refraining from certain bad behaviors so that the others are not bad in return. Evidently the rule "Do unto others as you would have others do unto you" applies to great apes as well.

Human weaknesses, aggressions, deceit, and selfishness are not the only holdovers of our distant past as apelike creatures; our "noble" characteristics are part of our initial biological nature as well. Rousseau surmised that the capacity to be good was a primeval instinct and that our natural self-love forces us to be good in accord with this instinct. For Rousseau, good behavior was the only conduct that came naturally to man. De Waal considers affection, consideration, and kindness typical primate instincts, but he finds that they are in steady competition with aggression, mistrust, and egoism. People and apes are therefore neither "good" nor "bad." They are capable of both behaviors, and the one comes as naturally as the other. But if the ability to be good is just one instinct among others, who or what ensures that people use that ability? What makes it a binding principle in human society?

The Law Within Me
Why Should I Be Good?

The year was 1730. A mother and her six-year-old son were taking an evening stroll near the gates of Königsberg (now Kaliningrad in Russia), a cosmopolitan town on the Baltic Sea. Lovingly and in great detail, the mother explained to her son what she knew about nature, about plants and herbs, animals and stones. The streets were dimly lit, and it grew dark out. The woman showed her attentive son the starry sky above them. They looked up, spellbound, into the infinite distance. The boy was fascinated. "Two things," he later wrote, "fill the mind with ever new and increasing wonder and awe, the oftener and more steadily we reflect on them: the starry heavens above me and the moral law within me. . . . I see them before me, and I associate them directly with the consciousness of my own existence." As it turned out, astronomy and moral philosophy were two areas in which he would make great strides.

The boy's name was Immanuel Kant, and his happy childhood under the care of his devout and well-educated mother came to an end when she died just after he had turned thirteen. The slender boy with clear blue eyes would grieve deeply for a long time to come. His father, a leather cutter, did everything in his power to give his sensitive son a good start in life. He sent him to the Friedrichskollegium, the best high school in their town. There, and later at the University of Königsberg, the young man proved to be a talented student. He could not tear himself away from the observatory on the roof of the school building, where he often spent long evenings gazing at the stars. At the age of sixteen, he passed the entrance examination for the University of Königsberg. Although he was supposed to be studying theology, he spent most of his time on mathematics, philosophy, and physics. In his spare time, he excelled as a cook and a gambler. He was an outstanding billiards player, and although he spoke softly and tended to mumble, he was a welcome guest at parties in Königsberg. His great passion, however, remained the cosmos. Kant's professor of logic and metaphysics, Martin Knutzen, supported him to the best of his ability. His reflecting telescope—the same kind the great physicist Isaac Newton had used—entranced Kant, who read Newton's seminal work about the structure of the universe; immersed himself in numbers, charts, and calculations; and derived his own model of the physical world. The slim volume he wrote on this subject had a colossal objective and a commanding title to match: *Universal Natural History and Theory of the Heavens.* Dispensing with mathematical calculations, he attempted to fathom the makeup of the world purely by means of his own deductions. The project was as strange as it was ambitious. Although scientists barely acknowledged his book, Kant judged his method a success, and he retained it for other areas of inquiry, certain that many of his insights were correct. Long after his death, his theories were indeed substantiated. He envisioned the solar system we have today as having originated solely by means of a process of attraction and repulsion of the elements—the first attempt to explain the genesis of the planetary system without the hand of God.

Although his published views were forceful and progressive, Kant was flummoxed when it came to planning his career. His postgraduate path was anything but straight and narrow. He frittered away nine years of his life as a private tutor and waited until what was then considered the ripe old age of thirty-one to complete his dissertation, which was on the subject of fire. He lectured at the university for minimal pay, and his professional development went nowhere until he reached the age of forty. Kant was highly gifted, fiercely intelligent, and interested in nearly everything: theology and pedagogy, natural law and geography, anthropology and logic, metaphysics and mathematics, mechanics and physics. Eventually the university offered him a professorship, but—to his horror—in the field of poetry, which would require him to hold ceremonial addresses interspersed with his own poems. Kant turned it down. It took him a full fifteen years of teaching to attain a coveted professorship in logic and metaphysics.

Realizing that his shaky health would not leave him much more time to make his mark on philosophy, Kant introduced rigid routines into his day. His life became the epitome of boredom. The writer Heinrich Heine later quipped that the life story of Kant is hard to describe, for he had neither a life nor a story. His servant was instructed to wake him up at five in the morning. He took a walk at the same time every day, and he went to bed at ten in the evening. He wound up living a long life, and was nearly eighty when he died. His daily routine seemed like one long protest song against life. But the books he wrote over the course of his thirty-four years as a philosopher were anything but boring. Many consider them the most significant oeuvre in German-language philosophy.

Kant did not regard the human mind the way a naturalist or a theologian would, as many philosophers had before him, but rather like a legal scholar in search of "laws." As a young man, he had attempted to decipher the "systematic constitution" of the cosmos. As a philosopher, he endeavored to find rules and patterns from which to derive binding laws of the human mind. To do so, he first had to address what may be the most important question in philosophy: What can I know, and how can I be sure of what I know? Like Descartes 150 years earlier, Kant decided to seek the certainty of knowledge not in things but in human thought. Kant called this philosophical approach, which explores the preconditions of our knowledge, transcendental idealism. But he stopped far short of Descartes in concluding where this knowledge could lead. Descartes had believed that human thought could discern the "true" nature of things, whereas Kant felt that this "true" nature was wholly inaccessible to man. And why should it be accessible? The "order of nature," he posited, is "ordered" by the human brain. Just as colors are produced not by nature, but by our eyes and our optic nerves, so the human mind creates an order and imposes it on nature. Man thus has a perceptive and cognitive capability to structure the world. "The understanding," he wrote in his *Prolegomena to Any Future Metaphysics*, "does not draw its (a priori) laws from nature, but prescribes them to it." Kant then applied this productive and modern idea to the question of morality.

He proceeded very cautiously at first. He did not think much of instincts, which Rousseau had believed in, and steered clear of simplistic classifications and the question of whether man was good or bad "by nature." Man, he argued, was equipped with a set of templates to grasp the world, and these evidently included a template for moral conduct.

Man's ability to be good made such a deep impression on Kant that he conferred a very special mark of distinction on man: "human dignity." He believed that man's freedom to act morally placed him above all other creatures. No other animal, Kant argued, is capable of deciding and acting freely. And because man is the greatest of all beings, there is nothing that counts more than a human life. The phrase "human dignity" was not Kant's invention; it had first been used three hundred years earlier by the Italian philosopher Giovanni Pico della Mirandola, one of the great Renaissance thinkers. Man, Pico della Mirandola asserted, is an autonomous being with the dignity to think and act freely, so his decisions and ambitions are of his own devising.

Kant was not concerned with whether man was good by nature, but rather with how the fact of being human *obliged* man to be good. Kant explored the faculty of human reason to discover a natural principle that makes morality possible. He reasoned that neither talent nor character nor life circumstances assured goodness—the will did. The only good thing about man was his good will. If people wish to get along, they need to abide by good will, not just as a motivation, but as an unshakable law. Kant called this adherence to good conduct the "categorical imperative." In its best known formulation in the *Critique of Practical Reason*, this imperative reads: "Act only according to that maxim whereby you can at the same time will that it should become a universal law."

In other words, Kant believed that since man is capable of *wanting* to be good, man *should* be good. For Kant, this conclusion did not reflect a morality that he himself had drawn up, but was simply a logical function of human reason. Moral law inhered within man, and Kant was merely analyzing it, the way he had analyzed the cosmos earlier in his life. For him, the obligation to be good was a natural phenomenon, like the sky and the stars, so the categorical imperative was universally valid, and it could and should be applied by all. People who heed the moral law within them are good people who do good deeds, even if their good intentions lead to bad outcomes. If the will is good, Kant believed, the action is morally justified.

Kant was quite satisfied with his system of thought, although he later worried whether the system he had worked out so carefully would stand up to biological scrutiny. He finally convinced himself that the "schematism of our understanding" is likely to be "an art concealed in the depths of the human soul, whose real modes of activity nature is hardly likely ever to allow us to discover, and to have open to our gaze." His regimented life offered him refuge from his relatively mild anxieties. At the age of sixty, he could afford his own house, a servant, and a cook, but in the years to follow, his formerly sharp brain was weakened by Alzheimer's, and he moved from increasing forgetfulness to a complete loss of orientation. On February 12, 1804, at 11:00 A.M., he died in an advanced state of dementia.

At the time of Kant's death, his renown was already considerable, and his fame would continue to grow. Many philosophers compare his achievements in philosophy to those of Copernicus, who showed that the earth revolves around the sun. Kant likewise overthrew previous conceptions of how we understand the world, demonstrating that our understanding scans the world according to its own set structures and claiming that each individual carries within him a logical scheme that obliges him to be good.

But is there actually a logical scheme of this kind, a "moral law" within us? If there is, how did it get there, and where is it? To find out why man should be good, we first need to know why man strives to be good in the first place. Kant was never able to address this point. Throughout his life, he was quite taken with science, and he would have loved to gain scientific insight into how the "schematism of our understanding" functions and have it "unveiled before our eyes." But in Kant's day, no one was studying primates, and neuroscience was in its infancy. The German physician Franz Joseph Gall had just begun to measure the brain, but his maps of brain functions were as bizarre as the nautical charts of the Atlantic before Columbus, and he could make only vague speculations about what occurred in the brain.

As a young man, Kant had been interested in the cosmos, and he tried to analyze the sky mathematically. Later he attempted to fathom the human mind and its laws. But his efforts were like those of a physicist trying to calculate the movements of planets and the laws of the universe without the benefit of even the tiniest telescope. Kant could speculate about the human brain, but he could not peer inside. Today, scientists do have the requisite telescope. They measure with electrodes, and they scan the human brain with magnetic resonance imaging. So we can again pose the questions that

Kant was unable to answer: Is there a center for morality in the brain? If so, how is it constructed, and how does it function? And how does it control our ability to act morally?

But before we turn to these fascinating questions, we have to shed light on a fundamental issue. Kant had declared reason the lord and master of the brain, and he was certain that reason dictated our actions. But as we saw in the first part of this book, the unconscious shapes us to a far greater extent than does the conscious, so we need to figure out to what extent the moral law within us is affected by drives other than reason—by our feeling, thinking, and volition.

The Libet Experiment
Can I Will What I Will?

This chapter will be on the long side, for two good reasons. One is that we will be meeting a man who was quite a character, and certainly one of the most inventive figures in philosophy. He himself once said: "The time will come when those who do not know what I have said on a given subject will be revealed as ignoramuses." Modesty was not his forte. And the other reason is that the chapter will address a very vital issue, one of the most hotly debated philosophical questions of his day.

Let us begin with our philosopher. Arthur Schopenhauer was the son of a wealthy merchant in Danzig (now Gdansk, Poland). In 1793, when little Arthur was five years old, the family moved to Hamburg. His ambitious father had big plans for him, and when he turned fifteen, his father sent him off to a series of day schools and boarding schools in Holland, France, Switzerland, Austria, Silesia, Prussia, and England. No sooner had Schopenhauer settled in somewhere than he had to leave again, which took a tremendous toll on him. He spoke fluent English and French, but he was withdrawn and distrustful of others and always felt like an outsider. When he was seventeen, his father made him enter the world of business. Then tragedy struck: His father died quite unexpectedly, likely a suicide. Schopenhauer suffered terribly from the death of his father, whom he feared but also respected and admired. Schopenhauer moved to Weimar with his mother, who was finally able to realize her dream of establishing a literary salon, which was a brilliant success. Weimar was only a small town in Thuringia, but all the major literary figures of the time—Goethe, Schiller, Wieland, Herder—lived and worked there.

The young Schopenhauer was aghast at the sight of Goethe and the other stars of the literary scene sprawled on his father's chairs and sofas. While his mother was entranced by her distinguished visitors, Schopenhauer reserved his most cutting remarks for the new salon. Despite his intelligence and good looks, he felt misunderstood. When he turned twenty-one, his mother asked him to move out. He was given part of his inheritance and he moved to Göttingen, and later to Berlin and Jena, to study medicine, science, and philosophy.

At the age of twenty-five, he wrote a skeptical, uncompromising, and radical dissertation explaining that man is incapable of gaining any objective knowledge of the world. Perception, he argued, is limited to what our mammalian brains allow us to see. He went well beyond Kant, who had assumed that human cognition was a highly refined and useful instrument. Schopenhauer, in contrast, did not give consciousness much credit. Schopenhauer's mother considered the book unrefined and boring and thought its title (*The Fourfold Root of the Principle of Sufficient Reason*) made it sound like "something for pharmacists." As luck would have it, Goethe, whom Schopenhauer did not hold in especially high regard, was impressed by the young man's clever reasoning, and he prophesied that this brilliant young man would have a distinguished literary career. Goethe sent Schopenhauer a copy of his *Theory of Colors*, of which he was proud. Schopenhauer, who knew quite a bit about the natural sciences, considered Goethe's book worthless prattle, and he had an unfortunate tendency to announce his opinions for all the world to hear. To add insult to injury, he proceeded to write his own theory of colors, whereupon Goethe broke off all contact with him. From then on, no one made the mistake of offering support to the arrogant young upstart.

In 1820, Schopenhauer held a series of philosophy lectures at the University of Berlin. To upstage the great star of the university, Georg Wilhelm Friedrich Hegel, Schopenhauer set the time of his lectures for the same hour as Hegel's; but his plan backfired. Hundreds of students flocked to Hegel, and only four or five to Schopenhauer. But he continued to regard himself as a genius, even as others were turned off by his arrogance. When the university chided him for his near-empty classroom, he left in a huff and moved to Frankfurt, where he churned out one book after another. His neighbors were intrigued by his habit of talking to himself on the street, his abiding love for his poodles but dislike of his fellow man, and his constant fear of being poisoned. Later in life he finally achieved some degree of renown, but he did not bask in his fame. His view of man had become rather grim, notwithstanding his smug satisfaction in the knowledge that "the world has learned something from me that it will never forget."

Schopenhauer's proudest achievement came very early on: at the age of thirty, he published his magnum opus, *The World as Will and Representation.* It did not attract much attention at first, but it focused on an issue that Kant, Hegel, and many other philosophers had disregarded. Nearly all of them worked on the assumption that the mind or reason guides human actions and that man's sole mission in life is to adhere to the dictates of reason. Schopenhauer was deeply mistrustful of that assumption, and he posed one of the most challenging questions in philosophy: "Can I will what I will?"

It was a provocative question that had enormous implications. If it is *not* true that we can really will what we will—that our intentions are not really formed freely and rationally—then our will is not free and the faculty of reason is rendered superfluous. And what becomes of the categorical imperative, the "moral law" underlying the faculty of reason? It becomes immaterial, because the laws governing my actions are determined not by rationality but by the irrational will. Schopenhauer went on to assert that the command headquarters in the brain is not reason but the will. It is the unconscious that determines our existence and our character. The will is the master and the mind is its servant. The mind is excluded from the actual decisions and hidden resolutions of the will, and it has no idea what is going on behind the scenes. The will says what to do, and the mind follows suit. The operative point, Schopenhauer tells us, is this: "What opposes the heart is not admitted by the head."

Is that true? Let's try an example. Think back to your childhood and imagine a day when you didn't feel like going to sixth-period math class and thought about skipping it. You struggled with the decision for a bit. You were bad at math, and that's why you didn't want to go, but if you didn't go, you could fall even further behind; still, the idea of sitting in that classroom was loathsome. So you dithered, unaware of just how determined you were not to go, even with all your misgivings about staying away. Your conscious mind didn't realize that your will had already made its decision. Then you learned that a couple of classmates didn't want to go to sixth period either. Regardless of their actions, your decision to stay away would likely compromise your performance in math. But when you heard that your friends planned to cut class, an inescapable feeling of joy arose within you, almost to your own astonishment, and any remaining desire to go to math class vanished. Only then did your mind notice how committed your will already was to skipping class, even while your mind was still wavering and grappling with misgivings. So were you exercising free will? Not really. Your will knew in advance what it wanted, and it tacked on a specious argument to ease your mind. You told yourself that the others weren't going either, as though that mattered. Your will had done as it wished, and your mind just gave it the suitable justification.

Schopenhauer's emphasis on the will was a pointed attack on "thousands of years of philosophizing" that had assumed reason to be man's guiding principle. He claimed to have recognized the "fundamental error of all philosophers" and the "greatest of all illusions" to which they clung, namely, that knowing what constitutes goodness is all that is needed to lead a good life. Immanuel Kant had contended that reason dictates the will. But wasn't it really just the other way around: that reason *follows* the dictates of the will?

Doubt had crept into the citadel of reason, and this doubt would continue to grow. Let us now jump ahead to 1964, about a hundred years after Schopenhauer's death. Pope Paul VI enters the great hall, clad in formal robes for an official reception; the cardinals kneel down in their red robes and kiss his ring. Only the biologists, physicists, and neuroscientists remain seated and shake hands with Christ's representative on earth. The Pontifical Academy of Sciences has invited a group of the world's leading experts to the grand Renaissance edifice, the residence of Paul VI, to ponder the brain, a topic of great fascination to the scientists of the day. One new discovery in particular holds the attention of the researchers and bishops alike. A hitherto unknown neuroscientist from San Francisco has conducted a pioneering experiment that is amazing the leading brain researchers of the era, among them three Nobel Prize winners.

Benjamin Libet was born in 1916 in Chicago and earned his doctorate at the University of Chicago in physiology (rather than in neuroscience, which was rarely part of college curricula back in the 1930s). Libet's interest in whether the events that take place in our consciousness could be measured scientifically began when he was a young man. In the late 1950s, he experimented on several patients who had received only local anesthesia at the neurosurgical unit of Mount Zion Hospital in San Francisco. The patients were in the operating room with their brains partially exposed. Libet attached cables to their brains and applied weak electrical impulses, observing how and when the patients reacted. The result was spectacular: More than half a second elapsed from the time the cortex was stimulated to when the patients responded. When Libet's experiments came to the attention of the Vatican in 1964, he was unaware of two of his colleagues' similar achievement: they, too, had noted a time lag. Libet was astonished to find that nearly a second had elapsed between the intention to make a hand movement and the actual movement, a delay that defied common sense. Someone who intends to reach for a cup of tea does so right away, so how could this time lag be explained?

Libet concluded that there is always such a lag but it goes unnoticed. In 1979, he began a new experiment that became associated with his name and brought him international renown. Libet sat a test subject in an easy chair facing a large clocklike disk with a green dot that circled rapidly around it. Then he attached two cables, one reaching from the subject's wrist to an electric measuring device, and the other leading from a helmet on her head to another measuring device. He gave the subject the following instructions: *Look at the green dot on the clock. At a time that you select yourself, decide to flex your wrist. Notice where the green dot is when you decide to do it.* The subject did as she was told. She decided to flex her wrist and noted the position of the green dot. Libet asked her where the green dot was when she made her decision, and he wrote it down. His excitement mounted as he looked at his two instruments. The change in voltage of the electrodes on her wrist showed him the exact time of the movement, and the electrodes on her head indicated the brain's readiness to act. What was the chronological succession? First the electrodes on her head registered activity, then—a half-second later—came the moment of the test subject's decision, and about 0.2 seconds later the hand movement followed. Libet could not believe his eyes: The subject had decided to act a half-second *before* she was aware of her own decision! The preconscious reflex of wanting or doing something is quicker than conscious action. Did this mean that the brain introduces processes involving the will *before* the person is in any way aware of this will? And didn't this also spell the end of the philosophical idea of free will in humans?

Let us travel through time and have Arthur Schopenhauer and Benjamin Libet settle the issue together. We'll go back to, say, 1850, and head to Schopenhauer's apartment in Frankfurt, at Schöne Aussicht 17. It is early in the morning. Hold on! He is unavailable at that hour. We'll have to wait a bit. Schopenhauer always got up between 7:00 and 8:00 A.M. and washed the upper part of his body with cold water and a huge sponge, then bathed his eyes, which he regarded as the most valuable sense organ, by dunking them underwater repeatedly so as to strengthen the optic nerves. Then he sat down for coffee, which he brewed himself. His housekeeper was not allowed to show her face in the early morning; Schopenhauer considered it vital to direct his full attention to thinking at that time of day, when the brain is like a freshly tuned instrument. So, let's wait one more hour and then ring the bell. Libet, who is sympathetic to Schopenhauer's ideas, gets a fairly cordial reception, at least by Schopenhauer's standards. Schopenhauer hates small talk, so the men come straight to the point:

"So, Mr. Libet, what's the verdict? Can I will what I will?"

"To put it bluntly: No. I cannot will what I will."

"So it is just as I said? The will is the master, and the mind is his servant?"

"More or less."

"What?"

"Just as I said, 'more or less.'"

"What are you saying? What does it mean to say 'more or less'?"

"'More or less' means that one can never be quite sure."

"Why? The case is clear as day. You showed that the will precedes the conscious mind chronologically, by . . . ?"

"Roughly half a second."

"Exactly, Mr. Libet, half a second. And that means that the will dictates and the conscious mind lags behind. Isn't that so? And if the mind lags behind, there is no free will, because the will is not steered, but only registered and remarked upon. And all moral philosophy is down the drain."

"Well . . ."

"The conscious or reasonable view of things is not the essence of man, but only a decorative frill added after the fact, a rhetorical justification or a belated commentary."

"May I say something?"

"Please do."

"A half-second elapses between the impulse of the will and the conscious decision—that is correct. But an additional half-second elapses before the patient moves his wrist, which is to say, until he acts . . ."

"So?"

"That means he still has the option of breaking off his action."

"So?"

"That means that although there is no free will, there is something we might want to call a 'free won't,' which I can use to prevent bad things from happening."

"A 'free won't'? You have some weird ideas."

"Maybe that sounds strange, but I think that's how it is. The will may not be free, but the 'free won't' is! Whatever drives us to do something, we still have the option of saying 'Stop!' "

"And you think you proved that with the clock? That there is an unconscious nonfreedom and a conscious freedom?"

"Well, 'proved' may be overstating it. But that is what I believe."

"All on the basis of those simple experiments?"

"Now, Mr. Schopenhauer, I freely admit that my experiments were quite simple. But I believe they were significant. Also, it is good to believe that there is something that controls our will, which is, I argue, the 'free won't.' Have you ever thought what it would mean for society if we were to accept the idea that no one is responsible for his will and cannot be called to account for his actions? What do I do with a murderer, if all he has to do is to say: 'I didn't know what I was doing; my unconscious will made me do it, and I had no control over it. Just take a look at the writings of Schopenhauer and Libet!' "

"Mankind is in a devilish mess either way, with criminal trials or without them, with or without prisons."

"That is your opinion, Mr. Schopenhauer, but it won't get us anywhere."

We had better leave the conversation at this somewhat unpleasant juncture. Not much more is likely to come of it anyway. The positions are clear, and no compromise appears imminent. Benjamin Libet is surely right not to dispose of man's responsibility for his actions. And isn't Arthur Schopenhauer right to doubt that Libet's measurements are really all we need to propose grand theories about the will, the "won't," and consciousness? Neuroscience is still far from a full understanding of the complex interaction that constitutes human consciousness, including feelings of spirituality, creativity, conscious will, and imagination, let alone able to measure them. And every neuroscientist still seems to have his or her own theory about the relationship of the material to the intellectual. The actual problem in Libet's measurements is that he had to translate the measurements of electrodes attached at the brain into language. For example, he had to assign his measurements to the "subconsciousness" or "preconsciousness" while using the terms "consciousness" or "unconsciousness" for marking the dot on the clock. But what is "preconsciousness"? It seems reasonable enough to call a will that makes a wrist flex "preconscious," but what about the will that uses a series of varying impulses to solve a complex mathematical problem or design a philosophical argument? As revealing as Libet's measurements appear to be, they do not yield simple answers but instead raise new questions. The major issue of the freedom of the will cannot be addressed simply by ascertaining how much or how little time elapses between an impulse from the brain and the awareness of this impulse. Moreover, there are many different kinds of forces driving the will. Some are simple and intense, such as hunger, thirst, exhaustion, and sex drive; others are more intricate. The will to pass your final exams, study law, or throw a big birthday bash is more multifaceted than feeling hunger and the consequent will to eat.

What does all this mean for morality? Today, tens of thousands of brain researchers at hundreds of institutes around the world are hard at work exploring the brain, many of them also bent on learning about the instincts and driving forces behind moral actions. If all moral prescriptions ultimately spring from moral desires, there must be something in the human brain that triggers this will to be good. But what might that be?

The Case of Gage
Is There Morality in the Brain?

September 13, 1848, was a lovely day. The afternoon sun shone bright and hot, and Phineas Gage had been at work since the morning hours. Gage was an explosives expert, "the most efficient and capable man" in the employ of the Rutland & Burlington Railroad, as his bosses later noted. His job was to level a rocky piece of land for the new railroad line. The workers in Vermont were outside the town of Cavendish, and soon the tracks would be laid through the New England states and passengers could look forward to train travel from Rutland to Boston. Gage had just filled a new blast hole with explosive powder and a detonator and asked his assistant to plug the entrance to the hole with sand. He was reaching for the three-foot-seven-inch-long iron rod to tamp down the sand over the explosive when someone spoke to him from behind. He turned around and exchanged a few words while continuing to push the iron rod into the hole, but he failed to notice that his assistant had not filled in the sand. While Gage was talking and laughing, sparks started flying from the rocks. An explosion sent the iron rod hurling through Gage's left cheek into his brain; it pierced his skull and exited through the top of his head. Some eighty feet away the rod crashed to the ground, covered with blood and brain tissue. Gage lay there unmoving. The afternoon sun was shimmering over the rocks, and the horror-stricken railroad workers stood rooted to the spot. When a few of them ventured up to him, they were astonished to see that Phineas Gage was alive. Although he had a hole straight through his skull, and blood was gushing out of the open wound, he regained consciousness and was able to explain to his fellow workers what had happened. They lifted him onto an oxcart and took him to a nearby hotel. He sat upright and maintained his composure throughout this mile-long ride. The other railroad workers were flabbergasted to see Gage climb off the cart himself. He sat down on a chair in the hotel and waited for the doctor, whom he greeted with the jaunty remark, "Doctor, here is business enough for you."

Today, Gage's skull is housed at Harvard Medical School's Warren Anatomical Museum, and his case has proved to be quite the head-scratcher for the scientific establishment. Phineas Gage, who was twenty-five years old at the time of his accident, lived another thirteen years with his terrible head injury. The injured foreman could feel, hear, and see. He had no trace of paralysis in his limbs or his tongue. He lost vision in his left eye, but everything else was fully functional. He was steady on his feet, his hands were as dexterous as ever, and his speech was unimpaired. But he was no longer the same. His bosses were alarmed at the radical change in his personality and felt they could not keep him on the job. Gage found work on a series of horse farms, but after a short time at each job he either quit or was let go. He finally resorted to appearing as a circus attraction and as a museum curiosity, where he was put on display along with his iron rod. Eventually he emigrated to Chile, where he remained until shortly before his death. There, too, he worked on horse farms and as a stagecoach driver. In 1860, he returned to the United States, but he languished in dark alleys in San Francisco with hopeless drunks, suffering a series of epileptic attacks until he died at the age of thirty-eight. Gage was buried with his iron rod, which he had carried by his side until the end of his life. The newspapers that had once given headline coverage to his accident made no mention of his death.

Why had Gage's life gone so terribly awry? According to neuroscientists Hanna and Antonio Damasio, who studied his case, Gage learned and spoke normally for the rest of his life, with one notable exception: Several witnesses reported that Gage had lost all regard for the rules of social conduct. He lied and cheated shamelessly, was prone to angry outbursts and brawls, and no longer showed any sense of responsibility. What had happened? Was it possible that the injury to his brain had introduced serious character flaws into this formerly upstanding citizen? De Waal remarks that in in-

juries of this sort, "it is as if the moral compass of these people has been de-
magnetized, causing it to spin out of control." But wouldn't that imply that
there is a biological center for morality in the human brain?

Hanna Damasio and her team made a thorough examination of Gage's
skull and concluded that parts of his brain responsible for key human
traits, such as those involved in honoring his commitments to others, had
been destroyed. They believe that Gage had lost his sense of responsibility
and was no longer able to structure his life on his own. One specific region
in the brain, the ventromedial region of the frontal lobe, appeared to have
ceased functioning, while all other parts of the brain continued to work
normally. If the Damasios were correct, Gage's consciousness was compromised after the accident. The relationship between thinking and feeling,
decision making and perception, was no longer intact.

It should be noted that not everyone who studies Gage's story shares this
interpretation. Some have cast doubt on Gage's medical evaluation and
conclude that Gage's character had not changed as much as the Damasios
were assuming. After all, Gage did lose the job he had been trained for, and
thus his professional standing, as well as his basic physical appearance.
People react quite differently to a dapper foreman than to someone with a
grossly disfigured face. Might some of his odd behavior be attributable
quite simply to his deformity? Couldn't we just say that the accident may
have traumatized Gage, and leave it at that?

Justified as these doubts may be, they do little to alter the neurobiological findings. The Damasios confirmed their results in many experiments
with animals, and established that the ventromedial region is a key part of
the brain where feelings are processed and plans and decisions are made.
But while it might be nice to picture the ventromedial region as a little
computer center that prints our moral judgments on command, in actual-
ity it is much more complicated.

In *Finn Family Moomintroll*, a Finnish children's book by Tove Jansson
that I often read to my son Oskar before bed, the Hobgoblin grants the
Snork a wish, and the Snork asks for "a machine that tells you whether
things are right or wrong, good or bad." The Hobgoblin replies ruefully that
he is unable to produce a machine of that kind. Likewise, there is no single
mechanism in the brain that governs morality. It is not a self-contained
system in one particular region of the brain, but rather a highly complex
network involving several different regions. Thus, while there are certainly

places in the brain responsible for morality, no one specific part of the brain is the seat of moral feelings and decision making.

I made a point of differentiating between feelings and decision making in the last sentence, even though Benjamin Libet had linked the two in claiming that our feelings dictate our decisions. While that is true to some extent, brain research has now established that so many different regions of the brain are involved in our feelings and decision making that it is quite difficult to ascertain how the process of making decisions functions. Feelings, abstract thinking, and all the regions of the brain associated with interpersonal relations work in concert and constantly overlap. The chain of command appears to fluctuate considerably, which can make people display markedly different reactions to a given situation.

Moral *feelings*—for example, sympathy for the needy, as when I see a beggar on the street and automatically feel sorry for him—arise unintentionally. Moral *assessments* are altogether different. Tempted as I am to hand the man money, I think about whether that is the right thing to do, whether he'll look for work if he gets a constant stream of handouts, or whether he'll spend the money on alcohol instead of food. Or I might decide that the decision is his own business, as long as he gets the money he obviously needs. It is often hard to differentiate feelings from assessments, but there is a clear distinction between *why* we act and *how* we judge an action morally. Feelings—as well as intentions, thoughts, and force of habit—have a major role in actions, but when we pass moral judgment, their influence seems to recede. Before we take a look at moral intuition—the next big peak in our mountain range of morality—let us peer one last time into the workshop of brain research.

I Feel What You Feel
Does It Pay to Be Good?

For some of us, it's the scene where Ruth dies in *Fried Green Tomatoes*, and for others, it's when Dumbledore is murdered in *Harry Potter*. We cry when watching sad movies or reading sad books because we identify with the feelings of the characters and feel their pain as if it were our own. We laugh along with them, and we get scared when we watch horror movies as though we're in immediate danger ourselves. All of us have experienced this emotional pull. But why is it that we understand other people's feelings? Why do we get goose bumps at the movies even though we're watching from a safe distance? Why do other people's feelings transfer to us?

The answer is simple: We empathize because the feelings of others (whether genuine or simulated in a movie) give rise to the same feelings in us. And that is most likely the case for other animals as well. The sister of Fawn, the rhesus monkey Frans de Waal observed in the research center in Madison, clearly felt Fawn's pain and fear. But as natural as empathy and understanding others' feelings may be, scientists were baffled by this phenomenon until just a few years ago.

The person who provided the first persuasive scientific reason for why we feel empathy remains astonishingly unknown to the general public. Giacomo Rizzolatti's appearance is often compared to Albert Einstein's: white hair sticking out every which way, a bushy white mustache, and an impish grin. But the similarities go beyond the surface. For many neuroscientists, the sprightly Italian is one of the greatest in his field, a man who ventured into new dimensions even as many colleagues considered his field of research relatively unappealing. For more than twenty years, Rizzolatti has been examining the function of neurons that control our actions. It seemed like a rather dry subject when he started out because the motor cortex, which initiates voluntary motor functions, was considered a fairly dull region of the brain. Why bother with simple motions, people thought, when we could research the complex areas of language, intelligence, and the emotional world?

This perception changed drastically in the wake of a startling development in 1992. Rizzolatti was working in Parma, at one of Europe's oldest universities, but in its snow-white ultramodern medical complex. In the early 1990s, Rizzolatti's team was engaged in an unusual project. The group knew that some types of behavior can be "contagious." If someone laughs or yawns, or even assumes a particular posture, others tend to simulate that behavior. The same is true in some species of apes, who are indeed known for "aping" what they see. But the researchers chose to work with *Macaca nemestrina*, a species of monkey that normally does not imitate the behavior of its fellow monkeys. Rizzolatti and his younger colleagues Vittorio Gallese, Leonardo Fogassi, and Giuseppe di Pellegrino placed electrodes on the brain of a *Macaca nemestrina*. Then they placed a peanut on the floor and watched a neuron fire as the monkey snatched up the peanut, as they had anticipated. The big surprise came when the research team put the same monkey behind a pane of glass, where it could not grab the peanut but instead watched one of Rizzolatti's colleagues grab it. Remarkably, the same neuron fired as when the monkey itself had grabbed the peanut. Although the monkey's paw did not move, it performed the action in its head. The scientists were amazed to realize that the neurons reacted in exactly the same way whether the monkey carried out certain movements on its own or simply reenacted the movements of its trainers mentally.

Never before had scientists observed the brain simulating movements that the body did not perform. Leonardo Fogassi was the first to grasp the significance of what had happened, but the whole team deserved the credit. Rizzolatti coined the term "mirror neurons" to designate the neurons that trigger the same reactions in the brain by passive reenactment of actual actions. The term caught on right away, and neuroscientists in Italy, and then at universities and research institutes around the globe, delved into research on this phenomenon. Might the fact that the human brain does not differentiate between what we experience ourselves and what we merely observe closely and empathize with be the key to understanding social behavior?

While mirror neurons, which are located in the prefrontal cortex of the frontal lobe, in an area known as the insula, are an important component, this insula is separate from the "social center," the ventromedial region we discussed earlier. Although mirror neurons are associated with unconscious empathy, they are not involved in more comprehensive planning, decision making, or volition. It is still largely unknown how those regions in the brain interact. The experts were stunned when Rizzolatti produced images that clearly indicated that mirror neurons are located in Broca's area in humans, one of the two regions responsible for speech. And neuroscientists at the University of Groningen in the Netherlands recently discovered an intriguing link between hearing and mirror neuron firing. The sound of a soda can popping open in the distance causes the brain to react as if a person were opening the can himself. The mere sound evokes the entire experience. Test subjects whose brains were particularly active in this process also claimed to be unusually adept at seeing others' points of view. Several American researchers have examined children with limited interactive skills and found that in autistic children, mirror neurons are activated weakly or not at all.

It remains to be seen whether experiments will confirm that mirror neurons are the directors of our feelings. This research is still in its infancy. But the hope is that mirror neurons will provide the key to understanding the nature of empathy, language, social behavior, and morality. If mirror neurons fire both when we act and when we observe the actions of others, we may conclude that the ability to share the feelings of other people depends on our own sensitivity. People who are in touch with their own feelings are more sensitive to those of others. Whether an individual puts this advantage to good use is, of course, an entirely different matter. Mirror neurons explain the "technical" side of our overall moral capability, and they might reveal a great deal about how empathy functions—a process Kant had regarded as indescribable. But we still need to figure out why empathy is so rewarding as to result in general behavioral guidelines or even binding rules of conduct.

As we saw earlier, morality has regulated the social life of groups during the course of evolution. In order for this regulation to function, the members of a group have to be able to imagine what others are experiencing and share their feelings and even their thoughts. Mirror neurons clearly foster altruism. The roots of altruistic behavior run so deep that people not only want to help others but also find this behavior rewarding. It fills us with delight when we hug, cuddle, and soothe a crying child and maybe even coax out a smile. Empathy is an instinct in every healthy person. It would seem that moral sensations of this kind preceded moral principles.

But where does that rewarding feeling come from? What is it about making others happy that makes us happy? And what is so satisfying about acting morally? Most neuroscientists will say it is the amygdala, the small but significant region we described in the chapter "Mr. Spock in Love." It is the seat of emotions in the brain, and it has been the subject of far more research than have mirror neurons. Research groups have established that friendly faces evoke stronger reactions in the left amygdala and generate a good mood and pleasure. Grim or threatening expressions activate primarily the right amygdala and produce fear and displeasure. These results, which are visible on MRI scans, are quite informative. Of course, MRIs produce only snapshots, not films. But it is plain to see that giving pleasure to others brightens our mood. Smiles and beaming faces reward us for our good deeds, especially when we see—or think we see—the results of our actions on the faces of others.

Altruistic behavior is thus based in large part on self-reward. It is rewarding for me to be good, and it is rewarding for the community when it is rewarding for the individual. Perhaps that is the point that Kant underestimated. He felt that kindness based on a feeling of duty has greater moral value than kindness that stems from affection or temperament. Kant's idea that one cannot rely on feelings of pleasure is not entirely false, but can we rely on a sense of duty? Merely fulfilling one's duty engenders a relatively weak feeling of pleasure compared to the pleasure of spreading happiness.

Before Kant, many philosophers had explained morality as an obligation to God. Those who led a pious life and acted accordingly were moral. But Kant liberated morality from man's obligation to God and redirected this obligation to man himself. That was the point of his idea of the "moral law within me." Kant was undoubtedly right on this point. While I may find the pleasure in doing good more natural than the duty to do good, my conduct rises to the level of morality only when I make these experiences of pleasure the basis for general rules for friendly conduct. Of course, the degree to which an individual benefits from being good has a strong environmental component. The categorical imperative won't get you very far if you're in prison or in a similarly hostile situation. But as a general rule, the ability to act morally goes to the core of what it means to be human. A society that has no concept of right or wrong is about the worst thing we could imagine—if it is imaginable at all.

The notion of "humanity" is a Judeo-Christian legacy that persuades us to see morality as the essential trait of our species. By nature, it seems, man is neither fundamentally brutal nor fundamentally noble—but rather both. The hole in Phineas Gage's skull reveals something about the control centers of morality in the brain. And mirror neurons show how empathy seems to work on the neuronal level. But no chemical process produces affection, love, and responsibility of its own accord. We do that ourselves—in large part because we reap the rewards. But now we need to address the big question of whether we attain the knowledge that being good is rewarding by way of practical experience or whether this knowledge is innate. Do we come into this world with a kind of "moral law," as Kant thought? Most of us can probably tell whether an action is good or bad without much thought. We feel it intuitively. But what is "intuitive morality"?

The Man on the Bridge
Is Morality Innate?

Picture yourself in the following situation: An out-of-control trolley is racing directly toward five men standing on the track. You, dear reader, are standing at the controls and watching the driverless trolley zoom toward them. If you flip the switch to divert the trolley onto a side track to the left, you can save the lives of the five men at the last possible second. The only catch is that if the trolley veers left, it will run over one man on the track. What would you do?

Before you reply, take a minute to mull over a second question. Once again we're dealing with a driverless trolley, and once again it is racing toward the five men on the track. But this time you are on a footbridge above the track, looking for something to throw down onto the tracks to stop the trolley. The only thing you see is a large man standing next to you on the bridge. The railing is low. All you would have to do is give the man a good hard push from behind, and his heavy body would stop the racing trolley. The five men on the track would be spared. Would you do it?

More than 300,000 people have now pondered these questions, which were devised by the British philosopher Philippa Foot and augmented over the years by Judith Jarvis Thomson and others. Harvard psychologist Marc Hauser posted a "Moral Sense Test" on the Internet (http://moral.wjh.harvard.edu) with the "trolley problem" and a series of similar ethical quandaries. And MIT's John Mikhail tested out trolley problems on chil-

dren and adults, atheists and believers, women and men, blue-collar workers and academics from a variety of backgrounds, including Chinese immigrants and Native Americans. The answers were surprisingly unvarying,
regardless of a respondent's religion, age, gender, education, or country of
origin.

For the two original trolley problems, nearly all respondents would flip
the switch and accept the death of a single man to save the lives of five, but
only one in six would push the man from the footbridge to save the lives of
the five.

Isn't that a strange result? Whether I flip the switch or push the man
from the bridge, the outcome is the same: One man dies, and five are saved.
There is no difference in the number of victims and survivors; yet there
apparently *is* a striking difference of some kind. Clearly it is one thing to
accept the death of a person and quite another to cause that death. Psychologically there is a substantial difference between being actively and passively responsible for the death of another human being. In the case of
being actively responsible for one man's death, I feel as though I have murdered someone, even if by doing so I have saved the lives of other people.
Being passively responsible for one man's death, as in the case with the
switch, is more like steering the hand of fate. Direct and indirect action are
emotional worlds apart.

From a moral standpoint, action differs from, say, giving a command or
instructions. The soldiers who dropped the bombs on Hiroshima and Nagasaki did not get past the emotional trauma; their superiors, however,
right up through President Truman, who had given the orders, appeared to
have fewer problems with it. We draw a distinction between intentional and
predicted damage, and between direct and indirect actions. Most people
consider damage that arises by physical contact more reprehensible than
when there is no contact involved. It is easier to press a button to kill someone than to thrust a knife into someone's heart. The more abstract a brutal
deed is, the easier it seems to be to commit.

Let us recall the origin of our morality from the social conduct of primates. In the realm of primates, there are no abstract actions, but there is
still a difference between action and failure to act. If someone fails to act,
we cannot be certain whether this lack of action was intentional, which is
why we hesitate to pronounce moral judgment on it. Deliberate action, by
contrast, seems unequivocal.

But Marc Hauser thinks there is much more to it. If most people in a given situation assess the moral implications quite similarly and behave the same way, isn't that proof that we have a common moral foundation that transcends individual cultures? Don't we all go by the same complex of rules and principles, such as "Be fair," "Do no harm," and "Don't be aggressive"? Hauser is convinced that there are moral rules within us. Since people are normally not aware of these rules, the rules do not get passed from one generation to the next in our upbringing, but rather are in our genes and are internalized in the first years of our lives. Hauser imagines that we acquire a sense of morality the way we do language. As Noam Chomsky has shown, there is a universal grammar in the brain from which children develop their mother tongue in response to their linguistic environment. We do not *learn* our native language; it *grows* like any part of the body. Morality, Hauser argues, has a similar kind of deep grammar that allows us to internalize the structure of our particular environment. Every person is born with a sense of good and evil, with a "moral instinct." Mores are not merely instilled in us by religious and judicial systems and by our parents and teachers; a baby emerges from the birth canal with a sense of morality, which is why all of us— even criminals—can usually tell right from wrong instantaneously.

Is Hauser correct? Does psychological testing prove that there is such a thing as morality? Is it the key that has yet to emerge from any abstract philosophical imperatives and laws or from brain imaging?

Kant had nothing but contempt for feelings. His categorical imperative was the diametrical opposite, a morality that can dispense with feelings. Feelings, he thought, were not partners of reason but its adversary; he believed they cloud our moral judgment instead of fostering it. Hauser bases his theory of moral feelings on the opposite premise, arguing that emotions are not necessarily lower instincts and can lead to lofty feelings. To be quite sure that there is a moral sense of this kind in every healthy and normal person, Hauser sought help from an old friend, Antonio Damasio. Together they examined patients with injuries to the ventromedial region of the frontal lobe, people with injuries similar to those of Phineas Gage. These people were also asked about the trolley example. The result was clear and unequivocal: Like most healthy people, the brain-damaged patients flipped the switch to save the five men on the track. But in contrast to the other respondents, the large man invariably fell victim to their distorted logic. The sociopaths with Phineas Gage syndrome were unhesitatingly prepared to push him off the footbridge. Where other people were held back by their intuitive moral instinct, these respondents obviously lacked this moral sense and judged the situation solely on the basis of intellect.

If this test is a reliable indicator, the intuitive moral sense is located in the human frontal lobe, and an innate universal grammar of morality is hidden away in the ventromedial region. But a few important qualifications need to be mentioned. The test question about the trolley and the switch seems clear and unequivocal, but the one about the man on the footbridge does not. Let us again picture ourselves in the situation of actually pushing a man off a footbridge to stop a trolley. If the man has his back to us, we find it easier to push him, but if he looks at us, it gets much more difficult. We don't like the looks of him? Well, then, okay—we could sacrifice him. Is he likable? Does he have a friendly smile? Then we probably won't push him. None of this refutes Hauser's theory of the moral instinct, but it does add layers of complexity. Our personal feelings of sympathy and antipathy help shape our intuitive morality.

The same applies to the example with the side track. Five out of six respondents say they would let a man on a track be run over to save five others. But what happens if I know that man, if he is a good friend of mine? Do I flip the switch even then? What if it is not a worker standing on the tracks, but my own mother, brother, son, or daughter? Who would flip the switch if faced with the choice between five adult men on the one track and a child playing on the other? In the example with the footbridge, many school-children might push their hated math teacher off the bridge to save the life of the men on the track.

In the case of the footbridge, many aspects that have nothing whatsoever to do with instincts come into play. If I push the large man now, it flashes across my mind, who's to say that he will fall right onto the track? And even if he does, can I be sure that he will stop the trolley? What happens if he doesn't? Then not only will the five men on the track die, but I will also have committed murder. Who would believe that I had only the best of intentions? All these questions are important for how I act. And they are not the result of long contemplation—they come quick as lightning, and are like social and cultural reflexes humans acquire as they go through life.

Genetic dispositions and cultural knowledge are not easy to tell apart. The two are inextricably linked. That specific decisions, as in Hauser's test questions, are the same across many different cultures does not prove that moral ideas are innate. Moral ideas may have developed quite similarly in these cultures because they proved to be good, or at least rewarding. In most cases, the correct answer to the question "Nature or nurture?" is probably "You can't really tell them apart." Some children and adolescents who were raised in the Hitler years had no qualms about killing people, including defenseless women and small children, when they later became SS officers. As in the case of language acquisition, our moral feelings are not fully innate. We are not born with a set of values, but only with guidelines as to which information we can absorb and a set of conditions for sorting things out.

The great variety of human moral constructs reveals the many ways in which this moral capability can be implemented. Ownership rights, sexual morality, religious precepts, and strategies for dealing with aggression are approached so differently in different cultures throughout history that it is difficult to determine what is "typically" human. Our society subdivides morality every which way, into everyday morality; ethical morality; the morality of responsibility, of class, and of contracts; maximal and minimal morality; initial morality; supervisory morality; female and male morality; business morality; morality for managers, for feminists, for theologians. Whenever a society recognizes a new problem, a new morality arises to address it. Still, every new morality draws on traditional values and appeals to our conscience and sense of responsibility, demanding greater equality and democracy and brotherly and sisterly love.

People who see the world in moral terms draw a sharp distinction between what they do and do not respect. For more than two millennia, philosophers have struggled to find definitive and irrefutable indications of how these criteria are implemented. The evidence is disquieting: A modern moral system like the constitutional state was crafted over the centuries under the guidance of philosophers, yet the whole construction was so flimsy that in Germany it could come undone by a National Socialist government without so much as a major moral uprising. In all likelihood, the most effective way to effect moral progress is not by way of reason but by sensitizing large segments of the population to specific issues. Emotions steer social development. As Richard Rorty wrote, "Moral progress is a matter of wider and wider sympathy. It is not a matter of rising above the sentimental to the rational. Nor is it a matter of appealing from lower, possibly corrupt, local courts to a higher court which administers an ahistorical, incorruptible, transcultural moral law."

To sum up our findings thus far: Humankind is endowed with an innate capacity for morality, but it is hard to determine the extent of this capacity. The primate brain makes it possible for us to empathize with others, and there are (neurochemical) rewards for "good" deeds. Ethical behavior is a complex altruism, comprising both feelings and logic. There is no "moral law" in man in the Kantian sense that obliges man to be good. But moral actions often reward the individual and the group to which the individual belongs. Morality is largely an outgrowth of how we regard ourselves, which, in turn, reflects our upbringing.

Now that we have the tools of the trade in hand, we should be ready to move ahead to the concrete moral issues facing our society. There is, as we have seen, the perceived moral right to be allowed to kill under very specific circumstances, such as the case of the man on the footbridge. But is there also a moral *obligation* to kill?

Aunt Bertha Shall Live
Are We Entitled to Kill?

Oh, my aunt Bertha! Throughout her life, she has tyrannized my family with her horrid ways. She has no children, thank God, so she drove her brother (my father) crazy instead. She has also aggravated her neighbors with a decades-long fuss about the property line, and her dog does his business in the neighbors' yards. On top of that, she always sics that vicious little yapper on the mailman. In short, Bertha is dreadful.

Did I mention that she is rich? Filthy rich. Albert, her husband, who died young, left her quite a fortune. And she invested it well, in real estate, securities, and stocks. Aunt Bertha has millions. And the best part is: I'm her heir. Unfortunately, old Bertha is made of iron. She is only seventy and fit as a fiddle. She doesn't drink or smoke; she doesn't even eat cake. Aunt Bertha does not like anything at all, aside from money. She'll easily live to ninety or a hundred. But if she really does make it to a hundred, I'll be over seventy. Who knows what I'll be doing then and whether I'll still be able to do anything with her money. Sometimes I wish ol' Bertha would kick the bucket tomorrow. Or make that today.

Couldn't we cook up some reasons to kill off a horrendous individual in order to do good? Maybe there's a plausible theory to justify Aunt Bertha's premature departure from this world. As a matter of fact, I've just thought of one: philosophical utilitarianism.

Jeremy Bentham was born in 1748 in Spitalfields, in the East End of

London. He came from a rich, politically conservative family, and attended the renowned Westminster School for the offspring of the city's finest families. The philosopher John Locke, the architect Christopher Wren, and the composer Henry Purcell all went to school here. In 1760, when Jeremy was twelve, his parents enrolled their highly gifted son in Queen's College at Oxford, and when he turned fifteen he was awarded his bachelor's degree in law. At the age of twenty-four, he set up a law practice in London, but his career went in a direction altogether different from what his parents had hoped. Bentham complained bitterly about the state of British law and the British courts. Instead of practicing law, he focused on reforming the legal system to make it more sensible and democratic, a path he could pursue without financial worries after 1792, when his father died and left him a substantial inheritance. For the next forty years, he worked exclusively on writing, turning out some ten to twenty pages per day. When he found the legal trivia tiresome, he had a student write up his suggestions for reforming civil law and formalize them as a legal code. Bentham was both a remarkable and a likable man. Just as the French Revolution had done away with the old class privileges of the Church and the nobility, Bentham dedicated himself to making British society more liberal and tolerant. He came up with social reforms, fought for freedom of expression, sketched out a model for a more humane system of incarceration, and supported the incipient women's movement.

His basic principle was as simple as it was persuasive: Pleasure is good, pain is bad. If that was correct, he thought, then philosophy and the state should act accordingly. The aim of society should be to reduce the amount of pain to whatever extent possible and to augment the pleasure of as many people as possible. The more pleasure something brings about, the more useful and better it is. Bentham called this principle utilitarianism. When he died in 1832 at a ripe old age, he was a famous man. Although he thought of himself as merely liberal, the French revolutionaries—and later also the French communists—were delighted by his philosophy. And three American states—New York, South Carolina, and Louisiana—adopted the civil code that Bentham had proposed.

The principle that pleasure is good and pain is bad seems convincing enough. Why not use it on Aunt Bertha? One thing is for sure: My aunt does not bring any pleasure into the world. She causes nothing but pain for her neighbors, the mailman, and others. The money she has in the bank does no good either. But something could be done about that, of course. If I had that much money, I could do so much good—and not only for myself! For example, a friend of mine is a doctor, the chief of staff at a pediatric hospital for leukemia patients. Another friend works with needy children. If I had Aunt Bertha's money, I could give them each more than a million euros, which would create so much pleasure right there! Here I am, picturing children receiving the best of medical care and the smiling faces of Brazilian schoolchildren—all from the money I have donated from Bertha's estate.

The only thing needed to make this dream come true is . . . Wait a minute—if Bentham is right, I have no choice *but* to bump off the old bag! The only thing I have to figure out is how to send Auntie to meet her maker in the kindest way possible: painlessly and without her catching on. My friend the doctor could surely think of some way to make her pass away peacefully. Who knows—maybe this will even spare her a far more painful death. No one would shed a tear for her, to put it mildly. In fact, most people would be absolutely delighted if the nasty old witch were out of the picture. The neighbors would finally have their peace and a clean yard, and the mailman could look forward to nicer people moving into her house. My friend the doctor would just have to happen onto her body and issue the death certificate and no one would investigate the case. Isn't the matter clear and simple? Don't I have a moral obligation to carry out this murder?

Let us run through the argument one more time: If I kill Aunt Bertha to save the lives of needy children, I would certainly achieve an optimal balance between pleasure and pain for all concerned and demonstrate that evil inflicted on an individual is excusable if there is a better outcome for society as a whole. But what would Bentham say if I were to use his philosophy to justify a murder? Oddly, he did not mention this very obvious implication of utilitarianism. He does not appear to have poisoned any rich aunts, but then again, he had no need to. And he did not issue any appeals to murder tyrants, ruthless slumlords, or any other exploiters. He was a liberal spirit, and as such he drew the line at heinous acts.

But that's not enough for me to go on. I still wonder what might have made Bentham hold back from drawing the simple conclusion that in weighing pain against pleasure, murder might be justified. The idea was in perfect accord with his philosophy.

I must have been about twelve when my parents first told me about the

Nazi concentration camps and about the millions of people who had been brutally murdered in the Holocaust. Right then and there, I began to wonder why so few people considered it their duty to kill Hitler to put a stop to this terrible suffering. Bentham would have argued that the case is clear as day: A tyrant who runs death camps and destroys world peace can be killed because the sum of the unhappiness an aggressor of this sort generates outweighs the personal pain of his death.

Doesn't the same consideration apply to the case of Aunt Bertha? The pleasure her death would cause would far exceed the pain inflicted on her. But Jeremy Bentham might have laughed off any such notion. He would ask whether I'd given any thought to what would happen to society if my example with Aunt Bertha were to set a precedent. Millions of people—rich aunts, creeps, politicians, big businessmen, and many convicts or people with learning disabilities without family—would have to count on being killed painlessly in their sleep. Just imagine the panic, the alarm, and the havoc that would ensue!

Maybe I'd be lucky and my murder of Aunt Bertha would not come to light. But if I consider my action just, it would have to be in accordance with sound principles, and if so, it would apply to anyone, maybe even to me, if my nephews one day thought as little of me as I do of Aunt Bertha, in which case I would have to have eyes in the back of my head. To be able to apply Bentham's principle of good pleasure and bad pain meaningfully, we must bear in mind that performing mathematical calculations to weigh pain against pleasure in order to make life-and-death decisions about people cannot be tolerated. Acceptance of murder on utilitarian grounds would spell the demise of civil society.

But do the two basic principles of Bentham's philosophy really mesh? On the one hand, the intended sum of pleasure determines whether an action is good. On the other, Bentham doesn't go so far as to allow for killing people, even though his philosophy fails to provide a convincing moral foundation for this exception. The argument against killing thousands of disagreeable people—and against torture, for that matter—might be to maintain law and order, but it does not address individual morality. By contrast, Immanuel Kant had ascribed human dignity to every individual as a fundamental unparalleled value. He would have found my calculations about Aunt Bertha appalling. He would have insisted that one human life cannot be weighed against another.

Bentham's calculus of pleasure and pain is irreconcilably opposed to Kant's notion that human life is the highest good. But which of the two is more convincing? Shouldn't Hitler have been killed for moral reasons to prevent a great deal of suffering and tragedy? Can Kant's dogma of human dignity stand as an inviolable principle? In more innocuous cases, such as that of Aunt Bertha, we might argue that at least she doesn't cause much harm. And this difference between active perpetration and passive nastiness is not trivial, as the previous chapter has shown, in assessing both the victim and the perpetrator. But Bentham did not draw this distinction—at least not when it came to the perpetrator. He would surely have both flipped the switch *and* pushed the large man from the bridge, because his utilitarianism restricts its inquiry to the moral usefulness of an action. But as logical as Bentham's equation is, man does not live by logic alone. There are more important moral principles than justice—particularly as utilitarianism has to grapple with the fact that everyone interprets justice according to his own beliefs. At any rate, people often make judgments based on their intuition, a fact that cannot be dismissed out of hand or fail to factor into a system of morality. Although morality and law shouldn't be founded on intuition, it would be inhuman to dispense with intuition altogether.

So Aunt Bertha shall live. And we must make sure not to gauge the value of a human life by its usefulness. But we have yet to clarify the tricky question of how else to explain the value of life. Where does this value really come from? And where does it begin?

The Birth of Dignity
Is Abortion Moral?

Imagine the following situation: You go to the hospital to visit a sick friend. You enter the elevator and press the wrong button. When you get out, you find yourself on a ward where volunteer donors are hooked up to patients who will not survive without the donors' help, but you don't really understand what is going on. After sitting in the waiting room for a while, you are called in, and a doctor inserts an IV with an anesthetic. When you wake up, you're lying in a hospital bed, and in the next bed you see an unconscious man to whom you're hooked up with all kinds of contraptions. You call for the doctor, who tells you that the man you're hooked up to is a famous violinist with a serious kidney ailment who will survive only if his circulatory system is plugged into someone else's with the same blood type, and you are the only person whose blood is a match. The staff at this renowned hospital apologize profusely for the misunderstanding—they thought you'd volunteered—and they offer to unhook you from the violinist, who won't survive if you take them up on their offer. If you agree to remain hooked up to the man for nine months, he will recover, and you will then be freed from him without endangering his life. What would you do?

It's an outrageous story, of course, nightmarish and unrealistic. After all, what visitor to a hospital would fail to notice that he is being hooked up to an IV? But as is always the case with moral dilemmas from the workshops of philosophers and psychologists, the point is not the details but the principle involved. This particular scenario is adapted from Judith Jarvis Thomson, a philosophy professor emerita at MIT, whose point is this: While it might be nice of you to make your kidneys available to the violinist and be confined to a hospital bed, you are in no way morally obliged to do so. As you can tell from the subtitle of this chapter, this example is not about fictional violinists but about a subject of more universal import: You have been put into a situation—involuntarily, unintentionally, and perhaps even by force—that makes you directly—physically—responsible for another human being. This is most likely to occur not by being hooked up to renally challenged violinists, but to women facing unplanned pregnancies.

According to Thomson, a woman with an unwanted pregnancy is in a situation quite similar to the involuntary bonding with the violinist. Just as you would not be forced to assume responsibility for the life of the violinist, neither would a pregnant woman be responsible for the embryo in her unwanted pregnancy. The right to decide what happens to her body, Thomson argues, outweighs an obligation to another life that she entered into involuntarily. This argument, which became very popular, inspired feminism to adopt the slogan "My body is my own!"

But even if one subscribes to this idea, Thomson's justification seems rather flimsy. Let us picture a starving man at our doorstep, knocking at the door with his last ounce of strength and begging for food. Thomson might argue that while it would be nice of us to give him something, we are in no way obliged to take responsibility for the starving man, since the situation was not of our own making.

Certainly not everyone would buy this argument. Indeed, the German penal code rightly includes a paragraph condemning "failure to render assistance." The fact that a situation was not initiated by us and that we do not wish to deal with it is not a sustainable argument against meeting our obligations. The morality of helping someone or not depends on the specifics of the scenario. The dilemma with the violinist leads to an impasse, because it does not illustrate a convincing, overarching principle. The greatest drawback of this example, however, is its crucial mismatch: The violinist is a grown man with all the psychic and intellectual capabilities that go with adulthood, but what about the embryo and the fetus? Do they, too, have an unconditional and inviolable right to life? To answer this question, we can look to the ideas of three thinkers we've discussed so far: Kant's concept of "human dignity," Bentham's "utilitarianism," and Hauser's intuitive "moral sense."

Let us begin with Kant. There is only a single sentence about embryos in his voluminous writings, and it is found in his discussion of matrimonial law. Kant writes that the embryo is a being already endowed with the full complement of human dignity. If it weren't, we would face the problem of specifying the point at which freedom and the dignity of man commence in the womb. According to Kant, self-awareness and freedom are specifically human qualities and do not exist anywhere else in nature. But how and when does freedom—and, with it, dignity—enter into a human being? Kant's answer can be understood only against the backdrop of his era: The freedom of the embryo, he contended, depends on its parents' freedom, because the parents conceived it of their own free will within a framework that they freely chose, marriage. The fruit of their union is an embryo. The flip side of his argument would state that embryos conceived by parents out of wedlock without their intention to create a child are not free and fully dignified human beings. This definition, which implies that children born out of wedlock don't have "human dignity," was Kant's reaction to a widespread problem in his era. In 1780, Adrian von Lamezon, a court official in Mannheim, Germany, posed a question and offered one hundred ducats for the essay that best answered it. The question was: "What is the most feasible means to put a stop to infanticide?" The overwhelming response—four hundred submissions—reflected the fact that abortion was a common practice in the eighteenth century, and infanticide even more so. In the great majority of these cases, the pregnancy had resulted from an employer taking advantage of his maid. Homicide of illegitimate newborns occurred regularly, even though nobody talked openly about it. In another passage in his *Metaphysics of Morals*, Kant showed some sympathy for infanticide. Since the illegitimate newborn is not free in Kant's full sense of the term, but rather "stolen into the commonwealth (like contraband merchandise)," Kant wasn't too concerned about infanticide, placing it on a par with other trivial offenses like killing in a duel and arguing for extenuating circumstances.

It is difficult to endorse Kant's argument today. After all, embryos can be conceived unintentionally within marriage or intentionally outside of marriage. Moreover, Kant's line of reasoning implies that the homicide of children conceived out of wedlock—or, for that matter, even the murder of adults conceived out of wedlock!—can be justified. Today we tend to look askance at Kant's advocacy of the unconditional need to protect embryos conceived in marriage. Surely no one who invokes Kant in the current discussions about abortion shares his conclusion that we should regard illegitimate embryos and newborns in a lesser light, so why give credence to Kant's line of reasoning, which is simply outdated and can only be understood within the context of his era?

Let us move along to the second route, utilitarianism. Utilitarians pose two basic questions. First: How capable of pleasure or pain is an embryo or fetus? And second: What carries more weight, the pleasure and pain of the child in the womb, or the pleasure and pain of the mother?

To answer these questions, we need to agree on the value of an embryo. No utilitarian would share Kant's view that the worth of an embryo depends on the marital status of its parents. According to utilitarianism, an embryo isn't unconditionally worthy of protection. The embryo is a human being in the sense that it belongs to the species *Homo sapiens,* but it isn't a human in the full moral sense, and hence is not a person. But what *are* people? How can I identify them? The notion of what constitutes a person does not come from Bentham himself. In his view, the action that was morally best was the one that resulted in the greatest possible happiness for the greatest number of human beings, but he was not judging the inherent value of individuals. His successors discovered two weak points and tried to remedy them, beginning with the question of how to define happiness. For Bentham, happiness was the experience of pleasure in the broadest sense of the term. But utilitarianism's most effective exponent after Bentham, the philosopher and liberal politician John Stuart Mill, found that explanation wanting. He sought to liberate the utilitarian notion of happiness from its whiff of inanity and dullness by equating happiness with mental pleasure rather than with physical pleasure: "Better to be Socrates dissatisfied than a fool satisfied." But if the mind stands above purely physical pleasure, an adult human endowed with a highly developed mind is a more valuable entity than a newborn or a horse, and only a complex human being counts as a "person." A later generation of utilitarians incorporated this notion into their theory, which took into account not only the basic desires of sentient beings but also complex human ideals. This approach is known as preference utilitarianism, and virtually all modern successors of Bentham subscribe to it. For utilitarians who take highly developed desires and preferences into consideration, no one can kill a person (not even Aunt Bertha!) as long as the person desires to remain alive.

Embryos, by contrast, lack complex desires and preferences. Presumably they have an instinct to stay alive, but that does not distinguish them from salamanders. For preference utilitarians, there is nothing that in and of itself forbids killing an embryo or fetus. Of course fetuses begin developing a consciousness before they are born, but so do pigs and cattle, and we kill them to obtain food. Consciousness is not the same as a desire to live. As far as we know, fetuses do not possess self-awareness in the sense of having complex preferences and desires. Thus a fetus may on principle be killed at any stage of its development—at least when it decreases the suffering of the mother or substantially increases her happiness.

This utilitarian argument makes more sense than Kant's unconditional human dignity for fetuses conceived in wedlock, but it also has shortcomings. While an embryo's intellectual level is about that of a salamander, it has the potential to become an Albert Einstein, and if it were not aborted, it would one day become a human being with desires and preferences.

This position, however, is not quite as persuasive as it first appears, because potentiality is not applied universally as a decisive moral criterion. If you held potential human life sacred, you would have to condemn masturbation and contraception, as the Catholic Church does (although only for the past 140 years). Consider this example to highlight the difference: Is boiling an egg really the same thing as putting a living chicken into boiling water? Potentiality tells us nothing about current feelings of happiness or pain, nor does it produce a state of consciousness, so it shouldn't be a true criterion in deciding questions of morality.

There are other grounds for objection as well. A major drawback of utilitarianism is its impact assessment. In order to strike a meaningful balance between pleasure and pain, I have to have a good idea of, and factor in, the consequences of my decision, which isn't always so easy. Even when it comes to simple personal questions, I often have a hard time figuring out what makes better sense for me: Should I go to my friend's birthday party or to a reading by my favorite writer? How can I know what will ultimately give me more pleasure? It's even harder to weigh complex moral situations and their potential chain of consequences. Who knows whether a woman who has an abortion will eventually regret it? Maybe it will take a heavier psychological toll on her than she had anticipated. And how about the father? Perhaps the decision will place a greater strain on the relationship than the couple had thought. That is one of life's many risks, a utilitarian would argue, but not an argument for a blanket ban on abortion.

The weightiest objection to the utilitarian view lies elsewhere. If no absolute protection can be accorded to a fetus because it lacks complex preferences and desires and is thus not a person, doesn't the same apply to a newborn infant? A baby becomes a self-aware free individual somewhere between the ages of two and three. Doesn't preference utilitarianism throw the baby out with the bathwater and open the door not only to abortion but also to infanticide as late as in the third year of life?

There are preference utilitarians for whom the unconditional worth of a baby's life does not begin until after the first birthday. Naturally, they do not endorse killing infants without compelling grounds, but their assessments of the infants' value are not based on the value the person represents per se, but rather on the consequences for society. Small children are nearly always of great value to their parents and other family members. And even small children who do not have families and live in orphanages are needy individuals entitled to societal protection. But it isn't easy for a preference utilitarian to say why we should go out of our way to protect infants but not animals. In the case of both infants and animals, you can argue that a society that deals with living creatures irresponsibly heads down a slippery slope. But that is not a compelling basis for the right to life of small children. This is preference utilitarianism's Achilles' heel.

At this point we come to the third route and take up Marc Hauser's idea that every normal person has a moral sense, an "intuitive" morality. As we have seen, utilitarianism takes a clear stand on the abortion question, but the consequences of this position—a lack of unconditional protection for small children—can be alarming. Moral philosophers generally balk at the concept of "intuition." Both Kantians and utilitarians argue that feelings are unreliable, differ from one person to the next, depend on a given milieu, and vary by culture and issue. Western philosophy in general has striven to establish a rational and universally comprehensible basis for its arguments. This determined rejection of feeling in moral philosophy is a legacy of the battle between philosophy and the Church. To free themselves from religion, most philosophers sought rational explanations that were as free from feelings as possible and defined human beings by way of intellect and reason. But as we saw in the first part of the book, this view of human beings is wrong. Body and mind cannot be cleanly divided, nor can the unconscious and the conscious. If our morality invariably entails feelings, we cannot simply disregard them. Naturally, feelings cannot be used as the exclusive barometer of a satisfactory morality. But a morality that makes no attempt to mesh with our intuition and hence with the biological foundations of our sense of morality is surely worse than one that incorporates intuition.

Is it really such a good idea to disregard feelings, as in the case of the utilitarian response to the question of small children, because they do not fit into the explanatory model? Moreover, does it make sense to grant the highest priority to fairness, as utilitarianism does? Is that in line with our nature? If a woman standing in front of a burning house with her infant and her German shepherd inside can save only one of the two, should she ignore her instincts and feelings of love to save the German shepherd for reasons of fairness, because it may have more strongly developed preferences?

If we want our rules of conduct to make sense, we can't disregard intuition. That is true of any half-reasonable moral philosophy. Philosophy cannot exist without values. And values are by nature an outgrowth not of reason but of feelings. If I, like utilitarians, declare the common good an important value, that is certainly easy to understand. It is not the outcome of logical deliberation, however, but rather a value, as is evident when someone claims to be an egotist and declares that the common good does not interest him in the slightest. I cannot supply a reason for my interest in other people that is based purely in logic. And my desire to do good deeds is a personal value judgment. The ultimate basis for any moral rule is hopes and wishes, not insights or knowledge.

Many philosophers today reject the notion of an intuitive moral sense because it appears to be based on religious sentiment. If the Catholic Church today would like to see all members of the species *Homo sapiens* granted universal and unconditional protection from the moment the egg and sperm combine, it is not invoking rational arguments but rather an emotional element, namely, God's will. Oddly, God's will is subject to change. In 1869, Pope Pius IX declared that embryos have a fully developed soul from the moment of conception, but before his statement, the first movements of the fetus, the first perceptible signs of life, were considered the point that it was imbued with a soul. That makes much more sense as an intuitive feeling, because life felt within the body has a different intuitive importance from life that is defined only biologically yet imperceptibly; even today, many women are not aware of their pregnancy at an early stage. But Pope Pius's decree was a reaction to recent medical advances. In the 1860s, it became possible to diagnose pregnancy reliably right from the start. Boldly and incautiously, the pope extended the Church's sphere of influence then and there to all fruit of the mother's womb.

From its very origins, religion has entailed translating intuition into images and commandments. The next step has been regulating the social order. But the religious dogma that the soul enters the body at conception is counterintuitive and makes no positive contribution to the social order. The perceived meaning of early human life is dependent upon the value that the mother and, to a lesser extent, the father and other family members accord to it. The further the fetus develops, the stronger the parent-child bond normally becomes. An all-important development is, of course, the moment of birth. For the fetus, it is the entry into a new dimension. It has now become biologically independent, its environment has changed completely, and a revolution is taking place in its brain. And for the mother and father, siblings, grandparents, and extended family, a new dimension of feelings arises upon seeing, hearing, and feeling the infant. As close as the bond to the fetus was in the womb, very few women would say that the bond after birth has the exact same dimension as before. Our moral sensibility is thus largely a question of the sensory experience and the power of imagination that is ignited with our feelings. Religions preserve this feeling of "intuitive morality"—with varying degrees of success.

Intuition offers a corrective to utilitarianism in two respects. It shows that the later an abortion occurs, the more problematic it becomes, which means that the upper limit of three months in Germany for an abortion exempt from punishment makes good sense. Even though the change from the ninety-first day of life to the ninety-second does not signify a step into a different dimension, as a general rule, after three months the natural limit of what can still be called a life without consciousness has been reached. Secondly, intuition confers an unconditional right to life on newborns and infants, because we feel intuitively that their lives are of full human value. The fact that there are people who lack these intuitions and are emotionally incompetent does not change that. Every system of morality has this problem. As we discussed earlier, not every person considers the common good important; even so, utilitarians assume that people possess these intuitive feelings. Biological instincts tend to be more reliable than derived social instincts.

The right to life, its value, and its dignity do not begin with the act of procreation, so there would seem to be no reason to prohibit abortions up until the third month. From each month to the next beyond these three months, the fetus's continued development makes ending its life increasingly problematic. The occasional defensible exception only proves the rule. Parents who learn that their child would run a very high risk of severe mental or physical disability and feel that they are not equal to the task may find no other choice than to abort the fetus. The utilitarian equation that weighs the intentions and the potential suffering of the parents against those of the fetus is distressing, but there is no alternative. The decision is even more difficult after birth if a child is comatose or requires machines to prolong its life, such as the case of an infant with a severe heart defect. In instances like these, what yardstick other than intense emotional deliberations can be applied? Questions like these, however, are no longer really issues of abortion. They're about the circumstances under which it is morally defensible to let a person die, or even to kill a person who expresses the wish to die.

End of Life
Should Euthanasia Be Allowed?

Warnemünde is a cheerful place—the choppy sea, the bright sky. Many years ago, Marie-Luise Nicht and her son were here at the Baltic. Soon she will be bringing him back. He would not have wanted to be buried under the heavy cemetery ground.

On the refrigerator is a brochure about burial at sea. Mrs. Nicht keeps leafing through it. The whole thing still seems unreal to her because her son is lying in the next room, in the larger and nicer of her two rooms. He is breathing, his heart is beating, and he is warm. Sometimes he opens his eyes. This is not what a dead person looks like.

"The person who was Alexander died four years ago," Mrs. Nicht says. "Another Alexander took his place." From a medical point of view, he is a person without a self, without sensation, without any chance of communicating—and without any hope of improving. But for Marie-Luise Nicht, he is her child, a child who needs her.

At first, she would sometimes clench her fist in her pocket, then smack him and shout: "Come back! You can't leave me here alone!" That phase is over.

Her son does not appear to be suffering. His muscles are slack, he is not sweating, and he appears to be resting comfortably. His mother is now used to his mouth hanging open with a string of saliva dribbling out. She can speak to him; she can massage and stroke him; she can put him in his wheelchair and take him outside if the weather is nice. She can easily imagine continuing a life with him. Even so, she would like him to be allowed to die. Marie-Luise Nicht is absolutely certain that Alexander would not want this life, which depends on an infusion of mush from a feeding tube.

———

In the fall of 2006, the German magazine *Der Spiegel* published this report about the plight of Alexander Nicht and his mother, Marie-Luise. One evening in October 2002, Alexander, then a high school senior, was in a car accident and was rushed to the intensive care unit with severe head injuries. A large portion of his cerebral cortex was destroyed. For nearly four years, Alexander remained in a persistent vegetative state, unresponsive and without any chance of recovering. Alexander's mother knew that her son would not have wanted to live that way, but the doctors treating him in Berlin insisted on having the machines keep Alexander artificially alive, and the courts emphatically rejected Mrs. Nicht's wish to end her son's life. The legal situation was more complicated than it appeared at first glance. Doctors in Germany are not allowed to prolong the life of a patient artificially against his will—but how can the doctor know the will of a comatose patient? Instead of trusting Marie-Luise Nicht's conviction that her son would not have wanted to live that way, the doctors continued to keep Alexander alive.

Patients like Alexander raise difficult legal and ethical issues concerning the will and rights of the terminally ill and comatose. Who is allowed to have a say and decide? And how much latitude does the doctor have to decide the fate of a patient? Can doctors induce the end of terminally ill patients by breaking off their treatment (passive euthanasia)? Can they act on the knowledge that treating a patient with strong pain medication will hasten the patient's death (indirect euthanasia)? Can doctors aid patients who explicitly seek to end their lives (assisted suicide)? And finally: Can doctors end a life at the patient's request by administering medicine or a lethal injection (active euthanasia)?

The major argument advanced by those who advocate permitting active euthanasia or exempting it from prosecution is the right of self-determination. People of sound mind should have the right to make decisions about their lives and thus about their deaths. Interestingly, both advocates and opponents of the right to active euthanasia have been known to cite Kant. Opponents emphasize the unconditional "sanctity" of human life, invoking Kant's insistence that man must be treated as an end unto himself and may not be "instrumentalized," or used as a means to an end. Authorizing someone else to carry out the death process would mean ceding control to another and sacrificing personal freedom and independence. Albin Eser, professor emeritus of international criminal law at the Max Planck Institute in Freiburg, argues that this counts as "instrumentalization."

But this argument doesn't hold water. Does it really matter whether I freely decide to kill myself or I—just as freely—ask someone to kill me because, for example, I am lying in a hospital bed and am unable to do so on my own? Am I not being "instrumentalized" to a far greater extent if I am kept alive against my free will? It appears that as Kant grew older, he was terrified of a possible onset of dementia and decided that his life in that condition would no longer have any value or meaning for him. Since the modern forms of indirect euthanasia did not exist in his day, and a cessation of treatment for a patient suffering from Alzheimer's or dementia would not result in immediate death, one could argue that had it been an option, Kant would have supported active euthanasia, at least for himself.

Those in favor of active euthanasia argue that it is a fundamental right of a free person, a part of one's right of self-determination. The following objections to allowing active euthanasia are advanced to counter this argument: (1) Does the fact that active euthanasia is permissible in certain cases undermine the bond of trust between doctor and patient? (2) Doesn't active euthanasia violate the physicians' code of honor "to help and to heal"? (3) Is it always possible to verify beyond the shadow of a doubt that a patient requested active euthanasia? (4) Who is going to safeguard a demented or comatose patient from relatives hoping to benefit from the patient's death? (5) Doesn't the legalization of active euthanasia lead society to rethink the question of how we should deal with terminally ill patients and thus pose a danger to the conditions of our coexistence? (6) Does it "open the floodgates" and force people to choose the option of active euthanasia to satisfy relatives or to avoid imposing additional strain on the health insurance system? (7) Doesn't the "freedom to die" eventually result in a "lack of freedom to live"? (8) Doesn't the authorization of active euthanasia relieve the healthcare system of the need to expand costly but more humane alternatives, such as a higher investment in palliative medicine?

Questions (1) and (2), concerning the relationship between physician and patient, can be answered quickly. They do not pose a philosophical problem but rather arise from a personal psychological situation with many possible variants. While it is possible for the relationship between doctor and patient to be strained by the option of active euthanasia, it need not be. And even if active euthanasia were legalized, no doctor would be obliged, or certainly ever forced, to perform the procedure. Questions (3) and (4), about possible abuse by family members, ask whether the legal system is able to craft the legal provisions to ensure maximal transparency. Questions (5), (6), and (7) are broadly defined philosophical questions pertaining to societal consequences and potential pressure on terminally ill patients. Here a key social and ethical dimension comes into play. But how can we assess the social consequences? In the Netherlands, three major studies of active euthanasia have been conducted since 2001. Of the approximately 140,000 men and women in the Netherlands who have since ended their lives in a hospital, about 4,500 were administered a lethal injection by a physician; four times as many died as a result of terminal sedation. Both numbers have remained fairly constant from year to year. The advocates of the right to active euthanasia see this as a confirmation that there has been no opening of the floodgates, because the number of requests to doctors for help in dying did not increase. But even opponents of the procedure find grist for their mill in these studies. Every year there were at least some cases that resulted in litigation, pitting family members against hospitals. Moreover, some critics assume that the statistics omit a number of cases that went unreported. The clinical data currently available do not provide an unequivocal picture of the ethics of euthanasia.

So only question (8) remains: whether the legalization of active euthanasia might undermine the implementation of more expensive alternatives. Most people would probably believe intuitively that palliative care, including terminal sedation, is better than a lethal injection. This intuitive feeling is ingrained in human nature, as the trolley questions (see "The Man on the Bridge," p. 112) demonstrate. Active killing differs from a failure to act even when the outcome is the same. The fundamental ban on taking a human life actively is not the result of a religious dogma of the "sanctity" of human life; rather, the dogma is the expression of a deeply rooted evolutionary intuition. For this reason, brushing aside the sanctity-of-life argument by pointing out that religious belief has declined in our era makes little sense. Our natural aversion to killing precedes even ancient religions. Interestingly, most advocates of the right to active euthanasia attach great importance to the difference between action and failure to act. Despite any criticism of the gray area of indirect euthanasia, an advocate of active euthanasia would be unlikely to argue that a lethal injection would be the fundamentally better route. Active euthanasia needs to remain a last resort when every other avenue has been exhausted.

The crucial problem in the question of the final days of life of terminally ill patients in excruciating pain is not medical in nature but psychological. As appropriate as it is to validate the right of an individual to decide for himself about his death, it is also of crucial importance to look into the circumstances that prompt a wish of this kind. The problem with active euthanasia is not the understandable legal claim of the patient, but rather the life circumstances that give rise to a decision to die. Palliative medicine is therefore the more humane path for both physician and patient.

If active euthanasia is permitted, what has been a last resort for a few hopeless cases becomes one "normal" resort among many. Some relatives might reduce their efforts on behalf of terminally ill patients, and hospitals might not bother to keep the final days and weeks of the patient's life as pain-free as possible. Even though the statistics from the Netherlands have not substantiated this fear, it is possible to imagine that people might begin to neglect their own right to choose the best possible end of life for themselves because of a societal pressure not to become a burden to the healthcare system.

The key question is therefore: What is a dignified death worth to society? In this light, the powerful argument for the right to self-determination takes on a new perspective. The gray areas of passive, indirect, and active euthanasia as they are currently practiced are surely still preferable to an unequivocal support for active euthanasia. Philosophers focus squarely on the rationality, consistency, and validity of a position, but politicians have a social and ethical responsibility to move beyond intolerable gray areas in theory and examine tolerable gray zones in practice.

We have seen in this chapter how the right to human self-determination comes up against its limits when it produces what are judged to be intolerable and inhumane consequences for society. But who is included in this "society"? How do we deal with living creatures—namely, animals—who have a capacity to suffer but cannot express their interests and cannot demand their rights?

Beyond Sausage and Cheese
May We Eat Animals?

In the fall of 1970, Peter Singer, a young man who had recently arrived in England to begin teaching at the University of Oxford after studying philosophy in Melbourne, sat in the large dining hall digging into a steak. Even as a teenager, Singer had been fascinated by philosophy and ethics. His parents were originally from Vienna, but the persecution of the Jews in Germany and Austria during Nazi rule forced them to leave the country in 1938. They were quite young at the time, and fled from Austria to Australia. Their own parents—Peter Singer's grandparents—were arrested by the Nazis and murdered in the Theresienstadt concentration camp.

Singer had taken his studies very seriously, particularly when it came to ethics. He wanted to plumb the nature of good and evil and find out what constitutes a good life. While eating his steak in the stately dining hall, he noticed a student pushing the meat on his plate to the side. Singer asked the student—whose name was Richard Keshen, and who later became a professor of philosophy at Cape Breton University in Canada—what was wrong with his food. Richard replied that he was a vegetarian and would never eat meat, because it was absolutely wrong to eat animals. Singer was astonished by Richard's resolute attitude. Richard challenged him to name a single good reason why it would be morally defensible to eat animals. Singer needed to think it over for a while, so they arranged to meet in the dining hall the following day, at which time Singer would give Richard a good reason why animals could be eaten. Then he polished off his steak, unaware as yet that it would be the last steak of his life.

On his way home from the university, Singer began to ponder the question. People had always eaten meat. Back in the days of aurochs and mammoths, humans had hunted and eaten animals. Later, herdsmen and farmers bred sheep and goats, cattle and pigs for the purpose of eating them. People in prehistoric times and in many nonindustrialized societies would never have survived if they had not included meat in their diets. But it became clear to Singer that none of those reasons applied to him personally. Eskimos might have to hunt seals to survive, but that was no reason for him, Peter Singer, to eat animals. In a country like England, a meatless diet would be easy to follow and wouldn't pose a threat to his health. Singer thought about the fact that wolves, lions, and crocodiles also ate meat. He realized that there wasn't a question of whether they ought to do so, because without meat, they would die. Singer knew that he would not die if he did not eat meat. In contrast to wolves, lions, and crocodiles, he could choose not to eat meat, and in that sense he was superior to them, and to the cattle, pigs, and chickens he ate in the university dining hall. Man is cleverer than animals; he has higher intelligence, a sophisticated language, reason, and understanding. Many philosophers in antiquity, the Middle Ages, and the modern era had offered this as the rationale for man to eat animals: People are endowed with reason, and animals are not. Humans are valuable, and animals are not. But can we really say that intelligent life is fundamentally more valuable than less intelligent life? Superior intelligence does not give you carte blanche to do as you like. Singer spent three years engrossed in the subject of how people should treat animals. In 1975, he published *Animal Liberation*, a bestseller that sold more than half a million copies.

The most important criterion for a living being's right to life, Singer wrote, is not intelligence or reason. A newborn baby is less developed in these faculties than a pig, but we are not entitled to eat a baby or to use it in experiments to test a new shampoo. The crucial reason for respecting a living being and acknowledging its right to live is its ability to feel pleasure or pain. On that point, Singer concurred with Bentham, who in 1789, the year of the French Revolution, had written:

The day *may* come, when the rest of the animal creation may acquire those rights which could never have been withholden from them but

by the hand of tyranny. . . . It may one day come to be recognized
that the number of legs, the villosity of the skin, or the termination
of the *os sacrum* are reasons equally insufficient for abandoning a
sensitive being to the same fate. What else is it that should trace the
insuperable line? Is it the faculty of reason, or perhaps the faculty of
discourse? But a full-grown horse or dog is beyond comparison a
more rational, as well as a more conversable animal, than an infant
of a day or a week or even a month old. But suppose they were otherwise, What would it avail? The question is not, Can they *reason*? nor
Can they *talk*? but, Can they *suffer*?

Singer adopted Bentham's utilitarian view that pleasure is good and
pain is bad, not only for humans but for all living creatures that can experience pleasure and pain, because animals, as sentient beings, are in essence
identical to people. The question of whether humans may eat the "other animals" is thus easy to decide: The simple human culinary pleasures are
ridiculously unimportant when compared to the unspeakable suffering of
the animals that had to forfeit their lives.

Singer's book on liberating animals from human domination caused
quite a stir and gave rise to an animal rights movement in England, the
United States, and Germany. The goals of organizations such as People for
the Ethical Treatment of Animals (PETA) and Animal Peace extend far beyond the platforms of traditional wildlife conservationists. Animal rights
activists protest not only mass animal farming, fur farms, and cruelty to
animals, but any exploitation of animals at all, arguing that people should
not be allowed to eat any animal products or cage animals in a zoo or the circus or use them for experiments. They insist on the right of animals to a
free and content life.

As persuasive as Singer's views might seem, they were attacked fiercely
by many philosophers. If the ability to feel pain, as opposed to the ability to
reason and reflect, or, for that matter, simply belonging to the species
Homo sapiens, forms the moral boundary, they argued, where exactly do we
draw the line? Pigs and chickens can suffer—we know that a pig squeals and
a chicken squawks if tortured or slaughtered. But what about fish? Can fish
feel pain? The latest studies suggest that they can, even if they are unable to
express it. And how about invertebrates, such as mussels? We know far too

little about their experience of pain to make any claims about it. Actually, we humans do not even know the extent to which plants might suffer. Does lettuce feel pain when we pull it out of the ground?

The perception of pain does not have a clear boundary. And this criterion is problematic because animal states of consciousness are not directly accessible to us. In the chapter about the brain we saw how difficult it is to pinpoint subjective experiences in humans. It is even more difficult to make statements about animals' subjective experiences. In 1974, when Singer was writing his book about animal liberation, Thomas Nagel, who is currently on the faculty at the NYU School of Law, published a now classic essay called "What Is It Like to Be a Bat?" Nagel was not particularly interested in animals but rather was making the point that trying to imagine how other living creatures, such as bats, view the world is simply impossible. We can only picture how we would feel if we flew through the night using echolocation to chase insects. But how could we tell whether this image meshes with the actual sensations of a bat? It probably does not. Consciousness—and this is what mattered to Nagel—always follows from the subjective character of experience and is thus fundamentally inaccessible to others.

Fair enough. But the fact that it is impossible to know exactly what goes through the minds of animals does not undermine Singer's argument. After all, we don't necessarily know the inner workings of the minds of our fellow humans, either, but that hardly gives us the right to torture them. No court permits torture, murder, and manslaughter on the grounds that the perpetrator could not have known precisely how the victim would feel during the crime. We ascribe a complex state of consciousness to our fellow humans and respect them on that basis alone. When it comes to animals, however, many scientists explain their psyches on purely biological grounds. But models based on observing animals' responses to stimuli are problematic. Do lions' dominance and submission rituals occur by accident or design? Who can say with any certainty? Human desire is also grounded in satisfying biological needs—avoiding pain, attaining sexual fulfillment—yet we do not reduce the quality of human experience to mere functional mechanisms, so why do so when considering animal experience? It would of course be naïve to project our own feelings and intentions onto animals, but it is equally naïve to regard animals as purely functional machines. How can we dismiss the possibility that the play instinct of animals goes beyond functionality? And although primate sexual activities and the sensations of pleasure they experience can be explained in functional terms, is that the whole story?

The ancient Chinese realized that it was impossible to know with any certainty what animals experience, but they used analogies to gain a sense of animals' inner lives, as we see in the following ancient Chinese story: Zhuangzi and Huizi are strolling across a bridge over the Hao River. Zhuangzi looks into the water and says to his friend: "Look at the slender fish darting about, so free and easy. That is the happiness of fish." "You are not a fish," Huizi replied. "How can you know that the fish are happy?" "You are not me," Zhuangzi responded. "How can you know that I don't know that the fish are happy?"

Modern neuroscience also employs analogies of this kind, examining reactions in our vertebrate brains and surmising that similar structures in the brains of other vertebrates are associated with comparable qualities of experience. In addition to establishing actual and apparent points of correspondence, they attempt to figure out why we identify more closely with some animals than with others. When we look at dolphins, we read their facial expression as a smile, and our mirror neurons engage. Most of us find dolphins likable. Animals with "strange" faces, by contrast, fail to stimulate our mirror neurons, and we can't locate a point of familiarity to arouse feelings of empathy. By contrast, we feel as though we can identify with some canine behavior; we enjoy dogs' playfulness and infer pleasure on their part. But there are limits. "We don't know," says Giacomo Rizzolatti, "what barking means, so we cannot mirror it. Barking does not figure in the human vocabulary of motor acts. People can imitate 'barking,' some of them even quite well, but we cannot really grasp what barking is."

Even after all this neuroscientific progress, we are still in the dark when it comes to the inner lives of animals, yet we persist in drawing a clear distinction between humans and animals in our legal and philosophical discourse and in everyday usage. In our society, no animal has a moral right to decent treatment. From a legal point of view, chimpanzees and plant lice are more closely related than man and chimpanzee. Humans have a constitution; chimpanzees have only animal welfare legislation with provisions that place them on the same level as moles and fail to take full account of the biological reality.

At the very minimum, highly developed vertebrates, such as primates and dolphins, should not be cast aside without rights. For Peter Singer, as for every preference utilitarian, "self-awareness" is the criterion that makes a life unconditionally worth protecting. That seems like a good basis, although we need to bear in mind that self-awareness cannot be determined neurologically by means of scanners. Some philosophers equate self-awareness with a sense of self, and conclude that even higher primates lack a morally relevant self-awareness. But neuroscience has shown that "sense of self" is not a hard-and-fast category. The chapter "Mach's Momentous Experience" discussed the many forms it can take. Some of them, for example, the corporal self, the locational self, and the perspectivist self, are clearly present in apes—if they weren't, apes would barely be able to function.

It is obvious that some vertebrates have at least a rudimentary self-awareness, but what moral value should we ascribe to this? Take elephants, for example. When local hunters in Africa kill these highly developed and sensitive animals to sell their ivory, may these "poachers" be shot? In Kenya, it would be perfectly legal to do so. But Singer would argue that they may not, because people have a more highly developed self-awareness than elephants. But what about when someone kills three elephants, or five, or ten? And what if these are female elephants who leave behind calves half-mad with fear? Then, says Singer, the balance tips in favor of the elephants. But what about the hunters' families? One can evaluate all kinds of variations on this theme and still wind up with arbitrary assessments.

The greatest problem in using self-awareness as the sole yardstick of the worth of a living creature's life is, however, its counterintuitive consequences, as we saw in the chapter about abortion. If the worth of a living creature's life depends on the complexity of its feelings and behavior, newborns and severely mentally disabled adults are on the same level as or even a lower level than, say, a German shepherd. Singer's intention is not to belittle the lives of newborns or of severely mentally disabled individuals, but only to raise the status of animals. Still, he has unleashed a storm of controversy, and his philosophy continues to infuriate many disabled rights advocacy groups. Self-awareness is an inadequate measure of issues pertaining to animal rights or abortion guidelines. As we can see from the example of the mother who instinctively prefers her infant to a German shepherd, we should not attempt to exclude intuition and instincts from moral philosophy.

The question of how to treat animals thus needs to factor in not only rational considerations, but also instincts. It is a very natural instinct to assess the lives of people differently from those of animals. Mapping our moral feelings is like throwing a stone into the water and watching it form a series of concentric circles. The innermost circle contains our parents, siblings, children, and close friends, the next circle comprises the people we know (and perhaps even our beloved pet), then comes humanity as a whole. Trout and chickens bred for broiling are typically well beyond these circles. While these moral circles do not extend out indefinitely, the fact that so many edible animals are marginalized results not from a law of nature but rather from current practices of displacement and manipulation.

If we factor human feelings into the equation on the issue broached at the beginning of this chapter, the question becomes: Is it defensible for us to eat animals that we could not bring ourselves to kill with our own two hands? Western civilization today has many of us feeling that it would be very difficult to make ourselves slaughter a pig or a calf—assuming we even knew how to do it. Many people do not have the same aversion to killing fish, and most people seem to have no qualms about "killing" chicken eggs. People evidently agonized less over the issue of killing animals in the past, and this is still the case in many less industrialized nations today. Morality is more a reflection of our cultural sensibility than an outgrowth of an abstract definition. And the West appears to be experiencing an unprecedented resistance to killing animals at this time, which is why the meatpacking industry packages a knuckle of veal to make it look as unlike a calf as possible. We aren't horrified by the idea of eating packaged meat because we haven't experienced the suffering of the animals directly. Our mirror neurons fire at the sound of a calf bellowing in the slaughterhouse, but they do not react at the sight of a packaged cutlet in the supermarket.

It is up to each individual to decide whether logical arguments should dissuade him or her from eating meat. If we think it over rationally, we are likely to conclude that the case against eating meat—both utilitarian and moral—is more persuasive. The choice to forgo steak, hamburgers, and roast chicken altogether or simply to eat meat less often depends in large part on how strongly we are sensitized or are open to being sensitized on this issue.

Great Apes in the Cultural Arena
How Should We Treat Great Apes?

Jerom died on February 13, 1996, ten days shy of his fourteenth birthday. The teenager was dull, bloated, depressed, sapped, anemic, and plagued by diarrhea. He had not played in fresh air for eleven years. As a thirty-month-old infant, he had been intentionally infected with HIV virus SF2. At the age of four, he had been infected with another HIV strain, LAV-1. A month short of five, he was infected with yet a third strain, NDK.

———

This is the opening passage of a report by legal scholar Steven Wise, who teaches animal rights law at Harvard Law School and other universities, about the laboratory chimpanzee Jerom, who was one of eleven great apes kept in isolation in a windowless cell made of steel and concrete in the Chimpanzee Infectious Disease building of the Yerkes Regional Primate Research Center at Emory University, where he died. Wise, who is president of the Center for the Expansion of Fundamental Rights in Boston, has championed the cause of extending three essential human rights to the great apes: the inalienable right to life, the right to bodily integrity, and the right to free personal development.

The call to grant chimpanzees, bonobos, gorillas, and orangutans fundamental human rights began in a movement initiated by Peter Singer and

the Italian animal rights activist Paola Cavalieri in 1993, when they published a book that functioned as a manifesto of a newly formed organization: *The Great Ape Project*. Their view of primates is clearly formulated in
their book: Apes have a social and emotional life similar to that of man, and
their intelligence closely approaches ours, yet they do not enjoy full legal
protection.

Were Peter Singer and Paola Cavalieri onto something? Do we need to
change our relationship with the great apes? Back in the eighteenth century, Carl Linnaeus of Sweden, the inventor of scientific nomenclature, had
initially classified man and chimpanzee, *Homo sapiens* and *Homo troglodytes*, as members of the same genus. Two hundred thirty years later, it
turned out that he was not entirely wrong. In 1984, Charles Sibley and Jon
Ahlquist, both molecular biologists at Yale, published the results of their
long-term DNA studies of humans and apes, results that are still considered core scientific knowledge. The genetic makeup of orangutans and humans, the studies found, differs by about 3.6 percent; gorillas and humans
by approximately 2.3 percent; and chimpanzees and humans (and also
bonobos and humans) by about 1.6 percent. These abstract numbers really
jump out when we consider that the difference between chimpanzee and
gorilla is more than 2 percent and that the two gibbon species under examination differ from each other by about 2.2 percent. The likely genetic difference between *Homo sapiens* and *Pan troglodytes* (as the chimpanzee is
called today) is astonishingly small: 98.4 percent of the human DNA is
chimpanzee DNA. The two species are about as closely related as horses and
donkeys. On a biomolecular level they are closer than mice are to rats or
camels are to llamas. In light of these results, the evolutionary biologist
Jared Diamond at UCLA has advocated a new classification system for the
apes. "Now, future taxonomists may see things from the chimpanzees' perspective," Diamond argues, "a weak dichotomy between slightly higher
apes (the *three* chimpanzees, including the 'human chimpanzee') and
slightly lower apes (gorillas, orangutans, gibbons). The traditional distinction between 'apes' (defined as chimps, gorillas, etc.) and humans misrep-
resents the facts." The significance of the biological facts seems
overwhelming. Can there be any doubt that great apes and humans are
nearly identical and hence must be treated in more or less the same way?

Doubts do exist, and they come from evolutionary biology itself. Genetic proximity is not the only biological criterion that comes into play.

From a phylogenetic point of view, crocodiles and pigeons are more closely related than crocodiles and tortoises. Even so, biologists include crocodiles and tortoises in the reptile family, but not pigeons. These classifications factor in adaptation to the environment and way of life as well as the degree of relationship. But to what degree do apes and humans differ in this respect? Maybe the German zoologist Alfred Brehm was right when he commented in the mid-nineteenth century, "Our aversion to the apes is based on both their physical and their mental abilities. They resemble man both too much and too little."

Japanese ethologists in the 1950s and '60s claimed to have found evidence of cultural activity in monkeys when they observed a colony of red-faced macaques on Koshima Island. Without human guidance, several juvenile macaques learned behaviors that had never been observed among apes living in the wild. Highly publicized studies reported that the macaques washed sweet potatoes before eating them, removed sand from wheat by floating the mixture in the water, and tapped new food sources, such as seaweed and shellfish. Significantly, these practices were copied by other members of the colony and passed on to future generations "culturally." And great apes have exhibited still more evidence of cultural behavior. The famous British primatologist Jane Goodall reported in the late 1960s that chimpanzees in nature use crumpled leaves to suck water from narrow crevices, fish for termites with blades of grass, and even strip the leaves from twigs to fashion tools. When Jane Goodall reported these findings to the paleoanthropologist Louis Leakey, she received a now legendary telegram in reply: "Now we must redefine tool, redefine man, or accept chimpanzees as humans."

The most striking and significant difference in comparing man and ape is obviously human language. No one seriously disputes that apes use a complex system of sounds to communicate. Apes also have Wernicke's area in the temporal lobe, which is linked to understanding words, and Broca's area in the prefrontal cortex, which is used to produce language and grammar. But why aren't they able to use a sophisticated oral language to communicate the way humans do? The answer is quite simple. As we saw earlier (in "The Fly in the Bottle," p. 66), the secret of human language lies in the larynx, which is situated several centimeters lower in humans than in all other primates, including the great apes. Most likely there was a reciprocal influence between the changes in the laryngeal area of the early *Homo sapi-*

ens and the subsequent development of the brain centers for symbolic communication, a process that did not occur in the other primates.

Even so, there have been some successes in language experiments. In the 1960s, Beatrice and Allen Gardner at the University of Nevada made headlines when they taught two chimpanzees, Washoe and Lucy, Ameslan, an American sign language used by the hearing-impaired. The Gardners reported that the two young chimpanzees learned a vocabulary of several hundred words. Great apes are capable of using abstract symbols for objects, situations, and actions, and associating them with specific people, animals, and items, as the psychologist Sue Savage-Rumbaugh noted in the 1980s while experimenting with a bonobo named Kanzi. Within the space of two years, Kanzi mastered a keyboard with 256 word symbols and used it routinely to make requests, confirm facts, reenact events, choose among options, or express feelings. Moreover, Kanzi reacted to several hundred words of spoken English. Experiments by Lyn White Miles at the University of Tennessee in Chattanooga yielded comparable results for orangutans.

All these achievements, though, are far surpassed by Koko, a female gorilla in Woodside, California, south of San Francisco. After twenty-five years of intensive training, Koko has mastered more than a thousand American Sign Language concepts and understands about two thousand English words. In 1998, the Internet carried the first live chat with Koko. Her sentences ranged between three and six words long, included references to time, and even featured jokes. Koko's IQ, which has been professionally tested, falls between 70 and 95. (One hundred points is considered normal human intelligence.) Koko can rhyme words—"do" and "blue," "squash" and "wash"—and invent metaphors, such as "horse tiger" for a zebra and "elephant baby" for a Pinocchio doll. She responds to the question "Why Koko not be like other people?" with this clever and accurate reply: "Koko gorilla." In more than three decades of regular training, Koko, who is now advanced in years, has acquired a greater virtuosity in human language than any other nonhuman living being to date. Learning from Koko means learning something about the psychology of gorillas in general, according to the zoologist and animal rights activist Francine "Penny" Patterson. For example, what might gorillas say when they are happy? "Gorilla hug." And how might gorillas retaliate when someone scolds them? With the insult "dirty toilet devil."

Koko's successes are possible only under isolated laboratory conditions. Gorillas living in the wild or the zoo have other things to do besides worry about human grammar. Still, to all appearances, gorillas are more intelligent than their natural orientation to their habitat and finding food would require. As with humans, primate intelligence arises from the needs and necessities of social behavior. Of all the challenges in the primate world, the rules governing hordes are the most complex. The intelligence of the great apes arises from a social structure, which shows why any language experiments involving great apes are problematic. Only the meanings that occur within or in reference to their realm can be learned; everything else remains beyond their range by nature, just as people are stymied by much of what great apes do. Intelligence is thus closely tied to species-specific social interaction. Still, experiments with great apes measure their achievements not by their own yardstick but by the yardstick of the human species. Seen in this way, their linguistic prowess approximates that of a two-year-old, and their mathematical abilities, as shown in an in-depth study of the female chimpanzee Ai in Kyoto published a few years ago, can rise to the achievement level of preschool children. It became evident that when great apes learn to use language and the numerical system, they forgo many of their normal species-specific forms of behavior and communication.

Meanwhile, humans are not defined solely by their ability to use language and perform mathematical operations. Babies and adults with severe mental disabilities may display minimal capabilities in these areas, but they rightly enjoy complete moral protection—which is virtually always denied to the great apes. Paradoxically, the fact that chimpanzees and gorillas display mathematical and linguistic prowess in the laboratory is regarded as their ticket of admission to the human moral community, yet humans themselves have no need to prove intelligence in order to receive moral consideration.

Even so, the Great Ape Project harps on the intellectual achievements of great apes, arguing that not only genes but also fundamental qualities of the mind such as self-awareness, intelligence, complex forms of communication, and social systems make great apes eligible to join a moral community that comprises "humans and non-human great apes." The admission criterion is the preference utilitarian concept of the "person," and because great apes have desires and preferences and pursue interests just as humans do, they are considered "persons." They are therefore entitled not only to unconditional protection but also to basic rights, such as the right not to be exploited in animal experiments or be put on display in the zoo or at the circus. They also have the right to a natural habitat, somewhat analogously to the rights of an endangered culture. According to the Great Ape Project, the United Nations, rather than wildlife conservationists, needs to step up to protect them.

There are obvious objections to demands of this kind. Does it really make sense to speak of great apes' "rights" to freedom from bodily harm, freedom to live up to their full potential, and so forth, without at the same time thinking about how they might fulfill their accompanying "responsibilities"? How, for example, should great apes, once integrated into the human community, pay taxes or complete their military service? All irony aside, we still need to ask what happens if an ape violates human rights that it did not accept on its own behalf but that were granted to it. How would we judge "war" among chimpanzees or "murder" and "cannibalism" among great apes? What would be done with an ape that injures or even kills a human—would it be sentenced according to the legal guidelines for humans?

A second sticking point in the Great Ape Project is its logical inconsistency. On the one hand, animal rights activists are intent on blurring the distinction between man and animal, which is branded "speciesism." A criterion of morality, it is argued, is not that man belongs to the human species, but that man has complex sensations and possesses at least a basic set of interests. People, it is claimed, have to learn not to use their own species as a measure, but instead must accept every living creature that fulfills the condition of being a "person." That is all well and good, but in that case, how can the Great Ape Project argue that great apes are entitled to preferential moral treatment precisely because they are the animals most similar to humans? This is the reason some animal rights activists consider the Great Ape Project far too weak, inconsistent, or "anthropocentric." Like conservative critics who reject the whole idea of shifting the line between man and animal, they ask what would be gained from setting the new line between orangutan and gibbon instead of between man and chimpanzee.

Advocates of the Great Ape Project stress the symbolic nature of their demands. Peter Singer would like to see the line shifted beyond the gibbon and have rights granted to all animals that experience pain and pleasure. In this view, the call for human rights for the great apes is only the first step, and it has already enjoyed its first successes. In October 1999, the government of New Zealand granted all great apes there—about thirty in all—an inalienable right to life. Since 1997, Great Britain has also outlawed animal experiments with great apes. Could these developments signal the beginning of a major shift in thinking and the end of the age-old distinction between animal and man? Maybe it is time for cognitive science to take over from traditional ethics. As we have seen, brain research has established entirely new hierarchies in the relationship between impulses and reflexes, reactions and processing. We now know that reason is only one limited component of human consciousness. Most things in our world are prelinguistically determined, as a result of capabilities that man and other animals have in common. The idea that reason is a distinguishing feature of human behavior is pure fiction. Classifying the great apes as closer to humans or to animals is a question of definition. As the Japanese primatologist Toshisada Nishida sums up this issue: "Chimpanzees are charming in their own right. They are inferior to us in some aspects, but superior in others." In any case, the current state of knowledge about humans and great apes has forced us to adjust our thinking, whatever the fine print of the law. It is clear that the more we learn from brain research, the nearer we move to our closest living relatives. The results of behavioral psychology are quickly being dwarfed by neurological advances. Perhaps it's a pity: Behavioral psychology has coaxed out wise, witty, and soothing insights like this one offered by Koko, which gives the lie to the common preconception that animals have no notion of death. "Where do gorillas go when they die?" Patterson's colleague Maureen Sheehan asked Koko. Koko thought it over, then pointed to three signs: "Comfortable hole bye."

When Charles Darwin proved the origin of man in the animal kingdom, he still stopped short of characterizing man as an "intelligent animal" for quite some time. Even in the twentieth century, the famous evolutionary biologist Julian Huxley, a grandson of Darwin's contemporary Thomas Henry Huxley, called man *Psychozoa* ("mind-animal") to highlight man's uniquely gifted grade of life. Neuroscience is now pulling us out of this noble enclave and back to our relatives, who are neither mindless creatures nor "lower" beings and have a value that must be acknowledged. But where does this value begin, and is all of nature worth protecting and preserving?

The Wail of the Whale
Why Should We Protect Nature?

They are intelligent, musical, and sensitive. Mothers nurse their babies for eight months and care for them for several years. At the age of thirteen, they reach sexual maturity. Few other animals have such social and varied lives. Their language is intricate and complex, and they take care of one another in an exemplary manner. Their playful nature is engaging and enchanting. They live a long life, to the age of seventy and beyond, because their only natural enemies are the Norwegians, Icelanders, and Japanese. Over the past twenty years, twenty-five thousand whales have been harpooned by whalers, bleeding to death with their internal organs shredded, or suffocating, half-butchered, on the decks of modern factory ships, with ruptured lungs or punctuated diaphragms. Twenty-five thousand dead whales—how can God, or a supposedly rational community of states, allow this to happen?

A 1986 resolution by the International Whaling Commission stipulates that no whales may be killed in the oceans unless they are hunted by indigenous peoples in the Arctic or will be used for research purposes. Since that time, many Japanese have been bent on researching whales, and they "study" up to a thousand whales a year. Norwegians have been declared an indigenous people, which allows them to skirt the resolution as well. In other words, anyone determined to kill whales can find a way to do so, while the International Whaling Commission sits back and watches or even casts a majority vote against the ban.

Whaling is a fairly unappetizing business—as the Japanese know full well, even though they insist that whaling is simply part of Nippon's medieval tradition and cannot be abolished just because the number of whales is declining. Interestingly, the declining population is the only argument invoked by opponents of whaling who serve on the commission. Their motive for preserving the whales is their rarity—not their right to life. The United Nations has a Human Rights Council for people, but there is no corresponding Animal Rights Council, only a whaling commission. There is no international agency to protect animals or ensure their rights. The highest authority is the Convention on International Trade in Endangered Species of Wild Fauna and Flora (CITES).

The first CITES conference convened in Washington, D.C., in 1973 and drew up an Endangered Species Act. But since 1973, people have nonetheless wiped out about half of all the species of animals and plants that existed then; that is a mass extinction of enormous magnitude. In the past few decades, people have inflicted greater damage on the earth than in all the preceding centuries, from the beginning of mankind until World War II. Each year, 5 percent of the land surface of the planet falls victim to flames. Only 6 percent of the planet's land surface still contains tropical forests, the most species-diverse biotopes on earth; within less than thirty years, the forests have dwindled to less than half their original size. If the current deforestation trends continue at this rate, the last tropical tree will have been felled by the year 2045. Day by day, several hundred animal species die out, most of them nameless and never discovered by science.

No one knows today how many species still exist. The number may be the oft-cited 30 million; then again, it may be as high as 100 million, or as low as 6 million. In contrast to the Cretaceous period, which began with the end of the dinosaurs and the beginning of the Age of Mammals, the current rate of extinction is about a million times higher than the rate at which new species emerge. One-fifth of all known bird species have already died out or are at the brink of extinction. With the loss of every species, the complex genetic makeup of 1 to 10 billion base pairs dies out forever. The failure of the mass media and politicians to address this issue means that future generations will be faced with an enormous problem. Remarkably, there is only a single professorship allocated to environmental ethics in all of Germany, in contrast to about forty for eighteenth-century philosophy. The indifference on the part of the universities is dismaying. It is hard to find any philosophical discipline that is as neglected as environmental ethics. But from what other discipline might we expect satisfactory answers to the basic questions of how and why endangered species can be protected from extinction?

The answer to why they should be protected might appear simple. Protecting nature means protecting ourselves. People say that once trees die, man is sure to follow. Maybe so. But the matter is not that straightforward. James Lovelock, a famous British chemist, doctor, and geophysiologist with many scientific publications and numerous patents, believes that all living things need to be respected, but his view of what constitutes a living creature is quite peculiar. Lovelock counts not only plants and animals, but also substances that are typically considered dead, such as crude oil, humus, lime rock, and oxygen. All of these arose from the interaction of dynamic biochemical processes. In the 1980s and '90s, environmental philosophers used similar arguments (though less flowery language) to contend that the time had come to extend reverence, responsibility, respect, and dignity to all of nature.

Those who, like Lovelock, declare everything in nature to be of value can easily draw a host of strange, or even antihuman, conclusions, in which man figures as a dangerous interloper in a wonderful world of equilibrium and harmony. Lovelock, who turned ninety in 2009, has managed to see a positive side to the nuclear reactor catastrophe in Chernobyl: Because people no longer venture into the contaminated areas, many trees and bushes now grow in the deserted region. Plants are generally more immune to radioactivity than humans. To Lovelock's utter delight, the new habitat is untouched by human hands. Clearly, this pleasure would not be shared by anyone who has been affected personally by the catastrophe. It would be impossible to imagine the mother of a cancer-stricken Chernobyl baby welcoming this development.

Beauty in nature cannot be equated with goodness, and once you have experienced the vicious side, it is hard to regard it as beautiful. Cliffs, canyons, deserts, and gorges, which today we view as magnificent, are the remains of enormous catastrophes. Cosmic explosions, meteorite collisions, devastating volcanic eruptions, and other geological disasters chronicle the history of a planet that began with a tremendous diversity of life forms and has retained only a single percent of that biodiversity. The rest dwindled away forever, buried in volcanic ash, frozen under the gray layer of dirt in the atmosphere, ensnared in insidious traps, jagged jaws, and vicious claws, losers in the cold battle for reproductive success. It takes quite a bit of romantic ignorance to reconcile the cruelties and dissonances of life with an image of a Garden of Paradise created in peaceful harmony. Nature is neither good nor bad per se; these categories simply do not come into play.

It is no easy matter to determine the inherent value of nature. If millions of animal species have died out without human intervention—and philosophers in the West even see this as a "harmonious process"—how can we decry man's eradication of the animal kingdom? Man is also an animal, and the fact that man displaces or wipes out other animal species is a "natural process" that occurs in nature on its own, albeit on a lesser scale. In this light, *Homo sapiens,* which in the past millennia has taken possession of the entire planet and multiplied into billions, is one natural catastrophe among many others. As a biological selection factor, humans even decide the direction evolution takes: who gets to survive, and who dies out.

Those who are uneasy with the idea of an intrinsic value in nature tend to argue instead that if nature has a value, that value is surely *for man,* and that it is in our ecological self-interest to retain the diversity of species. We need the rain forest for our atmosphere; we need clean oceans for our climate and our supply of drinking water. Everything on our planet, we're told, is interrelated; the world is one big ecosystem in which every species has an important place.

But is that really the case? The question of the ecological significance of the diversity of species has yet to be resolved. Ecologists are essentially split between two conflicting views. Let us picture the world as an airplane to help us visualize the two possible roles of the many plant and animal species. One group of ecologists believes that every species is a rivet needed to hold the plane together; the demise of any species compromises the airworthiness of the plane, and it eventually crashes. Other ecologists see the matter quite differently; for them, many species are simply superfluous passengers in a plane that could also fly quite nicely with a small crew.

Whatever the case, one thing seems certain: Not every animal or plant species is ecologically indispensable. This is particularly true of many of the most beautiful of nature's assets. Siberian tigers, okapis, pandas, orangutans, and certain species of dolphins are threatened with extinction. But the fate of the taiga of the Sikhote-Alin mountain range does not rest on the remaining three hundred tigers there. The same is true of the okapis in the Ituri rain forest, the pandas in China, and the last orangutans in Sumatra and Borneo. And friends of dolphins can rest assured that it won't be the end of the ocean just because whales disappear from it. Although the long-term consequences of human intervention are hard to predict, the extinction of particular species appears not to affect the big picture too drastically. It may well be that only a few tree species are needed to keep the carbon cycle in the tropical forests going. The pollution of drinking water and the destruction of the protective ozone layer wreak enormous damage on the biological cycles of nature, but the extinction of tigers, okapis, pandas, orangutans, or whales does not. We seem to want to prevent many animals from becoming extinct even when they are nonessential for their respective ecosystems. Indeed, humans sometimes raise much more money and devote more energy to saving animals that are relatively unimportant ecologically than to some extremely important insects, microbes, and bacteria. Ecology is certainly not the only motivation for aiding endangered species, and that is just as it should be, because if we were to judge the value of life only according to its function for the biological cycle, we would wind up with horrible results. Certain bacteria serve a more important and beneficial role in ecology than do humans, so should we favor them over man if required to choose? And surely it is not cause for celebration that the 7 million people who die of starvation on our planet every year will not consume our natural resources and thus conceivably prolong the longevity of the tropical forests.

A strictly defined ecology does not incorporate moral considerations. No sane person regards other people as mere biocatalysts or metabolic units—even a sociopath like Phineas Gage probably wouldn't think in those terms. If we acknowledge that people have a value that differs from that of rubber trees, it is because humans are capable of complex feelings. But a dog, a cat, a pig, a tiger, or an elephant can also experience pain or pleasure. The difference between the right to life of a human being and that of the other animals is thus gradualistic at best, measured by the complexity of what we perceive to be their ability to feel. Wildlife conservation that disregards the right to life of highly complex forms of life makes no sense from this perspective—this right to life is the only ethical argument, so the CITES discussion about hunting quotas for whales is not just about whether the gray and minke whales prized in Norway and Japan are actually endangered, nor can the question of whether it is permissible to shoot African elephants ignore this issue. Those who deem it legitimate to kill what are said to be excess numbers of animals in the national parks need to consider the defensibility of their solution in a clear case of human overpopulation.

The question of the point of species protection, now and in the future, cannot be resolved solely on the basis of ecological practicality. And rarity is not necessarily an ethical factor, because rarity of a species says nothing about its capacity for suffering. Without a doubt, okapis, tigers, and orangutans have an interest in living. But if we establish that this is true of a single individual within a species, does that make it apply to the species as a whole? Here, it would seem, the crucial difference is whether we argue in the name of morality or in the name of the creatures in question. How important is it to establish that an animal would know and suffer from the knowledge that it would be the final member of its species? Should the Siberian tiger someday vanish forever from the Manchurian birch forests, the extinction of this species would likely interest the tiger less than it would us. We save the tiger not in the interest of the tiger, but in the interest of humans who find tigers fascinating and do not want to stand by and watch poachers finish off the last of these beautiful animals for a handful of dollars. But do aesthetic criteria matter when it comes to protecting endangered animal and plant species from extinction? Why do there need to be tigers in the boreal forests of the Sikhote-Alin when they are procreating quite nicely in the zoos of the world? Maybe our aesthetic need to recognize "values" that we did not create ourselves would die out along with the species.

No philosopher or ecologist can provide unequivocally valid reasons for the existence of all the millions of animal species on this planet. For that matter, it would take quite a bit of philosophical rationalization to explain why there need to be humans. The most compelling argument for the value of humans is their complex capability for suffering and happiness. But if the same is also true of whales and elephants, they should be protected from being killed and from losing their means of subsistence, too, not because they are rare or beautiful, but because they have an interest in living that we cannot ignore. And we should also proceed cautiously in dealing with creatures about whose emotional lives we have even less evidence, such as frogs, birds, plants, or jellyfish. People still pit their allegedly "anthropocentric" interests against those of other creatures in rationalizing actions that contaminate the oceans, pollute the air, and ruthlessly plunder natural resources, even though it's clear that man loses out in the process.

So where do we draw the line in modifying and manipulating nature to promote man's interests, and how does our own nature factor in?

Tears of a Clone
Can People Be Copied?

What is the Raelian cult up to, anyway? That ominous mélange of killer capitalism, science fiction, hippie dream, and horror church that some years
back in Montreal announced the creation of the first human cloned baby
and with it the path to immortality? The baby Eve, if she was ever born,
would now be seven years old, as would cloned babies 2 and 3, announced
by the sect, who were purportedly born in January 2003. The answer is simple: The Raelian cult is not doing much of anything. The group's founder
and head, the French sports journalist Claude Vorilhon, now makes an-
nouncements that pale in comparison to the ones about human cloning,
such as the creation of genetically modified peanuts for people with peanut
allergies. If the French novelist Michel Houellebecq had not endorsed the
group and revived interest in it, no one would even be inquiring into its
whereabouts.

For example, what is the Italian gynecologist Severino Antinori—that
other mastermind of cloning—doing these days? You may recall that back in
2002 he claimed to have impregnated three women with cloned babies. In
late November 2002, Antinori was still confirming the pregnancies and
claiming that the first cloned baby would be born during the first week of
January 2003. But Antinori's cloned children vanished unseen in all the
hullabaloo surrounding Vorilhon and his sect, never to resurface. A hunger

strike, declared in late January 2003 as a protest against the Italian secre-
tary of health, was Antinori's last publicized sign of life.

And how about the scientist Panayiotis Zavos at the Andrology Institute
of America in Lexington, Kentucky? In the summer of 2004, he had verifi-
ably cloned a human embryo, but he killed it after four days. The whole
thing, Zavos said at the time, was just a means of preparing for the eventual
implantation of a cloned human embryo into its mother's uterus. It appears
highly unlikely that anything of this sort actually occurred, given the lack of
reports of success from the otherwise garrulous Zavos.

More than ten years after Dolly, the cloned sheep, first saw the light of
day in a Scottish barn, there is still no evidence of cloned human children
anywhere. The vision that some embraced enthusiastically but that most
others found dismaying or appalling has gone unrealized so far.

But why does the idea of cloned people really distress us? What is ethi-
cally objectionable or reprehensible about cloning? And at what point in
the cloning process does it cross the line into immorality?

The artificial reproduction of humans, say the critics of cloning, violates human dignity. Kant famously wrote that man is "an end in himself"
and must not be "instrumentalized." Cloning, it is claimed, instrumentalizes man and degrades human dignity. Let us examine the two categories
used by genetic engineers today—"reproductive cloning" and "therapeutic
cloning"—to better evaluate this claim.

Reproductive cloning, as the term is used here, means creating an organism that is largely genetically identical to its original. The cell nucleus
(which, like every cell nucleus, contains the complete genetic material) is
extracted from a human somatic cell, then an egg cell is selected and enucleated. The nucleus of the somatic cell is now infused into the enucleated
egg cell, and the altered egg cell is implanted in the uterus of a surrogate
mother. If the experiment were to succeed in humans, the surrogate
mother would bring a child into the world nine months later, and this
child's genetic makeup would match the donor of the somatic cell. To date,
this procedure has been used on mice, rats, cattle, goats, pigs, African
wildcats, white-tailed deer, bison, horses, dogs, and sheep—including, of
course, the world-famous Dolly. But the procedure has not been attempted
successfully with humans.

There are very few outspoken advocates of human reproductive cloning.
Most countries explicitly outlaw the creation of genetically identical hu-

mans, though the United Nations has yet to enforce a global ban. (International law has been far laxer when it comes to cloning plants and animals.) Since the 1990s, the uniform multiplication of useful plants and working animals has become routine. But why are there ethical misgivings, both rational and intuitive, that arise in connection with the reproductive cloning of humans, yet not of other animals?

Many people cringe at the thought of human genetic material being copied and transferred to another human being. Thrillers and horror stories are full of nightmarish scenarios involving cloning. It is evidently one of our most deeply held beliefs that each individual is unique. A deliberate violation of this "law" seems sacrilegious to us. When it comes to animals, however, we are less squeamish. We may consider our pet dog, cat, or horse unique, but not our goldfish, and few of us stop to think about whether the pork on our plate came from a unique pig. The feeling of uniqueness is thus reserved for only a narrow segment of the living world.

Our intuitive qualms are supported by several arguments, but they are plausible only if we accept the argument that uniqueness is intrinsically valuable. Cloning a living creature reproductively requires many egg cells, because very few of the thousands of enucleated and restored egg cells actually develop into advanced organisms and result in a healthy living creature. The yield for animals is therefore very small, and most of the egg cells die, as would certainly be the case for humans as well. Even if everything appeared to go well, the days of a human produced in this way could be numbered. Dolly the sheep made it to the age of six—half the average life expectancy of a normal sheep. Dolly succumbed to progressive lung disease and severe arthritis in February 2003, and her early death raised questions about the sturdiness of her genetic makeup.

Dolly's premature aging and frailty present a striking but ultimately weak case against the reproductive cloning of humans, as it would imply that if "technical" errors of this kind were eliminated, the production of genetically identical people would be acceptable. And pointing out that numerous egg cells die in an experiment of this sort will matter only to those who believe that a human egg cell already possesses a life with dignity and is unconditionally worthy of protection.

Let us pause here for a moment to turn to the second question raised by cloning, the question of the value and drawbacks of *therapeutic cloning* for man. We need to start by replacing this misleading term. (Even the term "reproductive cloning" is incorrect, because cloning is always reproductive, in that it is a reduplicating.) The term "therapeutic cloning" refers to a medical vision of using embryos to grow tissue, or perhaps even organs, to be implanted in diseased individuals. In the process, embryos would be destroyed in the very earliest stage, after just a few cell divisions, and individual cells expanded to produce functional tissue. One day it may be possible to infuse these stem cells directly into a patient's organ as a curative therapy to replace damaged or destroyed somatic cells.

Even if therapeutic cloning were someday to be realized, which, as we will see later in this discussion, is rather unlikely, it would be not "therapeutic," but just as "reproductive" as "reproductive cloning." The difference lies not in the *process* of cloning, but in the *goal* pursued: Is the aim to produce genetically identical humans or to serve medical purposes?

Scientists are eager to explore the enormous range of theoretical possibilities for embryonic stem cells. Embryonic stem cells are like fresh snowfall that can assume all conceivable shapes and colors. Genetic engineers call them "totipotent" (having unlimited capability). Although theoretically any conceivable tissue can be made from stem cells, there have been few practical successes so far. Another major obstacle is posed by the immune systems into which the foreign stem cell tissue is infused. In animal experiments, the rejection rate is extremely high, as is the probability of cancerous tumors.

So how should cloning be assessed? Let us begin with the argument of human dignity. To what extent is a person not regarded as an "intrinsic value" in cloning, but "instrumentalized" in a morally reprehensible manner? In reproductive cloning, the matter seems straightforward. Ernst Mach's doubts notwithstanding, man has a deep need to regard himself as unique, as an "I" standing apart from others. Our entire self-concept and that of our culture are based in large part on this uniqueness. People who have difficulty referring to themselves as "I" generally suffer from a severe psychological disorder, yet a cloned man would likely have problems experiencing himself as an "individual" (which denotes lack of divisibility), because his very origin results from divisibility. He would be consigned to the status of a copy, unless he never met the person whose genetic makeup had become his and never learned of his own status as a clone.

But why carry out such a dreadful psychological and sociological experiment? While inquisitive researchers interested in the interior and exterior views of a clone stand to benefit, a cloned human would likely suffer severe psychological anguish. This is a clear case of "instrumentalization." No wonder the great majority of people and nations reject and outlaw reproductive cloning, particularly since there is no apparent benefit at present to offset the enormous disadvantage.

Cloning for research purposes seems different, because the cons we have discussed do not apply. There would be no fully developed humans to sustain psychological damage, but rather preconscious embryos destroyed in the most primitive stage of development. Still, as we saw in the chapter "The Birth of Dignity," an embryo of this kind is without a doubt a *Homo sapiens*, a human life in the biological sense, and the Embryo Protection Law invokes this argument to ban research on embryos in Germany.

But even the law does not treat embryos like people. Destroying an embryo illegally and killing a born human being are two entirely different matters. The legal penalty when embryos are involved is much less severe. This difference between destroying embryos and murdering people is highlighted when German lawmakers grant researchers permission to conduct research using embryos. The state makes no other exceptions that allow researchers to kill, which shows that the lawmakers do not fully subscribe to their own argument that embryos are absolutely worthy of protection. Thus we find the same contradiction as with the regulation of abortions, which defines embryos as people in both the biological and moral sense, but nonetheless grants permission to kill them at an early stage.

Clearly the issue of the human dignity of embryos is highly complex. If we accept the arguments in the previous chapters—that the value and the dignity of a life are based not on membership in a genus or species, but on whether a living creature has a consciousness and an elementary self-awareness and interests (which is certainly not the case for a human egg cell divided six or eight times)—there is no reason to ascribe human dignity to an embryo. Embryonic stem cell research instrumentalizes man in a biological but not in a moral sense. Without human dignity, the embryo is a commodity that can be weighed against other commodities. If researchers' hopes of curing diseases such as diabetes, Parkinson's, and Alzheimer's with clone therapy are even remotely realistic, utilitarian criteria can be applied in all good conscience in weighing the nonexistent suffering of destroyed embryos against the immense happiness of hundreds of thousands or even millions of cured patients.

This argument carries a great deal of weight, and it would take solid counterarguments to refute it. The strongest objection to cloning for research purposes is, interestingly, not a fundamental objection but a utilitarian one. Research cloning over the past ten years has resulted in plenty of sound and fury, yet the successes of the purported gene therapists have been few and far between. Still, the idea of using manipulated cells to replace diseased tissue is sound, and the question is only whether embryonic stem cells are the ideal solution.

Stem cells are not limited to embryos. Our bone marrow, liver, brain, pancreas, and skin all contain stem cells, which scientists call "adult" stem cells. Adult stem cells are versatile ("pluripotent") and quite capable of development. Throughout the course of our lives, they continue to form new specialized cells for our body. In a petri dish, they can mature into many kinds of cell tissues. But in contrast to embryonic stem cells, there are limits. A stem cell from the brain can develop into all types of neuronal nervous tissue, but most likely not into a liver cell. Still, there may be exceptions in stem cells from amniotic fluid, from umbilical cord blood, and from deciduous teeth.

The immense advantage of adult stem cells over embryonic stem cells is clear. If biological and chemical stimulation could be used to cultivate stem cells from my own brain to form new brain tissue and to reimplant it in my brain in the place of diseased tissue, my immune system would be unlikely to reject it, and there would be no apparent elevated risks of cancer associated with the procedure. Since the 1960s, doctors have been using stem cells from the bone marrow that help to form blood in treating leukemia and lymphomas. There have been numerous clinical studies using adult stem cells to treat cardiac and vascular disease. Successes in clinical studies are emerging for patients suffering from paralysis and Parkinson's disease and those recovering from heart attacks. Rats with brain tumors are being treated quite successfully with injections of adult stem cells.

Research with adult stem cells appears promising. If the often heralded breakthrough in curing Parkinson's disease succeeds in the next couple of decades, more can be expected from stem cell research with adult cells than with embryonic cells. But often research projects in both areas wind up competing fiercely for public and private research funding. Supporting embryonic stem cell research inevitably means not investing the same money in the more fruitful field of adult stem cell research, which offers not only the far more realistic chance of a cure but also a path that is socially unproblematic. Adult stem cells can be harvested easily, whereas embryonic stem cells require human egg cells, usually as the result of artificial insemination. But the supply is limited. Egg donations may one day go commercial, with women from developing countries providing the supplies—and all the ethical problems that entails.

If we employ utilitarian calculus to weigh the projected happiness from a cure produced by embryonic stem cell research against a cure arising from adult stem cell research, the latter appears to be the far better route. We should not conclude, however, that research with embryonic stem cells should cease on moral grounds. The utilitarian calculus can only consider *predicted* successes, but it provides a perspective from which to evaluate the claims, image, and societal significance of this branch of research, which has given rise to such heated controversies in recent years.

Genetic engineering is thus not only a fundamental moral question but also has significant social and ethical dimensions, the same dimensions we encounter with the next problem in modern biomedicine: the question of preimplantation diagnostics.

Ready-made Children
Where Is Reproductive Medicine Heading?

Ghent is a lovely seaport city in East Flanders, famous for its flower market and quaint little streets. But in 2002 and 2003, young couples flocked there for another reason. Dr. Frank Comhaire, a specialist in reproductive medicine, offered couples a very special service for a hefty fee: the choice of gender for their future child. About four hundred couples left Ghent expecting a child of the gender of their choosing.

Comhaire's practice worked with a laboratory in Fairfax, Virginia, sending the sperm of the prospective father from Belgium to the United States, where machines sorted the sperm cells according to gender. Since male Y chromosomes glow less brightly than female X chromosomes under the light of the laser, they could be separated out using MicroSort technology. Back in Belgium, Comhaire fertilized an egg cell of the mother in a test tube with the sperm chosen by the parents, then implanted it. The Belgian doctor's practice was part of a large-scale medical experiment under the supervision of the FDA in the United States. Sixty clinics and seven international reproductive centers took part in this largest early-gender-selection enterprise of all time. The clients hailed from Spain, Belgium, the Netherlands, Great Britain, Scandinavia, France, and Germany.

The only firm requirement for participation in this gender selection was that the future mother be between eighteen and thirty-nine years of age. Preference was given to couples who already had a child, to comply with so-called family balancing. All other restrictions were dictated by the market. The cost of the blood analysis was 1,200 euros, the freight charges and laboratory expenses for the semen were 2,300 euros, and fertilization in the test tube and subsequent implantation came to 6,300 euros. An additional 6,000 euros would buy parents a guarantee of receiving the gender of choice. The high prices helped Comhaire uphold the morality of his operation by precluding any broad commercialization; the more exclusive the access, he argued, the smaller the ethical precariousness of the process. "Family balancing" had more to fear from the courts. In Belgium, the deliberate choice of gender for nonmedical reasons was not against the law, but the outcry of the mass media against Comhaire's family planning made the Belgian parliament impose a legal ban.

The American partners, by contrast, remained unruffled. American law still permits test tube gender selection of future children. The MicroSort technology, which was patented back in 1992, is a complete success. Its original purpose was to serve public health. It could be used, for example, to select girls in families in which hemophilia could be passed on only to boys. In 1995, the first child selected with this technology was born. Since 1998, the company has offered its costly service to healthy couples as well.

In 2003, a Scottish couple with three sons made headlines in Great Britain. The family's only daughter had died in an accident, and to restore their family's "female dimension," the couple applied for the right to conceive a child in a test tube and to select the gender. The authorities rejected the application because there were no medical grounds for the procedure. The case was taken up in the media, with the British tabloids siding with the parents (in contrast to the situation in Belgium). In March 2005, the Science and Technology Committee of the British parliament called for a change in the law that would allow parents to determine the gender of their embryos conceived in a test tube if there were compelling grounds to do so. Although the Review of the Human Fertilisation and Embryology Act of December 2006 upheld the general ban, it is likely that exceptions could be allowed in the future.

The desires of ambitious and intrepid parents expand with the greater array of technical options. Once you can select gender, you might turn your thoughts to other features, such as eye color or height, which is a source of great concern to many experts in reproductive medicine. Will children become products, sorted by the rules of quality management and inventory control? Critics warn of "consumer eugenics" and "designer babies." Like cosmetic surgery, reproductive medicine could become a rapidly growing market that introduces entirely new norms. Parents who do not submit their children to tests to safeguard their health and optimize their aesthetics could soon be regarded as either too poor or too uncaring to save their child from an uncertain fate of lesser attractiveness and diminished social opportunities in the brave new world of the beautiful. This scenario may well loom ahead.

Let us make our way through the wide-ranging ethical field of Preimplantation Genetic Diagnosis (PGD) and examine the many opportunities and risks it entails. One of the important questions of human self-awareness is the question of how one was conceived—the old-fashioned way or in a test tube? This need never matter to the individual in question, but it raises vital questions for legal scholars, doctors, and moral philosophers, who must ponder what criteria should come into play with test tube conception and what one should be permitted to determine in creating new life.

The fertilization of egg and sperm in a test tube has become a routine procedure. The physician uses hormone injections to stimulate the development of multiple follicles of the ovaries, each containing an egg. The quality of the sperm is also tested. Once the hormone treatment takes effect, the doctor extracts the follicular fluid with an optimal total of five to twelve mature egg cells from the individual follicles, and the extracted egg cells are fertilized with the man's sperm in the test tube. The success rate is about 70 percent.

A newer procedure entails injecting a single (selected) sperm into the egg cell with a micromanipulator. If the egg cell has divided twice on the second day, two embryos are implanted in the woman's womb. Another common option is implantation after the fifth day of fertilization. The spare fertilized eggs are either destroyed or frozen in liquid nitrogen (which only a few countries permit). About two weeks after the embryo has been implanted, the pregnancy can be ascertained. The rate of success of carrying a child to term is about 40 percent.

Test tube fertilization was originally intended for two major groups of couples: those with a high familial risk of devastating hereditary diseases (so that their offspring could be tested and selected), and those unable to fertilize an egg naturally. For the latter group, the sperm may come from a different man or the egg from a different woman if warranted by the medical situation. A surrogate mother might also carry the embryo to term.

Most critics of PGD concede that an isolated case is not immoral, with the exception of those who reject PGD on religious grounds, who argue that the decision should always be in God's hands, not in the hands of parents. The main argument against PGD is its social and ethical consequences. Early routine inspections of embryos could open the floodgates. The harshest critics of the procedure reject PGD as a matter of principle. They regard it as a selection of "life worth living" over "life not worth living," which they consider immoral. They feel that it is not a basic right to have a healthy, nondisabled child. Less adamant critics have no problem with selection according to medical criteria; for them, the immorality begins with all the nonmedical selection points, such as gender, height, or beauty traits.

Let us consider the opinion of those who universally reject PGD. The distinction between "life worth living" and "life not worth living" brings to mind the barbaric atrocities of the Nazis, who classified mentally and physically disabled people as unworthy of living and murdered them. The state set itself up as an arbiter of the worth of people's lives and murdered people who had an interest in staying alive. These actions must be condemned in the strongest possible terms as the ultimate affront to humanity.

But the Nazis' grave moral breaches aren't really equivalent to PGD. As mentioned several times earlier, four- or eight-celled embryos are not people. And it is not the state intervening here; this is a choice made by expectant parents. And how can one make the case—on anything other than religious grounds—that couples don't have a right to a healthy, nondisabled child, especially if their choice has no deleterious effects? The selection of healthy embryos may go against our traditional notion of medical unpredictability in pregnancy, but human society has already done a great deal to lessen this unpredictability by reducing infant mortality and improving obstetrics. Why cling to tradition in the case of PGD? Doesn't this medical progress offer more advantages than disadvantages?

Critics of the procedure argue that if this kind of choice were allowed, everyone would eventually opt for it, or at least anyone who could afford it would. The element of chance that is traditionally part of bringing children into the world would then be replaced by widespread parental caprice. Developing countries, these critics argue, would have more and more boys and fewer and fewer girls, as is already the case in China, where the one-child policy has resulted in abortions to ensure that the one child be a boy. In the rich countries of the West, critics warn, there would be a predominance of tall, thin, athletic children with a healthy set of genes. The situation would be especially dire if only the upper classes could pick and choose: The rich select their looks, and the lower-class children remain "ugly." But however the situation plays out, is it really so reprehensible that it ought to be nipped in the bud on principle?

Many people are uneasy contemplating these ideas. But is unease an adequate argument? All this is still the stuff of science fiction. But once the options are out there and people are allowed to use them, the uneasy feeling might change. Who knows whether a generation of children created by deliberate selection will one day regard this procedure without any sense of unease, as absolutely normal and natural?

Just ten short years ago, cosmetic surgery had a shady reputation; now it is—at least in some circles and social classes—virtually a matter of course. How many children will one day complain to their parents for not being "optimized" early on? In the foreseeable future, PGD is sure to be followed by PGR (Preimplantation Genetic Repair) and PGO (Preimplantation Genetic Optimization). Defective genes in embryos could be replaced by healthy genes in the near future, which might be easier, more promising, and less expensive than treating a person who is already ill and disabled. PGO begins with well-researched genes that are responsible for particular traits. As far as we know today, it's rare that a specific negative trait can be traced to a single gene, but it does occur. A single gene determines the color of our eyes. An exchange could bring about a change from blue to brown, or the other way around. The notion of PGO even inspires visionaries to picture the optimization of the human species as more peaceful and moral creatures, as though morality were no more than a genetic disposition that can be pinpointed on a single gene.

The array of conceivable options is vast. Thirty years after the birth of the first test tube baby, Louise Joy Brown, reproductive medicine has evolved into a "world of miracles." Defending the boundary between a medical and a nonmedical selection or optimization is the easy resolution. In the case of medical selection and genetic error correction, no one is harmed, and both parents and child benefit. Aesthetic selection and correction, in contrast, entail an incalculable risk for the child; after all, the child is being shaped to fit the aesthetics of the parents, not to its own aesthetics. There is little difference of opinion about the desirability of health, but a great deal about ideals of beauty. Something I consider beautiful today may strike me as tacky or generic twenty years from now. And even if my taste remains constant, my child will not necessarily share it. So why should society promote aesthetic selection by authorizing it? Wouldn't it be preferable to safeguard parents from themselves and children from the taste of their parents?

That is one way of looking at it. But we can also ask to what extent it should be a legislative duty to intervene. Since when is it the task of the state to protect people from themselves? Protecting children from the values of their parents is also a tricky matter. That is exactly what happens in the case of an abortion—the mother makes decisions about the embryo's right to life and thus about its value. We've seen how difficult it is to legally force the mother not to make that kind of decision.

It is far more likely that the world of reproductive medicine will generate entirely new kinds of dubious miracles. For one thing, reproductive medicine opens the door to very different timelines. In July 2005, a forty-five-year-old woman in California gave birth to a child that she had had frozen thirteen years earlier as an embryo. Her twelve-year-old twins thus got a triplet sister, because all three children come from the same fertilization process. Steve Katz, an American specialist in reproductive medicine, contends that this is only the beginning. He projects that in the future, frozen embryos could be thawed out after fifty to a hundred years, when the parents are long since dead.

Another question revolves around the issue of growing "replacement parts." In July 2004, the case of two-year-old Joshua Fletcher caused quite a stir in Great Britain. Joshua suffers from a rare blood disorder. His body does not produce enough red blood cells, and thus he is not expected to survive into adulthood. His life could be saved by the donation of stem cells from the body of a close relative. But because neither his parents nor his brother is a genetic match, a close relative would need to be conceived first, ideally in a test tube so that the most similar from among the potential future siblings could be selected. The idea is to implant a sibling in his mother's womb whose stem cells would save Joshua without harming the new child. The British Human Fertilization and Embryology Authority (HFEA) allowed the procedure as a well-founded exception. Nothing is known about the outcome.

Another new opportunity that has arisen from reproductive medicine is the shift of the age limit up to which women are fertile. The late 1990s saw the beginnings of so-called ooplasmic transfer. If an older woman undergoing artificial insemination was concerned about the fertility of her egg cells, she could enhance them by adding cell plasma from the egg cell of a younger woman. The father of this method is Dr. James Grifo, who practices reproductive medicine in New York. Grifo was the first to test ooplasmic transfer to produce embryos. The experiment was successful, and Grifo children now live in China. Grifo had chosen China, which was boundlessly supportive of research, so that he could circumvent long-drawn-out licensing procedures in the United States.

Soon it was no longer necessary to go all the way to China. In 2001, a research group led by Jacques Cohen at the Institute for Reproductive Medicine and Science of Saint Barnabas Medical Center in Livingston, New Jersey, reported fifteen births of children whose conception had been assisted using ooplasmic transfer. But Grifo neglected to inform his patients that the donated ooplasma from a young woman is not simply neutral raw material, but contains many of the donor's mitochondrial chromosomes, which carry genetic material. If the donor mitochondria blend with the genetic material of the treated egg cell, the embryos conceived by ooplasmic transfer have three parents: the mother and the father for the genes in the cell nucleus, and the mother and the plasma donor for the mitochondrial genes. The child is a genetic mix not of two but of three individuals.

In November 2005, Douglas Wallace, at the University of California, Irvine, discovered that ooplasmic transfer was associated with extremely high risks. Many of the mice created through ooplasmic transfer turned out to be infertile, leading him to conclude that the children created by Grifo and Cohen might also show a high rate of infertility. Studies indicate that in the United States, reproductive medical experiments do not require the prior extensive animal testing that would be demanded of a hand cream or cough syrup anywhere in the industrialized world. They also show how baffled legislative bodies can be when asked to draw up laws governing the implementation of the latest cures in reproductive medicine. Sometimes it takes a grim prognosis like the effects of ooplasmic transfer on mouse fertility to point the way.

Authorizing embryonic experiments and PGD in a somewhat broader framework will eventually make it hard to keep up with the changes in technology and to impose bans on new techniques that grow out of approved methods yet pose unforeseen consequences that could run afoul of the law. If a procedure that appears to be harmless produces harmful results, the ensuing legal problems are immense. We cannot even imagine the magnitude of the ethical confusion and litigation that lies ahead. Will the Grifo and Cohen children one day sue their medical birth facilitators because their infertility might have been avoidable? Will they even lay claim to an inheritance and other financial support from their genetically related "second mothers," who years earlier agreed to provide plasma to enhance someone else's egg cells? Or, last but not least, will these second mothers demand the right to see and care for the children they did not anticipate having?

As we saw earlier, it is not the job of the state to protect parents-to-be from their own taste and ideas. Legislation of that kind would invariably culminate in totalitarianism. On the other hand, it *is* the duty of government to ward off foreseeable harm to society. The new opportunities offered by reproductive medicine are mired in this moral and legal morass. If matters that used to be determined by chance become matters of choice, the consequences would be enormous, because this kind of society would lose a feature that had been inevitable and inescapable: making the best of the hand you are dealt.

Once cosmetic surgery holds out the promise of a pretty face and body for everyone, reproductive medicine looms as the next step in preventing or eliminating imperfections from the moment of conception, and health and beauty become double entitlements for parents and children. As a consequence, society loses its understanding of and tolerance for perceived imperfections and deviations from generally accepted norms, putting parents and children in a tenuous position. Will the children approve of the "corrections" their parents bestow on them? And will they accept their parents' decision to forgo these corrections and possibly mark them as misfits?

Every new opportunity forces the judicial system to reweigh potential benefits against possible harm. Isn't it right and proper for Joshua Fletcher to get a sister who saves his life without suffering harm in the process, even if the sister eventually learns why she was created? Most of us were not conceived out of purely selfless love anyway. And who can say whether the sister was created *only* for this purpose and not from her parents' wish for another child? Choosing not to avail oneself of an opportunity can also be morally reprehensible.

On the other hand, consumer eugenics—selection according to physical characteristics—gives free rein to an unwelcome societal development: profound and universal unease. Even if consumer eugenics cannot be firmly rejected on any solid moral principle in a particular case, if the common good is the main objective, we cannot help feeling troubled by what we would be setting in motion when bringing children into the world. Do we want to expand our parental obligations to ownership of an object of our own design? It is not necessarily a bad thing to accept that not everything in life is correctable. In any case, the potential for modification offered by genetic engineering and reproductive medicine may soon be dwarfed by a sleeping giant: neuroscience.

"Bridge into the Spirit World"
How Far Can Neuroscience Go?

"The monkey could see. His eyes followed you around the room. He could eat, and if you were stupid enough to put your finger in his mouth, he would have bitten it off." Robert White, a neurosurgeon from Cleveland who is now eighty-five years old, enjoys discussing his rhesus monkey experiments, which made him famous virtually overnight some thirty years ago. This bite-happy monkey was unique because its head was attached to a body that was not its own.

White cannot recall exactly how many primates he has decapitated in his laboratory at Case Western Reserve University in Cleveland since the 1970s, but the number appears to run in the several hundreds. He performed these procedures in a side wing of the medical school, an enormous wedding cake of a building with a classical columned doorway. White carefully removed a rhesus monkey's brain and attached it to the circulatory system of another living monkey. When the experiment succeeded, the neurosurgeon took to transplanting the heads by severing the skin, muscles, and tendons, then the windpipe, esophagus, spinal column, and marrow. Now only six vessels were supplying blood to the brain. Within a few minutes, White connected the blood supply of the monkey's head with a monkey's body that had been prepared for this purpose. The transplanted monkey's heads survived for several days, after which their faces swelled, their tongues became bloated, and their puffy eyelids closed for good. Their immune systems had rebelled against the foreign body and shut down. But the intrepid experimenter jumped for joy when he realized that the brain had evidently not been rejected.

Once the youngest professor of neurosurgery in America, he is now a father of ten. A practicing Catholic, he decided to seek support for his infamous experiments from way on high, and he talked at length with Pope Paul VI, then with Pope John Paul II, and he was invited to join the most exclusive research group in the world, the Vatican's Pontifical Academy of Sciences. The new pope, though, is likely to have grave reservations, particularly since White, who has been dubbed "the Frankenstein from Ohio," has been announcing plans to transplant heads and brains in humans as well.

The Catholic doctrine of the soul has helped the surgeon overcome his moral qualms about conducting experiments on primates. In his view, a monkey has "nothing in common with man, at least nothing having to do with the brain or soul." White's dream of providing new bodies for people with conditions like Christopher Reeve's (the late actor who was paralyzed in a riding accident) or Stephen Hawking's (the physicist suffering from amyotrophic lateral sclerosis) was daring in the extreme. "What's the difference whether I implant a liver, replace an arm, or transplant a body?" White asked me eight years ago. "No one would ever think of looking for the soul in the liver or in an arm. The soul is only in the brain."

The pope presumably sees the matter differently, but he does not have to finance the project. White told me that all he needed was the sum of $4 or $5 million, and he could go to Kiev in Ukraine and carry out his first human head transplantations. He conceded that the "greatest operation in the history of mankind" would have flaws; the patient would not be able to move his arms or legs, nor could he speak, swallow, or digest food. Still, White laughed, he couldn't really complain. It would take another twenty years to make the connection to the spinal cord work, which would eliminate these drawbacks. I asked White whether he would make his own body available for this procedure. Again, he laughed: "Of course—but I'd rather it be my head, which is worth more."

Robert White has made several trips to Ukraine, but the "greatest operation in the history of mankind" has yet to take place, so philosophers, physicians, and legal experts are spared for now from addressing the thorny issues of what is actually being transplanted, the head or the body, or whom the family of the donor body is encountering when visiting the recipient. But the fact that White's plans have so far come to naught should not put our minds at rest. His experiments are only the tip of the iceberg. Neuroscience poses the greatest scientific challenge of the twenty-first century—and a profound challenge to our morality. Successes in neurobiology are transforming our traditional view of humankind and at the same time producing entirely new prospects and perils.

Many of these prospects are clearly a blessing. A relatively new research discipline is neuroprosthetics, a combination of neuroscience and biomedical engineering. Its successes to date give rise to visions of fantastic opportunities. Neuroprosthetics stimulates human organs such as the heart, the bladder, and the ear and achieves impressive results. A notable example is cochlear implants for severely hearing impaired to nearly deaf individuals ("cochlea" being the scientific term for the auditory portion of the inner ear). Here is how it works: A small speech processor behind the ear of a severely hearing impaired person converts sounds into electrical signals, then a coil relays them through the skin to the implant. From there, the impulses are passed on via microelectrode arrays in the cochlea to the auditory nerve and finally processed in the brain. The trick to neurostimulation of this kind is that the processor behind the ear processes sounds to make brain neurons understand them without "hearing" them in the usual sense. Neurostimulation is the art of making electrical signal transmissions in the brain bypass impaired sensory functions in the body.

Retinal implants, aimed at restoring vision to the visually impaired and nearly blind, work in much the same way. Implant patients are already able to distinguish between light and dark, and clinical trials are showing promising results. Researchers have also gone to great lengths to find ways to help paraplegics walk. Here, too, the idea of artificially stimulating the body's electrical pathways shows great promise. In the early 1990s, researchers began using sensors to measure the precise mobility level of patients. The language of the neurons responsible for movement was known; the question was only whether it would be possible to guide movement. A research group in Munich achieved this breakthrough a few years ago. For the first time, a paraplegic, using the handles of his walking aids, was able to give orders to a computer he carried with him in a backpack: "Stand up!" "Walk!" or "Climb stairs!" The computer relayed impulses to electrodes fastened to the patient's legs, and the impulses made the muscles react accordingly while different sensors evaluated the process and reported the results to the computer. The computer, in turn, adjusted the commands to the requirements of walking.

Another option is a motion implant, which, like a cochlear implant, is placed under the patient's skin; here, too, the research to date looks quite promising. Paraplegic patients have been able to walk just a few steps so far, but significant advances are likely in the future.

Documentary films have captured amazing and impressive images of Parkinson's and epilepsy patients experiencing dramatic and instant relief from their symptoms with deep brain stimulation. Both ailments are associated with a precise region of the brain. Electrical signals from what is referred to as a "brain pacemaker" target pathologically overactive areas of the brain and alleviate symptoms on the spot. A Parkinson's patient previously unable to hold a cup in his trembling hands sits in his easy chair sipping his coffee, instantaneously free of all suffering. An epilepsy patient stops writhing in midseizure. And neuroprosthetic aids for hearing and walking might also be used to help patients with psychological disorders. Electrodes in the brain could intervene directly in neurochemical pathways to activate "positive" neurotransmitters and lift patients out of depression.

These are wonderful advances, and cures of downright biblical proportions are on the horizon, enabling the deaf to hear, the blind to see, and the lame to walk. So where is the problem? What do neural implants and deep brain stimulation have to do with head transplants à la Frankenstein? The answer is simple: All these new manipulations of our nervous system in the brain, which go far beyond what has been possible with biochemical medication, could be used for nefarious purposes and open the floodgates to alarming abuses.

The military or the CIA could use deep brain stimulation to interrogate prisoners. Who needs a traditional lie detector when you can use a modern brain scan? Daniel Langleben, a psychiatrist at the University of Pennsylvania, had this same idea seven years ago. Since MRIs make it possible for researchers to see what goes on inside the brain, it was just a matter of locating the spot where lying occurs. According to Langleben, a region in the premotor cortex is activated when resolving conflicts. Langleben claims that because lying is considerably more strenuous than telling the truth, lies are inevitably accompanied by increased brain activity. This may not always be the case, of course; in fact, seasoned liars might expend less energy telling their usual lies than straining to tell the truth. Two companies are now planning to market Langleben's lie brain scanner.

This kind of machine would be in high demand in the American legal system. Expert opinions based on MRIs are already used in the courtroom. Neuropsychiatrists use the device to ascertain whether felons are in full possession of their faculties. Grisly crimes and serial murders are often linked to breakdowns and impairments in the ventromedial region of the perpetrator—as in the case of the famous Phineas Gage. These snapshots of the mental state of murderers and rapists do not, however, make it easier to figure out whether perpetrators are in full possession of their faculties, and the courts have to decide how to handle these cases.

It is certainly possible that surgical remedies for some kinds of brain damage that result in severe behavioral disorders will soon be developed. Wouldn't it be better for both perpetrator and society to have brain-damaged criminals undergo brain surgery—perhaps even forcibly—instead of locking them up for life or sentencing them to death? But who has the last word in a case like this: the neuropsychiatrist, the judge, or the criminal or his or her family? And who will prevent abuse of a system that mandates surgical intervention to save the cost of financing a criminal's lifetime sentence behind bars?

The next potential source of abuse might be the drug mafia. The more we know about the brain, the more effectively it can be manipulated. Psychoactive substances that boost dementia patients' ability to focus may appeal to teenage drug users, but the effects on serotonin receptors and dopamine metabolism can be quite dangerous. (For a discussion of their function, see "Mr. Spock in Love," p. 42.) Dopamine, for which phenethylamine acts as a releasing agent, has the same chemical composition as mescaline and LSD, and stimulates—or overstimulates—specific regions of the brain. The more effectively we target the dopamine balance in the brain, the more potent the designer drugs that can be produced with it.

And even apart from the issue of criminal hard-core drugs, does the legitimate range of use of attention-enhancing psychoactive substances extend to patients suffering from dementia, forgetfulness, or even just a mild case of ADD? Will parents start popping a little pill into their children's cocoa to enhance their ability to concentrate on their important schoolwork? Who knows if we'll even need genetic engineering and reproductive

medicine if we can optimize our children's achievement this easily. Politicians and managers could plow through their sixteen-hour days without
drooping, and Tour de France cyclists' doping would maintain not only
their stamina but also their euphoria on even the steepest uphills.

Less deleterious, perhaps, but still frightening are the advertising
agencies, Web designers, and other marketing organizations that relentlessly milk every new neuropsychological discovery to manipulate their
target groups. No sooner do psychologists establish that people are naturally drawn to the right side of an unfamiliar space than supermarkets
scramble to rearrange their shelves and products. Color psychologists use
MRIs to put their catalogues to the test. And the manufacturers of home entertainment products and Internet games use brain scans to stay on top of
their customers' psychological preferences. Where we used to rely on
guesswork and surveys, now the human central nervous system is mined
for information.

But what are the repercussions of this enormous experiment beyond the
confines of the laboratory? The activities we engage in modify our neuronal
circuits, in some cases permanently. People who play a great deal of chess
optimize particular abilities, which appears to offer a clear benefit, but
what about kids devoted to Ego Shooter, who spend their time gunning
down thousands of virtual enemies a day? They, too, will become adept at
this task—but what other consequences will the thousands of shootings
produce in their brains? Does the incredibly rapid pacing of videos and
films really have no impact on the brains of our children? Anyone with any
understanding of neuroscience knows the answer.

The momentum to exploit neuropsychological discoveries to rev up the
excitement keeps building. Will we soon witness a war of home entertainment electronics technicians versus neuropsychiatrists, the former in hot
pursuit of ever greater thrills, the latter demanding regulations to fend off
potential or established short-term and long-term damage? It may soon be
time to make "attention theft" a punishable offense.

The philosopher Thomas Metzinger at the University of Mainz in Germany has coined the term "anthropology assessment" for a method of gaug-
ing the potential societal risks arising from brain research. Neuroscientific
advances are creating new hazards and new potential for what Metzinger calls
our "consciousness culture." Metzinger advocates introducing high school
classes in meditation to help children enhance and sustain their mindfulness

and fend off the increasing number of distractions with which they are confronted. He has drawn up a catalogue of proscriptions for neuroscientists and neurotechnologists: no collaboration with the military, no excessive commercialization of research results, no skirting strict guidelines for obtaining human tissue, no medical or commercial abuse of patients.

An exhaustive set of rules is essential. Even aside from Robert White's transplants in Cleveland, it is evident that many pitfalls lie ahead. Stroke research is poised to take its first steps in the direction of brain transplants to replace particular stricken regions of the brain, which can succeed only if medicine can restore destroyed nerve tracts and nerve contacts. But if it can, won't we have the knowledge to construct an actual brain? The idea of "artificial brains" has captured the human imagination since time immemorial, but the new arts of neuroprosthetics and neurobionics are fueling real hope for "brain prostheses" in the near future.

The implications of these advances for our view of man are vast, because a brain prosthesis—a machine with a mind—would not be mortal as we now understand the term. Wouldn't someone with a brain prosthesis be superhuman? Doesn't this sound like the artist Franz Marc's vision for Expressionist painting: "building a bridge into the spirit world"?

The moral challenge for neuroscience and its practical applications is thus at least a double one. It has to guard people against abuse, and to prepare society for deep-rooted changes in the way we view ourselves and the world that certain types of brain surgery would usher in. Here, too, we must heed the Kantian caution that man must not be instrumentalized, because any misuse by the military and the secret service, or by marketing and home entertainment electronics, has elements of instrumentalization.

The social consequences could be considerable, and the utilitarian calculus of pleasure and pain is sometimes quite problematic. Society is therefore well advised to implement ethical controls as early as possible and to bring in philosophers, psychologists, and sociologists to assess current neuroscientific research and anticipate future issues.

Before we leave our discussion of the traditional view of man and what constitutes humankind, we might wish to know something more about ourselves. We have learned about our cognitive faculties and considered some important moral questions. What remains is a look at human desires, yearnings, longings, and pleasures—in short, at faith, hope, and love, without which we would not be who we are.

What Can I Hope For?

Le Bec

The Greatest Conceivable Being
Does God Exist?

Does God exist? And can his existence be proved? The only meaningful conception we can make of God is that of an infinitely great and perfect being. Anything else would somehow not be God, at least not in the Judeo-Christian sense. One might say that God is the greatest conceivable being. But if God possesses all conceivable qualities of greatness, he exists. If he did not, he would lack at least one quality, namely, that of existing—and would thus not be God. A being that would be impossible to improve on in one's mind must therefore exist, because otherwise this conception would be absurd. Consequently, we can conclude that God does exist!

I don't know whether that convinces you, but if it doesn't, don't blame me; I wasn't the one who came up with it. The credit goes to Anselm of Canterbury, an Italian who spent most of his life in France yet bore the name of a city in England. He was born in about 1033 in the city of Aosta in northern Italy, and was named Anselmo. At the age of fifteen, he dreamed of joining a nearby monastery, but his ambitious father had bigger plans in mind for his talented son and wanted him to go into politics. When Anselm was twenty-three, he embarked on a three-year journey through France and was drawn in particular to the northern part of the country. For more than a hundred years, the Normans had displaced the Franks from northern France and developed a blossoming culture, adopting the French language and the Christian faith of their predecessors. More than 120 abbeys were built in the Norman period, and they became highly developed cultural, economic, and intellectual havens.

Religious art also flourished in Normandy. The most famous monasteries and abbeys were St.Wandrille, Mondaye, Jumièges, Hambye, the Trappist monastery in Soligny, and the Benedictine monastery of Bec. When Anselm arrived, Lanfranc, the pride of Normandy, had turned the abbey of Bec into one of the most important intellectual centers in Normandy. In 1060, Anselm—after some hesitation—also entered the abbey. Three years later, Lanfranc became the abbot in the larger commune of Caen, and Anselm succeeded him as prior in Bec. Lanfranc's close ties to William, Duke of Normandy, shaped his future path. In 1066, William conquered England, and Lanfranc became the archbishop of Canterbury. The cathedral, which later became world-famous, was at the time just a heap of rubble, having been burned down in the course of the Norman wars of conquest. Lanfranc repeated his Bec accomplishments in Canterbury. The framework of a magnificent Romanesque church with transept and choir arose from the rubble. While Lanfranc was building up the most important cultural and religious center of England in Canterbury, Anselm continued to develop Bec.

The only portrait of Anselm painted during the Middle Ages highlights his noble features: angular head, large nose, receding hairline, and long white hair running down the back of his neck. Anselm proved a brilliant choice for his new position. He became the abbot of an increasingly flourishing abbey, an elite training center with a monastery school and seminars in rhetoric. And he began to write his own philosophical and theological works. In about 1080, he completed *Monologion* and *Proslogion*. The latter work, a lengthy meditation on the nature of God, contains the proof of God that opened this chapter.

The proposition that God is the "being than which none greater can be conceived" has been one of the most widely discussed arguments in the history of philosophy. Anselm's discourse became famous as the first ontological argument for the existence of God. Ontology is the study of the nature of being, and an ontological proof of God uses intuition and reason to prove the existence of God directly. Let us recall the key point: Since God is the greatest conceivable being, it is not possible for him *not* to exist. If he did not exist, it would diminish God's greatness to an excessive degree. It would contradict the notion of something than which none greater can be conceived if something greater *could* be conceived. Consequently, it does not make sense for us to imagine that God does not exist.

Throughout the Middle Ages and into the early modern period, Anselm's proof for the existence of God—a single page in length—carried great weight. But of course it also provoked constant criticism. Its first critic was the Count of Montigny, known also as the monk Gaunilo, who lived in the monastery of Marmoutiers near the city of Tours on the Loire. Gaunilo wrote to Anselm that one could not use a convoluted definition to deduce that something exists. Gaunilo copied Anselm's proof, substituting "perfect island" for "perfect being," to show, using Anselm's own words, that this island necessarily existed. He wrote that just as unparalleled excellence proves God's existence, the unparalleled excellence of the island also proves *its* existence.

Anselm endeavored to defend himself, calmly pointing out that his argument did not apply to islands and things of that kind, but rather represented an exceptional case. The leap from perfection to existence applied only to something that is unconditionally perfect, namely to God. An island, by contrast, is never perfect, he argued, and is by its very nature not the greatest conceivable being. Anselm took Gaunilo so seriously that he insisted that his proof of God could be copied and distributed by other monks only in combination with Gaunilo's critique, and that Gaunilo's, in turn, would appear only with Anselm's response. Anselm's confident and generous reaction in the controversy surrounding the proof of the existence of God enhanced his fame.

When Lanfranc died in 1089, the famous abbot of Bec was the obvious successor for the office of archbishop of Canterbury. But William II, the son and heir of William the Conqueror, wavered for four years as to whether he should bring the intelligent and self-assured Anselm to England before deciding to do so. The king's doubts proved justified. The cathedral of Canterbury thrived in many ways under Anselm—the Church expanded and scholarship flourished—but it did not take long for the dithering king and his proud archbishop to become fierce competitors for the power of Church and Crown. After Anselm had been in office for four years, William refused to allow his disloyal archbishop to return home after a trip to Rome, and Anselm spent the next three years in Lyons. William's successor, Henry I, allowed Anselm to come back to England, then sent him into exile yet again in 1103, this time for four years. When he returned in 1107, Anselm spent two more years in Canterbury until his death at the ripe old age of seventy-six. In 1494, the man who believed he had proved the existence of God was canonized.

The most extensive dispute about Anselm's proof was launched 150 years later, by a theologian and philosopher who would far surpass the fame of the archbishop of Canterbury. Like Anselm, Thomas Aquinas was Italian. He was born the son of a duke in about 1225 in the castle of Roccasecca near Aquino. When he turned five, he was sent to a monastery, and at the age of nineteen, he resolved to join the Dominican order. He studied and taught in Cologne, Paris, Viterbo, and Orvieto, and in 1272 he established a Dominican school in Naples. Although he died in 1274 at the age of just forty-nine, he was extremely prolific, and it seems fair to say that no philosopher of the Middle Ages had a greater influence on the thinking of that era than Thomas.

After Anselm it became customary to introduce a theological treatise with a rational clarification of the question of God's existence. But Thomas had major problems with Anselm's proof. Without mentioning his predecessor by name, Thomas criticized the way Anselm made the leap from the conception of God to God's actual existence. The fact that I can conceive of a perfect God means only that God exists in my imagination, but not that he exists in reality. And Thomas did not stop there. He rejected the idea that it makes any sense to speak of the "greatest conceivable being." The greatest conceivable being is either so great that I cannot imagine it at all, or it is too small. Whatever I imagine, I can always add something to it to make it something even greater. The largest known number can always be followed by a +1. Anselm's proof of God thus fails right from the outset, because there is no such thing as the greatest conceivable being.

Thomas had no intention of disproving the existence of God; he wanted only to show how to furnish a better proof of God. In contrast to Anselm, he thought that God's existence was so great that it cannot be grasped by the human imagination at all. His own attempt to prove God's existence thus takes an entirely different route. Thomas explains God from the logic of cause and effect. His proof of God is a causal proof of God. Since the world exists, it must have originated at some point, because nothing comes from nothing. Some kind of "efficient cause" must have created everything or set it in motion. Whatever was right at the beginning of everything was itself unmoved—otherwise it would not be at the beginning, but would require an efficient cause as well. Thomas adopted the term "unmoved mover" from Aristotle to designate what came first.

But how should we imagine this unmoved mover, which is, after all, unimaginable? To be what it is, it has to have all the attributes that the world does not have. It has to be absolute, eternal, true, unimaginably intelligent, and perfect. To form an image of God, man has to cast off accustomed conceptions one by one. The more human conceptions I jettison, the less darkness surrounds me. I have to envision a being that does not consist of matter and that is not bound by time. God is almighty and omniscient, infinite and unfathomable. His will is absolute and perfect, infinite in his love and the quintessence of happiness.

For philosophers like Thomas Aquinas, the goal was to mediate persuasively between reason and faith, and to explain how man actually knows who or what God is. No prominent philosopher of the Middle Ages entertained any doubts about the actual existence of God; it was just a matter of showing how God was conveyed to the mind.

Yet this was precisely the route Immanuel Kant took in his *Critique of Pure Reason* (1781). All representations I devise of the world, Kant explained, are representations in my head (see "The Law Within Me," p. 89). My senses enable me to gain experiences, which my understanding turns into representations, and my reason helps me to sort out and assess them. But I know nothing of what lies completely outside the world of my sensory experience. And here, according to Kant, lies the quandary in any proof of God. If I construct the representation of an absolutely perfect being for myself, it is a representation in my head. Anselm had to concede that as well. Even if I use the representation in my head to deduce that it is part of God's perfection to exist in reality, it is still only a representation in my head. Anselm failed to see that. For him, God had leaped out of the head into the world. But in reality, Anselm had only shown how the representation that God must exist formed in his head; no more and no less.

When Kant confronted the ontological proof of God, which he knew in Descartes' variant (which is quite similar to Anselm's proof), his critique of the logic of proofs for God took off. His influence was enormous. Although people continued to offer various proofs of God, the ontological proof was laid to rest for quite some time.

Remarkably, new proofs of God have been emerging recently within the scientific community, specifically from the otherwise fairly levelheaded field of neuroscience. Some neuroscientists even believe that they have penetrated the mysteries of God. The first one to claim advances in this area was a Canadian neurologist named Michael Persinger, at Laurentian University in Sudbury. In the 1980s, Persinger, who is now in his sixties, undertook a series of strange-sounding experiments in which he placed his test subjects on chairs in a soundproof basement at the university and had them put on dark glasses. Then he outfitted them with a motorcycle helmet containing electromagnetic coils that emit relatively strong impulses, allowing him to measure and manipulate brain currents. Many of his test subjects claimed to have sensed a "higher reality" or a "presence," as though suddenly someone else were in the room. "Some say that they feel their guardian angel or God, or something along those lines," Persinger reported. The intrepid Canadian is convinced that religious feelings originate under the influence of magnetic fields. This phenomenon is especially evident when there are abrupt variations in the earth's magnetic field, for example, during earthquakes. How often does mystical experience accompany natural catastrophes? People with a high temporal lobe sensitivity are particularly susceptible to these kinds of magnetic influences. God and geomagnetism are thus quite closely linked, at least in Persinger's view. Unfortunately, no other neuroscientist has been able to replicate these experiments, and the neuroscientific community generally regards Persinger as an eccentric.

His younger colleague at the University of Pennsylvania, Andrew Newberg, has had more success in this area. In the late 1990s, Newberg, who is board certified in internal medicine, nuclear medicine, and nuclear cardiology, designed a whole series of experiments to fathom the mystery of faith. He chose deeply spiritual individuals—Franciscan nuns and Tibetan meditators—to be his test subjects, and he used SPECT imaging to observe the blood supply in their brains. The test subjects began to meditate and to immerse themselves in their faith. As they approached the transcendent peak of their meditative state, they tugged on a string, and Newberg released a radioactive dye into their IV line so he could study the resultant changes on a monitor. The parietal and frontal lobes were most clearly affected, with activity in the parietal lobe decreasing while increasing in the frontal lobe. Persinger had identified the place at which God touches us as the temporal lobe; Newberg situated it in the frontal lobe.

Persinger remained cautious about his findings—but not Newberg, who boldly and euphorically proclaimed that the existence of a religious center in the brain is highly significant; after all, it was clearly God himself who devised and instilled this center in us, and he is always right there within our brains. Newberg's book describing his experiments, *Why God Won't Go Away*, became a bestseller.

The philosopher Diogenes is said to have found illumination in a barrel; nowadays it is sought in a brain scanner. But the fact that Persinger locates the religious center in the temporal lobe and Newberg in the frontal lobe is quite revealing. The temporal lobe is responsible primarily for hearing and speech comprehension; it also plays a major role in explicit memory. The frontal lobe, by contrast, orchestrates actions. Both regions of the brain govern "higher" cognitive functions, but in very different ways. Like Persinger, Newberg was criticized for the sweeping conclusions he drew on the basis of relatively few experiments. Couldn't religious feelings engage far more than a single region of the brain? And even if there is a specific place in the brain responsible for spiritual feelings, who is to say it's really "God" conveying the insights and enlightenment? Maybe we're just inundating ourselves with feelings of enlightenment of our own devising, perhaps as the result of an evolutionary malfunction.

The neurotheological proof of God is far from persuasive. At best, it can show how perceived religious truths arise on a neurochemical level, but the notion that God actually speaks to man remains pure speculation. Even clear evidence that there are centers in the brain for religious experience would not mean that there is a bridge from the head to the world of the supernatural. Kant's contention that proofs of the existence of God do not extend from one's own realm of experience into a purportedly objective world applies here as well. Kant's critique was aimed only at an ontological proof of the existence of God, but it applies to any neurotheological proof equally well.

But what about a causal approach? The causal proof for the existence of God does not use representations as a starting point, but rather seeks to find out why the world exists. However, there isn't any need to assume that God was the First Cause that set everything in motion. The argument that nothing can arise from nothing posits a First Cause—but must the First Cause be God?

For some people it is easier to imagine an eternal God than eternal matter; for others, it is just the other way around. At least we know that matter does exist. We do not know that about God—at least not in a comparably sensory manner. Bertrand Russell's belief that matter is eternal made him doubt the need for a First Cause. If everything has a cause, there is no beginning of matter or "first" God. Russell took cynical pleasure in proposing the possibility of several Gods who create each other one after another.

Thomas's theory of God as the First Cause is not a very persuasive proof of the existence of God. Perhaps it would have been better if he had remained somewhat more consistent in the objection he raised to Anselm's proof: that any idea of God is inevitably too small. Something that is not fully accessible to our experience should not be set in stone. Many theologians have used this argument to reject *any* proof for the existence of God. The Protestant theologian Rudolf Bultmann claimed, for example: "Anyone who supposes that he can offer evidence for God's reality by proofs of the existence of God is arguing over a phantom." Our vertebrate brain was not designed to give us direct access to what lies beyond the senses—if it did, it would no longer be beyond the senses. Thus, it is in the very nature of the matter that God cannot be seen, but only—in whatever form—experienced, or not.

But those who would like to prove the existence of God anyway have another ace up their sleeve. If the existence of God cannot be shown directly, for the reasons we have discussed, can't it at least be demonstrated indirectly? This approach, which is the subject of lively discussions these days, especially in the United States, is taken up by "natural theology."

The Archdeacon's Watch
Does Nature Have Meaning?

The young Charles Robert Darwin was a big disappointment to his father. He was unfocused and slow to catch on when studying medicine in Edinburgh. The very idea of dissections turned his stomach. And every aspect of nature, from the starfish and crabs washed ashore to the birds in the field, held his interest more than his textbooks. After watching Charles go through the motions for two years, his father's patience ran out. Enough of medicine! He enrolled his lackadaisical son at the venerable Christ's College at the University of Cambridge. If Charles could not make it as a physician, maybe there was hope for him as a clergyman.

Soon after Darwin arrived at Cambridge in 1830, he was assigned a set of special rooms in Christ's College, the very rooms where the renowned philosopher and theologian William Paley had once lived. Twenty-five years after his death, Paley enjoyed saintlike status at the university. His works were on Darwin's required reading list. Even though the study of theology bored Darwin even more than medical school, the writings of Paley—unsurpassed and timeless masterpieces of theology—were a major exception. Darwin was spellbound by these books. In his free time, he roamed through the meadows and woods and collected beetles and plants, but back in his study, he read and reread Paley's *Natural Theology*—the book of the creative plan for the universe, the divine scheme of nature, devised by the Great Designer of all things and detectable in every beetle, bird's egg, and blade of grass. But who was this Paley, a writer who left an indelible impression on Darwin and whose proofs for the existence of God were considered comprehensive and authoritative through the mid-nineteenth century?

William Paley, born in July 1743 in Peterborough, came from a family of modest means in the service of the Church. His father scraped by on his salary as a minor canon of the cathedral church, supporting his wife, three daughters, and William as best he could, then put his solid grounding in Greek and Latin to good use when offered the position of headmaster at a small elementary school in Giggleswick, a village in North Yorkshire. The young William was soon at the top of his class, and his quick intellectual grasp and lively mind made people expect great things of him. When Paley turned fifteen, his father enrolled him at the University of Cambridge. Paley may have been frail and unathletic, but he was highly gifted. Christ's College was an elite training ground for British clergymen and politicians. William would make a name for himself and realize his father's dreams.

Paley was the youngest student at Cambridge, and his abilities were truly remarkable. He drew a great deal of attention to himself even as a student. His long, elaborately coiffed hair, his frilly shirt, and his expensive silk stockings were evidence of the young man's determination to stand out. In the public debates at the college he cut a colorful figure with his grand, effusive gestures and tremendous passion. Some may have considered him a crackpot, but most applauded him for his sharp mind and rhetorical talent. Paley earned the highest grades on his final examinations of all the students in his class.

But he did not reap the professional rewards he was anticipating, and he had no choice but to accept a job as a Latin teacher at an academy in Greenwich, until he was hired to lecture at his alma mater. In 1766, he returned to Christ's College at Cambridge, and a year later he was ordained as an Anglican priest. Paley had high aspirations, and he was willing to do whatever it took to get ahead. He fantasized that by the age of thirty, he would be an attorney at the royal court. In the solitude of his room, he delivered fiery closing statements, and he fancied himself engaging in verbal duels with Prime Minister William Pitt and the most gifted orators in the British parliament. But the only positions this ambitious man from a modest background was offered were at two small parishes. In September 1777 he was given the vicarage of Appleby. Paley had set his sights higher, but the parish income did ensure his livelihood. He married the daughter of a well-to-do liquor dealer; she bore him four daughters and four sons, though she did not see her husband very often. In 1780, the bishop of Carlisle, a county capital near the Scottish border, hired Paley for the cathedral there and two years later named him archdeacon.

At the age of forty, he was finally able to show the world what he was made of. Instead of rhetorical duels in parliament, he now published compelling arguments. His style was polished, persuasive, and easily understood. He was drawn to the writings of his famous contemporary and compatriot Jeremy Bentham and reconciled utilitarianism with the Church position. Like Bentham, Paley viewed the goal of all of philosophy in a single principle: the increase of happiness. Man does not become good in the Christian sense by his faith, but only by his deeds, by assuming responsibility and by serving his community. Just as God devised a great variety of mechanisms, combinations, and interlocking connections in nature, all of us must adapt to our specific social milieu to achieve our calling.

Paley enjoyed a string of successes. The bishop of London offered him a lucrative position in the cathedral of St. Paul's; the bishop of Lincoln appointed him deacon of his diocese; the bishop of Durham offered him a comfortable and well-paid parish in Bishop Wearmouth. But his criticism of the Church and his liberal political outlook prevented him from becoming a bishop. Paley was awarded an honorary doctorate at Cambridge and moved to Bishop Wearmouth, an idyllic town on the North Sea coast.

Here he found the time to write his last major work. He still considered the most important principle to be increasing pleasure and minimizing pain. The more purposefully a life revolved around realizing this individual and societal principle, the better. But how is the idea of purposefulness established in the world? What is the nature of the connection between the will of the Creator and the principles of the individual? In his study in Bishop Wearmouth, Paley wrote his most important book, *Natural Theology.*

Progress on the book was slow. A severe kidney ailment brought on bouts of pain that made it impossible for Paley to write for weeks on end. His plan to construct a theory of the universe based on a detailed study of natural phenomena proved exceedingly difficult. Paley explored everything he could amass in Bishop Wearmouth that would shed light on blueprints in nature. He collected the flight feathers of the chickens on the farms and the bones of fish at the beach, and he plucked grass and flowers at the wayside and immersed himself in anatomy books.

The key word in his new book was "adaptation." How did God arrange all the millions of living creatures in nature, and how did they accord with his will by intertwining physically and mentally to form a magnificent unity? In 1802, the book was finished, and it soon became a bestseller. Fifty years later, Paley's *Natural Theology* was still the best known teleological proof of God's existence in British theology; in the words of the book's subtitle, it provided *Evidences of the Existence and Attributes of the Deity, Collected from the Appearances of Nature.*

Paley was in awe of the great complexity of the living world, and he understood that it had to be presented in an extraordinary manner. His response was neither new nor original. More than a hundred years earlier, in 1691, the naturalist John Ray had attempted a very similar project, and many other philosophers and theologians had followed. But Paley formulated his views more clearly and persuasively than had any of his predecessors. The most famous passage in the book is its opening—the image of the watchmaker. What is more admirable than the precision with which the gears and springs of a watch are produced and the complexity with which they are assembled? If we found an object like a watch on the heath, its accuracy and elegant design would force us to conclude

> that the watch must have had a maker; that there must have existed, at some time, and at some place or other, an artificer or artificers, who formed it for the purpose which we find it actually to answer; who comprehended its construction and designed its use. . . . Every indication of contrivance, every manifestation of design, which existed in the watch, exists in the works of nature; with the difference, on the side of nature, of being greater and more, and that in a degree which exceeds all computation.

The image of the watchmaker of nature became inseparably linked to Paley's name. His *Natural Theology* enjoyed more than twenty printings and reached a broad readership. Paley did not invent this image; he found it in the writings of the Dutch theologian Bernard Nieuwentijdt. But Nieuwentijdt had not invented the metaphor either. Back in 1696, William Derham published a treatise called *The Artificial Clockmaker*. And Derham, in turn, was reworking and updating the image of the complex mechanism of nature in Cicero's *Nature of the Gods*.

But as unoriginal as the image of the watchmaker was in his day, Paley took it far more seriously than had any of his forerunners. He went through the whole body, head to toe, and showed how each and every part corresponded to the inner workings of a magnificently constructed watch. He reserved his greatest admiration for the human eye, which he compared to a telescope, and concluded that there is exactly the same proof that the eye was made to see as that the telescope was made to support the eye. The eye had to have had a creator, just like the telescope. Paley provided a great variety of examples to illustrate his arguments. "Make a change in any part of the human body, e.g. take a finger-nail, and instead of having it at the back of the finger, suppose it fixed on the forepart; how inconvenient for handling, and in many other respects would such a change be!"

Paley was in excruciating pain by the time he finished writing the book. Again and again he sought explanations for why the divine creation, which was exquisitely conceived, would include pain and suffering. If God created the kidneys, why didn't he prevent them from hurting and bleeding? Paley remained vague on that point, alternately defending God's creation by insisting that the good far outshines the bad and hoping that the process of creation would not be complete until evil and suffering ceased to exist. But Paley's own suffering did not cease; it only worsened. He was finally offered the position of bishop of Gloucester, which he had wanted for so long, but it was too late to accept it. He spent his final months bedridden, and in May 1805, blind but lucid, he succumbed to his kidney ailment in his house in Bishop Wearmouth.

Paley's work was complete. He felt he had unraveled the mystery of creation in the principle of adaptation of organisms to nature; all of biological nature was purposefully set up by its creator. But Paley could not know that he had not brought natural philosophy to an end; in fact, thirty years later, he became the impetus for a new theory that devised an entirely new framework for "adaptation."

Two years after reading Paley's *Natural Theology*, the newly minted Anglican clergyman Charles Darwin boarded the research vessel *Beagle* to travel to South America. The observations he made of both living animals and fossils shook the foundations of his view of life. The plants and animals adapted to their environment, just as Paley had written, but they evidently did so again and again. Paley's "general plan" of a watchmaker who had set the whole mechanism of nature in motion once and for all was not in evidence. The Church dogma of the existence of a personal God lost its credibility.

Darwin fretted and wavered for more than twenty years, until 1859, when he published *On the Origin of Species by Means of Natural Selection*, which moved away from Paley's argument. He reluctantly declared in his autobiography, "We can no longer argue that, for instance, the beautiful hinge of a bivalve shell must have been made by an intelligent being, like the hinge of a door by man." Where Paley had envisioned a grand harmony, Darwin saw only a "struggle for existence." If nature were indeed a watchmaker, this watchmaker would have had to be blind. As Richard Dawkins has commented in *The Blind Watchmaker*, "Natural selection, the blind, unconscious, automatic process which Darwin discovered . . . has no purpose in mind. It has no mind and no mind's eye. It does not plan for the future. It has no vision, no foresight, no sight at all . . . it is the blind watchmaker." Darwin's *Origin of Species* ultimately limited mention of Paley to a single passage: "Natural selection will never produce in a being anything injurious to itself, for natural selection acts solely by and for the good of each. No organ will be formed as Paley has remarked, for the purpose of causing pain or for doing an injury to its possessor. If a fair balance be struck between the good and evil caused by each part, each will be found on the whole advantageous."

Paley's influence on Darwin, while powerful, did not stop the latter from advancing a theory of evolution that insisted on autonomous species adaptation to nature. Instead of naming God as cause and operating principle, Darwin invoked nature itself. "Nature does" is one of his most frequent phrases. Darwin's contemporary Jean Pierre Marie Flourens (see "The Cosmos of the Mind," p. 18) was one of the first to scorn Darwin's use of nature as the subject of these claims. How, Flourens argued, can nature be goal-oriented without having goals? How can it conceive of purposefulness if it does not think? Although Darwin's theory of the autonomous adaptation of species had found widespread acceptance within about thirty years, fundamental doubts linger even today, especially among critics who rally around the concept of "intelligent design."

Darwin's contemporary and bitter adversary, the prominent Irish physicist William Thomson, known as Lord Kelvin, led the opposition to Darwin's theory. Darwin was stung by Kelvin's attack, because Kelvin, a physics professor at the University of Glasgow, enjoyed worldwide renown. Kelvin began by casting doubt on the timeline for Darwin's evolution, which he found insufficient for all the developments Darwin was outlining. He calculated the age of the earth at 98 million years, though he later reduced this number to 24 million years. If the earth were older, Kelvin argued, it could no longer be as hot in the interior as it is; but he failed to take into account that radioactivity retains the heat in the interior of the earth. In 1871, the same year that Darwin's *Descent of Man* appeared in print, Kelvin spoke of the "overpoweringly strong proofs of intelligent and benevolent design."

Even today, many people who wish to see God and not nature as the cause of the complexity of life invoke the slogan "intelligent design." The hub of intelligent design theory is the Discovery Institute, a Christian conservative think tank in Seattle. The many varied theories of intelligent design have two basic positions in common, namely, that physics and biology cannot adequately explain the world, and that there is only one truly convincing solution to this problem: the existence of an intelligent God with long-term designs. They use the idea that the constants of the physical world are so wonderfully attuned to one another as an indirect proof of the existence of God. Even the slightest deviation would make all life on earth— including man—impossible.

This observation is certainly correct, but the question of whether it points to God as a creator depends on how this fine-tuning is evaluated. The chain of events that gave rise to man is so colossal as not to appear random. But does that prove necessity? Even the most improbable coincidences are still possible. Some scientists believe that purposefulness in nature should not be overstated. Biologists in particular have problems with the idea that everything in nature is well organized, beautiful, and purposeful. After all, the history of our planet has featured five global disasters during the transition periods between major geological eras, with frightful mass extinctions of plant and animal species. And not every detail that evolution has allowed to exist is a blessing. All mammals have seven cervical vertebrae, but dolphins would be better off with one or two fewer. If you've ever watched a giraffe drinking, you might wish it had a couple of additional vertebrae. The male babirusa, a wild boar in Sulawesi, Indonesia, has two oddly curved tusks that do not offer any evident advantage. But the fact that it does have them is not a sign of purposefulness. It is more probable that they simply pose no problems.

A closer look reveals quite a bit that does not fit the category of intelligent design. Neither God's intelligence nor the intelligent adaptation of nature explains why deep-sea shrimp are bright red. The color looks nice, but for whom? There is no light in the pitch-black deep sea, and the red offers no advantages. Even Darwin's theory of evolution does nothing to explain the bright color. What higher purpose could be served by blackbirds imitating cellphone ring tones or warbling most tunefully when the mating season is over and their singing is no longer useful in evolutionary terms? How is it that humans fall in love with people of their own gender? Open questions of this kind show weaknesses in an evolutionary theory that interprets every phenomenon and every behavior pattern as optimal adaptation to the environment, yet they do not play into the hands of intelligent design either. Any objections to purposefulness in Darwin's theory apply equally well to the notion of a clever master plan. Biologists now tend to steer clear of the concept of unconditional purposefulness, which makes the whole idea of intelligent design even less tenable.

Organisms do not simply link together from atoms and molecules, like pieces in a Lego set; they originate in contact with their environment. A potato comes out white and leafless if it vegetates in a cellar, but turns green and leafy in the fields. The same occurs on a vast scale with all living creatures. Nature perpetually reinvents itself in this feedback process with the rest of the world. Life, it would seem, has such a complex structure that it represents its own very special form of organization and gives rise to a unique entity that is more than the sum of its parts. The terms and thought patterns of classical physics are as insufficient here as they would be in explaining cosmic origins.

Albert Einstein said in a 1929 interview:

We are in the position of a little child entering a huge library filled with books in many different languages. The child knows someone must have written those books. It does not know how. It does not understand the languages in which they are written. The child dimly suspects a mysterious order in the arrangement of the books but doesn't know what it is. That, it seems to me, is the attitude of even the most intelligent human being toward God. We see a universe marvelously arranged and obeying certain laws, but only dimly understand these laws. Our limited minds cannot grasp the mysterious force that moves the constellations.

Let us leave aside the fact that Einstein actually embraced the notion of an intelligent creator of universal constants—that is, of an *author* of the many books in the library—and focus instead on his insistence on the limitations of the human mind. Vertebrate brains and objective reality do not fit together like the pieces of a puzzle, for the simple reason that we ourselves create every idea from our own "objective reality." "Real reality," outside our perception, inevitably remains a construct, and each of us has to decide where God figures in it.

Biologists will continue to debate whether to explain the animate world on the basis of cause and effect or of self-organization. Remarkably, though, it was a scholar outside this discipline—a sociologist—who delved deeply into the biological concept of self-organization right from the start. In the following chapter, we will turn our attention to this sociologist, arguably the preeminent scholar in his field in the second half of the twentieth century, in particular to his explanation of one of the most mystical phenomena outside of religion: love.

"A Quite Normal Improbability"
What Is Love?

In 1968, it was anything but business as usual at most German universities. The student movement was in full swing, and its two major centers were Berlin and Frankfurt. Particularly in the field of sociology, there were heated confrontations between the students and their professors. Professors Jürgen Habermas and Theodor W. Adorno, teaching in Frankfurt, shared many of their students' political views but not their desire for revolution. Although Habermas and Adorno felt the students were justified in labeling the Federal Republic a "reactionary" and "late capitalist" state, they did not believe that the state could be changed by force.

In the fall semester of 1968, matters finally came to a head. Adorno's lectures were interrupted, the famous philosopher and sociologist was ridiculed, and the Institute for Social Research was occupied. In light of these events, Adorno canceled his lectures overnight, and the university scrambled to come up with a replacement for the rest of the semester, someone who was intrepid enough to leap into the pandemonium of the sociology department. To everyone's great surprise, a candidate was found, a virtually unknown forty-one-year-old public administration expert from Münster. His name was Niklas Luhmann. The topic of his lecture series was "Love as Passion."

A lecture series about love, at a time when the humanities and social sciences disciplines were focusing squarely on "late capitalism" and the future of society? Who was this valiant substitute teacher, laying out the finer points of a "theory of intimacy" for those twenty or so inquisitive students who had not joined the strikes and had made their way to the large third-floor auditorium of the main building?

He was born in 1927 in Lüneburg, a city in north-central Germany. His father owned a brewery, and his mother was from a family of Swiss hoteliers. Shortly before it came time to take his college entrance examinations, Luhmann was conscripted into the Wehrmacht as a *Luftwaffenhelfer* (a term for German students deployed as antiaircraft gunners), and in 1945 he was taken prisoner by American troops. In 1946, he completed his examinations and entered law school in Freiburg, but in 1953, after passing his state examinations, he switched over to public administration, first in Lüneburg and then in Hanover. In his spare time, he read his way through a mountain of scholarly literature from a variety of eras and in wide-ranging subjects, and noted every interesting idea on index cards.

In 1960 he applied for and was accepted to a yearlong program in public administration at Harvard University. Here he met the famous American social systems theorist Talcott Parsons, who divided society into separate functional systems—an idea Luhmann found immensely appealing. When he returned to Germany, he became an instructor at the University for Administrative Sciences in Speyer. No one seemed to notice that he was extremely overqualified for this position until his first book, *Functions and Consequences of Formal Organization*, was published in 1964 and a sociology professor in Münster took an interest in this unconventional and innovative public administrator. Helmut Schelsky, one of the leading German sociologists at the time, recognized Luhmann's undiscovered genius, just as Bertrand Russell had discovered the brilliant Wittgenstein in Cambridge, but Schelsky had quite a time persuading Luhmann to embark on an academic career and move to Münster so that Luhmann would not "go down in history as a senior civil servant without a doctorate." In 1966, the thirty-nine-year-old was granted a doctorate on the basis of the book he had published while in Speyer—another parallel to Wittgenstein and highly unusual in the German academic world. In the same year, something even less usual came to pass: He was granted his postdoctoral *Habilitation* degree. And Schelsky had arranged a professorship for Luhmann at the newly established University of Bielefeld, an appointment that became official in 1968. Since his duties there would not begin until the following spring, he spent the fall semester of 1968 in Frankfurt standing in for Adorno, then taught in Bielefeld until his retirement in 1993. He lived in Bielefeld for his first ten years on the faculty, and moved to the nearby town of Oerlinghausen in the Teutoburg Forest after the death of his wife. His daily routine was unvarying. From the early morning to the late evening he worked on his books, taking a little stroll with his dog only at lunchtime. In 1998, Luhmann died of leukemia at the age of seventy-one.

Schelsky's instincts were right on the mark. Luhmann, who had been trained in public administration, became a titan of sociology. To introduce him in this book as a philosopher of love is thus a bit odd—but Luhmann would have relished the thought. As his performance in Frankfurt in the fall of 1968 proved, Luhmann was a man with a fine sense of humor, and he surely would have chuckled at the label. Restricting our attention to Luhmann's ideas on love is like looking at Immanuel Kant as a philosopher of religion or René Descartes as a doctor. Still, Luhmann had truly important things to say about love, and his pronouncements on this subject shed light on his complex work as a whole. But a few introductory words on Luhmann's sociological approach are in order before we launch into his views on love.

Luhmann hoped to figure out how society functions. One promising point of departure was Parsons's systems theory, and another was biology. That was not unusual; after all, one of the founders of sociology, Darwin's contemporary Herbert Spencer, had derived sociology from psychology, and psychology from biology. But Luhmann did not think much of a model of this kind, which applies findings from simple organisms to society as a whole. The development of social systems, he argued, could be explained, as Parsons had, with concepts from the theory of evolution, but social systems are not just highly complex forms of biological systems, even though people are certainly living beings, because social systems depend not on the exchange of nutrients and energy among living creatures but on the exchange of communication and meaning. Communication and meaning differ so fundamentally from proteins that it is barely worthwhile for a sociologist to ponder biological foundations in this manner. It did not matter to Luhmann that humans were living creatures and thus "social animals" of a sort. Learning from biology meant something completely different to him.

The scientists who inspired him were the Chilean neuroscientist Humberto Maturana and his student Francisco Varela. Maturana was one of the founders of "theoretical biology" and a specialist in color perception in the brain. In the 1960s, Maturana and Varela explored the question of what constitutes life, and they determined that living beings "produce themselves and specify their own limits." Just as the brain itself constructs what it uses to function, organisms create themselves in the process of self-perpetuation. Maturana called this process *autopoiesis* (self-creation). In 1969, when he presented this idea at a conference in Chicago, Niklas Luhmann, who was the same age as Maturana, was just beginning his lecture series in Bielefeld. When he later heard about Maturana's concept of autopoiesis, he realized that Maturana had not only described the self-creation of life and the brain, but also redefined the term "communication." According to Maturana, communication is more than simply a means of conveying information; it constructs a system with whatever language is employed. Bacterial interaction forms an ecological system; brain regions communicate and create a system of neurons, namely, consciousness. Doesn't this mean, Luhmann mused, that social systems are also an autopoietic system that arises by means of linguistic (that is, symbolic) communication?

Luhmann had been planning for some time to provide a precise description of the social systems of a society based on the concept of communication. The idea of autopoiesis supplied a key missing component. Although Maturana later had serious doubts about stretching this approach so far, Luhmann's accomplishments went well beyond those of Maturana and all others in this field. Luhmann became one of the sharpest observers of social processes in the second half of the twentieth century. He was an "intellectual continent," an architectural theorist of superlatives. The very fact that he approached the subject on the basis of communication was revolutionary.

Before Luhmann, sociologists had framed their discourse around people, norms, social roles, institutions, and actions. But for Luhmann, the *incidence* of communication was the focus, and it was of little consequence *who* was doing the communicating. The important question was only: "With what result?" In human society, no nutrition and energies are exchanged as they are in bacteria, no neurons as in the brain, but rather *expectations*. But how are expectations exchanged? Which expectations are expected, and what are the results? In other words: How is communication able to exchange expectations in such a manner that modern social systems that are basically stable and functioning arise independently of other influences— systems like politics, economics, law, science, religion, education, art, or love?

Love is accordingly a social system, made up of expectations, that is, of predictable and set codes. Luhmann's book *Love as Passion*—which he did not publish until fifteen years after his lecture series on the subject—is about the history and current state of love codes. Luhmann argues that what we take to be love today is less a feeling than a code—and a very bourgeois code at that—that arose in the late eighteenth century. The declaration "I love you!" is far more than an expression of feelings, such as a statement like "I have a toothache." A declaration of love implies an entire system of promises and expectations. Assuring one's love promises that a person considers this feeling reliable and takes responsibility for the object of his or her affections, that he or she is prepared to act like a lover and all that implies in the eyes of the other in our society.

The need for love springs from a specific type of self-categorization. The less a person is part of a clearly defined milieu, the stronger the need to assert individuality. But modern societies don't make it easy for the individual. They are split into many individual social systems, autopoietic worlds concerned only with ensuring the perpetuation of the system. In Luhmann's descriptions, systems thus act like organisms under the conditions of Darwinism, introducing from the outside only what they need to preserve themselves. There is little place for individualism. Ten years of work in administration seem to have confirmed Luhmann's conviction that individuality is not what counts in social systems. The individual person is splintered into many different roles: mother or father, professional, competitive bowler or badminton player, member of an Internet community and neighbor, taxpayer and spouse. It is difficult to construct a unified identity in this manner. What is missing is a confirmation of how we experience ourselves as a whole—as an individual.

According to Luhmann, this "self-portrayal" is accomplished by love, and it constitutes the very function of love, which is a rare and therefore "improbable" form of communication, yet an altogether normal one. Love, Luhmann tells us, is the "quite normal improbability" of finding one's "own happiness in the other's happiness." The image of the beloved is so thoroughly transformed that he or she departs from a "normal" perspective. That is its unique and distinctive quality: The lover sees only the beloved's smile, not the crooked teeth; or, in Luhmann's sober formulation: "External supports are dismantled, and the internal tensions become more acute. The capacity for stability now depends on purely personal resources."

The ensuing process of lovers attuning their expectations is fraught with potential disappointments. Love is, paradoxically, the code that ought to ensure the greatest degree of stability, yet it is the most fragile of all codes. The more the lover finds expectations for stability fulfilled, the less nervous tension there is in love relationships—for better and for worse. Perfectly attuned "expected expectations" are dependable, but not terribly thrilling; the very improbability that constituted the attraction quickly fades. The romantic idea of love as a unity of feeling, sexual desire, and virtue, Luhmann explains, is quite a tall order. Finding meaning in the world of another—if only temporarily—is a colossal achievement.

At this point it is worth taking up the question of "why," for which Luhmann does not provide an answer. Why can't the strong desire that frequently marks the start of a romantic relationship be maintained? Why does it wear off? Is that really just a question of predictable "expected expectations"? Doesn't it also perhaps wear off in love relationships in which communication—that is, attuning of expectations—works poorly? In other words, in bad relationships? Maybe there is an altogether different reason for the erosion that lies totally outside Luhmann's focus: a biochemical reason, for example?

Luhmann was roundly criticized for disregarding biology and its influence on our emotional lives. For Gerhard Roth, a neuroscientist in Bremen, it is incomprehensible that a sociologist like Luhmann failed to consider man's role as a biological individual. To make matters worse, most neuroscientists were inclined to dismiss the views of Maturana and Varela, who were so influential for Luhmann, because their views could not be verified or refuted experimentally.

Luhmann replied quite simply that as long as brain research focused on neuron communication rather than on expectations, sociology could leave aside neurons and focus on how expectations are communicated. This is precisely the point of the functional independence of the systems of biology and sociology. Only what is relevant within a system is relevant. At the same time, it is interesting to note that from a biological point of view, Luhmann's concept of love integrates a series of very different states of consciousness. To be fair to Luhmann, discussions of love in a given societal context generally have clearly defined parameters, and everybody knows what is meant, but that does not change the fact that Luhmann's umbrella concept of "love" as the need for "self-portrayal" in the eyes of the other is—in both a biological and a social sense—only one segment of a far more comprehensive picture. This concept is not an adequate descriptor of a first blush of love; falling head over heels in love with someone does not necessarily mean that confirmation is being sought in the eyes of the other. If it did, a teenager's love for a pop idol might seem even more ridiculous than it already is. And the need for sex, which is often coupled with feelings of love, does not necessarily imply a quest for profound self-confirmation. The point of a sexual encounter for one person might be exactly what another person is trying to steer clear of. Actually, people may not be seeking self-confirmation at all; quite the contrary, the idea of adopting an uncharacteristic role or playing a charade might be exactly what constitutes the sexual attraction.

Another potential argument against Luhmann's concept is this: If love were truly only a social code, it would make no sense to apply the term to the animal kingdom. I will return to this point momentarily. By the same token, it would be absurd to use this sense of the term with respect to a human's love for a pet animal. The love of a parent for his or her offspring (in both the animal kingdom and in humans), sexual love, and love of family and friends have only one thing in common: The one experiencing love is deeply devoted to another living being. Furthermore, there are sensual and intellectual feelings of love, highly complex emotions, and even a moral imperative, such as the Judeo-Christian "Love thy neighbor as thyself." This commandment, which is found in other religions in similar form, is easier said than done; feelings of love cannot usually be conjured up on command, which makes requirements of this sort a questionable means of fostering morality. "Respect thy neighbor even if you don't love him" would surely be a less overwhelming alternative.

It is hard to say whether animals experience feelings of love. We have already established that we don't know what it is like to be a bat (see "Beyond Sausage and Cheese," p. 138), and we surely have no way of telling whether animals feel love. Behaviorism continues to skirt the term "love" altogether and restricts discussions of this issue to sexuality and bonding. Many behaviorists harp on man's long-lasting monogamous relationships as the sole means of defining the unique form of love experienced by humans, which presents at least three problems. First, parental love is absent from the discussion, and the deep connection between mothers and their children in some highly developed mammals is brushed aside as mere "bonding." Second, there is the question of why lasting monogamous relationships in the animal kingdom are not characterized as love relationships. If they were, gibbons and birds of prey would be regarded as capable of love, and chimpanzees and ducks would not. And finally, humans also have nonmonogamous love relationships—a practice that likely goes back to the beginnings of mankind. Nonmonogamous relationships can make it next to impossible to identify the biological father. It would appear that monogamy in humans is a far more recent phenomenon than feelings of love, not the other way around! The popular biological theory that evolution invented "love" as a "social bond" to safeguard the long period of parenting humans require has been called into question. Biologists are right to shrug their shoulders or knit their brows when asked to address the issue of love, because the term "love" is not defined in biology. Here again, neuroscientists have more to say on the subject, because they can identify the areas that govern our sexual desire—primarily the hypothalamus. But it is important to note that the nuclei in question differ by gender. In women, the ventromedial nucleus governs sexual arousal, but in men it is the medial preoptic nucleus. (Some neurobiologists consider this the reason that men typically react more strongly to optical stimuli than do women.) Recent imaging studies show that both have some connection to the feeling of love, so there is a biochemical tie between sexual desire and love—although a somewhat tenuous one, because in real life, they often appear separately. Even if love often goes hand in hand with sexual arousal, the reverse is certainly not always true. If it were, anyone who enjoyed pornography would be ceaselessly in love.

The hormone oxytocin plays a key role in love. During sexual arousal, oxytocin is released in both women and men. It acts like an opiate: invigorating and intoxicating, yet soothing. It was dubbed the "fidelity hormone" or "bonding hormone" in studies of prairie voles. In contrast to mountain voles, which have fewer oxytocin receptors, the closely related prairie voles live monogamously. Researchers working with Thomas Insel, the director of the notorious Yerkes Regional Primate Research Center at Emory University in Atlanta (see "Great Apes in the Cultural Arena," p. 145), undid a whole series of happy prairie vole relationships by injecting them with oxytocin blockers. Their fidelity was over in a flash, and they became as promiscuous as mountain voles, displaying random copulative behavior. The wanton mountain voles, in turn, happily settled into life as faithful couples when given vasopressin.

Researchers today consider it highly likely that oxytocin receptors have a significant effect on human desire and the ability to bond. Seth Pollack, a psychologist at California State University at Monterey Bay, has found lower levels of oxytocin in orphans than in children who have a close relationship with their parents. Oxytocin is thus a glue that binds. In mothers, it brings on contractions, initiates the milk supply, and enhances bonding with the baby. In couples it enables a relationship to progress from initial sexual encounters to a long-term relationship.

Altogether different centers and biochemical agents are also at work in the brain when we are in love, most likely in the cingular cortex, an area that has to do with attentiveness, and the mesolimbic system, which works like a reward center. Phenethylamines generate feelings of elation. And let us not forget the usual suspects (see "Mr. Spock in Love," p. 42): noradrenaline for rushes of excitement and dopamine for euphoria. Their level rises while soothing serotonin falls, thus triggering some degree of mental incapacity. And the body produces intoxicants such as endorphins and cortisol. After a while, this whole business ebbs away naturally. Three years is considered the maximum period that we experience feelings of love for a partner, and the average is closer to three to twelve months. International statistics indicate that the average divorce occurs after four years of marriage. The crooked teeth that went unnoticed at first now stick out. From a biochemical point of view, only oxytocin has any relevance for whether the romantic relationship lasts.

What does this tell us about love? What have we learned from all this information about oxytocin receptors and "self-portrayal in the eyes of the other"? Where along the spectrum of brain research and Luhmann does the truth lie? Everything new excites, everything surprising stimulates—both negatively and positively. The improbable arouses more excitement than the probable. Uncertainty throws us off balance whether the occasion is good or bad. On these points, neuroscience and systems theory are in agreement. Love is "a quite normal improbability" in both the biochemical and the sociological sense, an improbable experience that functions according to biochemically and socially identifiable patterns. Our brains fear boredom, and for this reason alone, it would seem, they love love. Nothing is more suspect than the seemingly innocuous Christian motto once formulated by the remarkable Lutheran pastor Dietrich Bonhoeffer: "Love wants nothing *from* the other; it wants everything *for* the other." We might well ask: For what purpose? Love is supposedly selfless, yet if it is true that love is self-portrayal in the eyes of the other, it really just reflects back to us the most exciting image we know—that of ourselves.

Of course we still do not know who or what this "self" is, but it clearly has a profound impact on the decisions we make. As Luhmann tells us, decisions are the differences that transform our lives. But how free are we to make them?

Do Be Do Be Do
What Is Freedom?

In the harbor of the old town on the island of Naxos, which, like many towns in Greece, stretches from the sea up a hill of yellowish brown rock formations, there is a small square with a taverna about halfway up. The russet tops of eucalyptus trees tilt toward the light between the narrow houses. The food is not bad, and it is relatively inexpensive, so every evening the taverna fills up with backpackers and young families. People hold forth on all kinds of causes, girls giggle, and a chorus of children's voices fills the place. At least that's how it was in the summer of 1985, during that vacation in the Cyclades that awakened my interest in philosophy. I had fallen in love with biology as a small child, when I wondered why cherry trees don't grow in our bellies if we swallow a cherry pit. But my journey into philosophy began with an adage. The very first evening at the taverna I noticed a stone tablet inserted into the wall like a tombstone, which carried this inscription:

To be is to do—Socrates
To do is to be—Sartre
Do be do be do—Sinatra

I later found out that the taverna was not the birthplace of this well-known saying, but it was new to me, so it held my attention far longer than the little joke merited. As I mentioned earlier, it was during this vacation that I got to know Socrates. I didn't know whether he had literally said that being means doing something, but I didn't really care, because the idea that being signifies doing made sense to me. I spent far more time pondering the second statement, *To do is to be*, which I thought was truly puzzling. I had heard of Sartre, and I knew that he was deeply devoted to politics and that he had visited Fidel Castro in Cuba and the terrorist Andreas Baader in his prison cell, but none of that told me why doing means being. Didn't you have to be, that is, exist, in order to be able to do something? I had a hard time understanding that saying, probably because I sensed what I now know, namely, they were probably both wrong: Sartre *and* Socrates. The only one to get it right was Sinatra. And that is what this chapter is about.

After my vacation in Greece, I began studying philosophy in Cologne. I met a girl my own age who had dark curly hair, big eyes, and a remarkably deep voice. I don't know whether she would want me to use her name, so let's just call her Rosalie. The first time I went to her apartment—which had the standard IKEA shelves, hanging plants in macramé holders, and a futon—I noticed that she kept Simone de Beauvoir's *The Mandarins* at her bedside. In this novel, Beauvoir, the prominent French philosopher, feminist, and companion of Sartre, recounts the wonderfully pessimistic years in postwar Paris. The major figures of the French intelligentsia, including characters modeled on Sartre and Beauvoir themselves, spend long nights discussing the meaninglessness of existence and the lack of understanding between people, and they dream up a way out that would entail a great deed. The book was a bestseller, and Rosalie was quite taken with it. She was of course fascinated by Paris. In the 1980s, Paris was still the most exciting city in Europe—at least in the imagination of us students. That changed in 1989, when the Berlin Wall came down and drew our attention there instead. Rosalie was also captivated by the notion of the absolute freedom of the individual in Sartre's philosophy. Sartre wrote that people are not predestined by society and psychological disposition but rather are free to do as they wish and are fully and boundlessly responsible for themselves. Individuals "invent" who they are. The claim that you can keep reinventing yourself (now trumpeted relentlessly by the consumerism industry) originated with Sartre: "In life, a man commits himself and draws his own portrait." *To do is to be.*

I was also intrigued by the idea that all my decisions were determined solely by my free will, although neither I nor Rosalie had made much use of our free will up to that point. Compared with the Mandarins of Paris, our life in Cologne was pretty boring. Was I merely afraid to take my fate into my hands? The idea did not sit well with me. Was it really just my lack of courage, or was there more to it? Rosalie did in fact change her life. She left the university and went to acting school in Stuttgart. She also signed up for self-discovery groups, on the quest for the elusive "I." When we got together, I took her to task, quoting Niklas Luhmann, who was quite popular at the University of Cologne back then. My future dissertation adviser had brought Luhmann's theory to the philosophy department when he came from Bielefeld. The question "Who am I?" I insisted, echoing Luhmann, "leaves you groping in the dark, and the only way out is by resorting to devious tricks." Rosalie was not impressed. Then she went into therapy. I had a response right out of Luhmann for that as well: "The influence of therapists on morals . . . is difficult to estimate, but it is surely to be feared." Back then I thought that therapy was essentially the opposite of Sartre's *To do is to be*, a hunt for a straw man that supposedly set the stage for everything else.

Today I think that I judged Rosalie too harshly. Without realizing it, I had applied a precept to her that I myself had nagging doubts about, namely, that we are free of internal and external constraints if we are strong enough to liberate ourselves from them, and that deeds are the only thing that matter when judging a person: "In life, a man commits himself and draws his own portrait." Wasn't that asking too much of man? How had Sartre come up with this?

Sartre wrote that man is "condemned to be free" in *Being and Nothingness*, which analyzes the philosophies of Edmund Husserl, the founder of phenomenology, and Martin Heidegger, who set the stage for Sartre's own philosophical inquiry. Husserl's innovation was to move away from explaining man and the world from an "inner essence" with rules and laws, as Kant had. He went the opposite route and, like a modern neuroscientist, probed the conditions of our experience. Kant had explored the conditions of cognition but not of experience, which he simply presupposed without much elucidation. Husserl, by contrast, focused squarely on experience: How do my senses communicate the world to me? Since he was not a biologist, he used many vivid images and concepts for sense perception, especially when describing the connection between seeing and knowing. His contentious student Martin Heidegger developed Husserl's idea into a philosophy of life, an attitude toward the world. In contrast to Husserl's pithy terms, Heidegger's words were mystical and obscure—which is exactly what made them fascinating for many readers, including Sartre.

When Sartre published *Being and Nothingness* in 1943, he was thirty-eight years old. France was occupied by the German Wehrmacht. The Nazis with whom Heidegger sympathized were Sartre's adversaries when he joined the French Resistance. An analysis and critique of Heidegger, who continued to impress him, is one of the subtexts of *Being and Nothingness*. The contrast between the leading intellectual of the Third Reich and the rising star of the French cultural scene was stark. On the one side was Heidegger, who was bourgeois through and through and deeply rooted in his homeland, with the political double standard of the opportunist and the sexual double standard of the petit bourgeoisie, and on the other was Sartre, who stood at five feet one inch and found the bourgeois milieu deeply repugnant, and who liberated himself from all political and sexual double standards, directing all his efforts at an uncompromising morality.

Sartre, the son of a French navy officer who died at a young age and an Alsatian mother, spent his childhood in his grandfather's bourgeois household. Educated by private tutors and at elitist schools, he acquired an impressive range of knowledge in a self-prescribed strict work regimen. He read widely and held to an unvarying daily work schedule (9:00 A.M. to 1:00 P.M. and 3:00 P.M. to 7:00 P.M.) for the rest of his life. In the realm of philosophy, he was persuaded that there was no reliable higher power or moral law within man. As a child, he had felt out of place living with his grandfather's family, and now he asserted that mankind as a whole was out of place and lost. Heidegger had regarded human existence as "thrown into the world," an outlook that Sartre confirmed from his own experience. While working as a high school teacher, Sartre traveled through a series of French cities, sometimes joined by his companion Simone de Beauvoir, with whom he had an on-again, off-again love affair. In 1933, the year of Hitler's accession to power, Sartre and Beauvoir were enjoying their "free" life as an unmarried couple in two rooms of a small hotel in Paris. At the beginning of World War II, Sartre, who was briefly serving in the military, found time to work on a book about the Age of Enlightenment. He also fared quite well during his captivity as a prisoner of war in Trier. In 1941, after his early discharge because of problems with his eyes, he and Beauvoir orga-

nized a resistance group against the Vichy regime, the French military dic-
tatorship allied with the Germans. Sartre wrote plays and novels and began
work on his major philosophical treatise. After the defeat of the German
Wehrmacht in Stalingrad, he renewed his contacts to the Resistance and
stepped up his political activities. When *Being and Nothingness* was published in the spring of 1943 during a severe paper shortage, Sartre was already a famous man, a well-connected key figure in French intellectual life.

Sartre's *Being and Nothingness* highlighted his view that man is the only
animal that can ponder things that do not exist, as is evident in the book's
title. Other animals' limited imagination prevents them from picturing
something that once was or has yet to be. Humans, by contrast, can invent
things that *never* exist—they can lie. Imagination is liberating. By the same
token, Sartre argues, man has no substance at all as a naked being. Unlike
animals that are determined by fixed instincts and behavioral patterns,
man has to set his own patterns of behavior: "Existence precedes essence."
Theologians and philosophers had always failed to appreciate this fact
while looking for rules and patterns to define man. But in a world without
God, these definitions of man based on philosophical values and binding
moral maxims would no longer make any sense. The only truly existential
facet of man is in the realm of feelings: revulsion, fear, worry, boredom,
and sense of the absurd. Sartre called his philosophy "existentialism."

The relentlessness with which Sartre eradicated his predecessors' assumptions about man, and his emphasis on negative feelings, need to be
understood against the backdrop of his war experience. Sartre's spirit of
rebellion against inertia and emptiness was similarly adamant. What mattered was to offer resistance (to the Nazis) and to construct something new.
This feeling is expressed philosophically in Sartre's countless exhortations
to act: "Man is what he does," or "The only reality is in action." There is no
excuse for people who daydream aimlessly, because they are only fleeing
themselves and their responsibility. All this, Sartre claimed, is self-
deception.

Sartre went on to outline an ambitious mission in his next book, *Existentialism Is a Humanism*, which was published shortly thereafter and defined the philosopher as an agent of enlightenment, exhorting others to
embrace their freedom and thus realize themselves as human beings. For
Sartre it essentially comes down to the "project" that man makes of himself: "Man is nothing other than his own project. He exists only to the ex-

tent that he realizes himself, therefore he is nothing more than the sum of his actions, nothing more than his life." The will, by contrast, is only a consequence of a preceding project of this kind: First man draws up a design of himself, then he acquires a will that accords with this design. In Sartre's words: "What we usually understand by 'will' is a conscious decision that most of us take after we have made ourselves what we are." This idea captivated my friend Rosalie, and it inspired an entire generation of postwar intellectuals to lead life as a "project." Of course, these supposedly highly individualistic projects were often strikingly similar: Clad in black and melancholy, existentialists roamed from jazz clubs to campus to movie theaters to cafés, indistinguishable in their fashionable conformity.

Sartre's life remained exciting and heady all the way to his death in 1980. He was the preeminent French intellectual of the twentieth century and a well-regarded moral authority. But was his notion of man's freedom realistic? Is the individual truly so free of internal and external constraints that he can draw himself, the way an artist draws a work of art? If Sartre were right in claiming that the "plan" we draw up of ourselves precedes the will, man would be capable not only of liberating himself from all social expectations but also of rising above his instincts, habits, wishes, behavior patterns, moral precepts, and reactions formed in early childhood. All it would take is the courage to reassess and change one's life circumstances inside and out. "Self-realization" in Sartre's sense would begin with an inventory of our psyches, clearing out unwanted merchandise and restocking the shelves with more enticing goods. Is my petit bourgeois education holding me back? Out with it! I'll go for the exciting, carefree life of an artist and man about town! Kant had also believed that the will was capable of making free and rational decisions, though he insisted that free deeds needed to be good deeds, which is an enormous restriction. Sartre felt much the same way. Although he did not believe in Kant's "moral law" in our psyche, Sartre's equation also held that freedom is self-determination, and that self-determination is good.

However, freedom of the will is no easy matter to achieve. As we saw earlier (in "The Libet Experiment," p. 95), most neuroscientists disagree with Sartre and contend that man is *not* free. First, man is a product of his aptitudes, experiences, and upbringing, and second, it is not our consciousness in the light of day that tells us what to do, but rather our *subconsciousness* in the dark of night. Even if I liberate myself from many external constraints, my desires, preferences, and longings remain unfree. I am not the one determining my needs—they are determining me! And that is why many neuroscientists claim that people are utterly incapable of "reinventing" themselves.

That is certainly depressing news, especially because Sartre's philosophy of freedom is so enticing. An early passage in Robert Musil's novel *The Man Without Qualities*, which I found riveting when I was a student, suggests that life offers not only a "sense of reality" but also a "sense of possibility." I have felt a deep need to keep my eye out for alternative options since my childhood in the none-too-enticing rural region of North Rhine—Westphalia. But what is the good of this sense of possibility if I have no free will to act on it? If my experience, upbringing, and education really predestine me for social servitude, then all my actions do is replicate social programming, play roles, fulfill norms, and adhere to a social script. What I regard as *my* will, *my* ideas, and *my* esprit is nothing but the reflex of ideologies and cultural patterns. In other words, I have no will at all and no ideas of my own—I merely *ascribe* them to myself.

Gerhard Roth tells us that this is the neuroscientific way of regarding the will and ideas. I cannot really take credit for what I consider my freedom of will, and the fact that I do so anyway stems from my boundless overestimation of the capabilities of my consciousness. What the prefrontal cortex regards as its own attainment is in fact only an auxiliary service. Roth explains: "Our intellect can be regarded as a team of expert advisers used by the limbic system in governing our behavior." The actual decision makers that "set off" our actions are thus located in the interbrain. They are experts in experiences and emotions, administrators in the domain of feelings, even if they have no grasp of complex reflections and considerations. Nevertheless, only the limbic system decides what we ultimately do, namely, what it considers "emotionally acceptable."

It is hard to deny the pull of the dark power of the unconscious. The question is only: What does it mean for us? For Gerhard Roth, freedom is purely an illusion. That is one way of looking at it, but does freedom of will really hinge on whether I have a clear picture of my motives? In other words: How well would I have to understand and have power over myself for Gerhard Roth to concede that I have at least some modicum of free will?

Let us look at an example: In the framework of my limited parameters I believe that I know myself very well. I used to have a great deal of difficulty keeping my feelings in check when someone's political or philosophical opinion riled me up, so I was often quick-tempered and emotional back in college. These days I resolve to stay calm in controversies, and it often works quite well. I had trouble keeping my feelings from getting the better of me when I was younger, but now they heed my will. It's a matter of experience. When I go to a debate today, I am determined to keep my cool, and as a rule I succeed, so I would say that my feelings have learned to submit to my intellect. Isn't that proof that my mind guides my feelings as well as the other way around? Once you get down to specifics, of course, the matter is never so clear-cut; my ability to temper my emotions entails my feelings as well. How often have I been annoyed with myself after such heated discussions? The decision to calm down fit the bill of "emotionally acceptable," or emotionally desired, but I am still convinced that my free will had an effect on my temper. I keep my cool even when certain things seem "emotionally unacceptable" to me.

The point of this example is that feelings can be learned. Things that frightened me as a child no longer do so. Things that I found appealing months ago now bore me. And learning feelings certainly engages my mind, so in this respect, my feelings and mind work together, each shaping the other. Even when my feelings win out in a given situation, my mind helps steer my feelings from behind. Just because this laborious process has yet to be described with the tools of neuroscience does not mean that it does not exist. If we were unable to learn feelings, adults would continue to react like small children, and all hell would break loose.

We are free to some degree, because we certainly chart our own courses, but our freedom is limited by our life circumstances. Still, changes are certainly possible within these parameters. We should be wary of portraying this freedom too modestly or too ambitiously. Those who lack self-confidence do not develop, and those who wish to live out their inner freedom to the fullest according to Sartre's ideas will soon be in over their heads. Man does not in fact design a plan for life and then tack on a will to suit this plan. It is no wonder that the overwhelming challenges of existentialism eventually fell out of favor, much like the Judeo-Christian model of loving others "as thyself," or the exaggerated psychological challenges of socialism.

The powerful and reciprocal dependency of thoughts and feelings explains why people are so marvelously unpredictable, and why so many fine ideas and good intentions are never put into action—the alcoholic who resolves to give up the bottle, the office worker determined to tell off his boss, life's many unrealized dreams. As unfortunate as that may be for the individual, it may work out better for society as a whole. A world in which all people attain complete self-fulfillment would probably not be a paradise. And we should also keep in mind that many external constraints serve the positive purpose of furnishing stability and security, and liberation from them does not pave the way to happiness. We don't necessarily want to be stripped of family ties, fondness for our homes, and cherished memories.

The answer to the question of whether our basic psychological makeup determines our actions or our actions our psyche is thus: It does and it doesn't. My actions and my frame of mind keep crisscrossing, forming an endless succession of doing and being, being and doing: *Do be do be do.* The degree of latitude we have in realizing ourselves varies quite significantly from one person to the next and depends in large part on our material freedom, which is to say our financial opportunities. And this brings us to the next topic we need to examine in connection with happiness and desires: how property and possessions both liberate and limit us.

Robinson's Used Oil
Do We Need Possessions?

I'm a nice guy—and very generous. I have decided to make you a present of the trees in my backyard: a gnarled old cherry tree, which I've always been quite fond of, and a beautiful weeping willow. You can have both of them. There's just one catch: You have to promise me not to cut them down or do anything else to them.

What's that you say? This present disappoints you? Why? Because you get nothing out of it? True. But why is that? Because the only way it makes sense to have or possess something is if you can do what you want with it, at least to some extent, you say. And why can you? Because it belongs to you. The whole purpose of property, you say, is being able to do what you like with a thing. Something with which you cannot do anything doesn't belong to you. Maybe you're right. I'm taking back my trees. It doesn't help to own something if you can't do what you like with it. But why?

Property, you say, is something that belongs to you. It is the relationship between oneself and a thing and is nobody else's business. Is that right too? Of course, you say. You point to your bicycle and say: That is *my* bicycle! You point to your jacket and say: That is *my* jacket! The principle underlying your understanding of property was laid out clearly and unequivocally in 1766 by Sir William Blackstone, in the second volume of his famous *Commentaries on the Laws of England:* "There is nothing which so generally strikes the imagination, and engages the affections of mankind, as the right of property; or that sole and despotic dominion which one man claims and exercises over the external things of the world, in total exclusion of the right of any other individual in the universe."

Blackstone was a progressive man and very popular in his day. His book went through eight editions in his lifetime and was still considered authoritative an entire century after publication. Blackstone's aim was to base the judicial system not on traditional ideas, but on "nature and reason." And for him, property was a "relationship between a person and a thing." I suppose you see the matter the same way. It is nobody's business what happens between you and your jacket. But is that really true?

Let us take a look at a book by a second British author, written in 1719, just about fifty years before Blackstone's *Commentaries*. The author was an unsuccessful merchant named Daniel Foe, and the title of the book was *The Life and Strange Surprising Adventures of Robinson Crusoe*. Foe had led a very eventful life by the time he published his novel at the age of sixty. He was part of an ill-fated rebellion against the king and spent time in prison, then became quite wealthy in the wine and tobacco trade. But his economic good fortune was not to last. The war between England and France cost him a great deal of valuable cargo and drove him to insolvency. Foe opened a brick factory and supplemented his income with journalism.

His two major themes were religion and economics. He was a Presbyterian at a time when non-Anglican Protestants in England were known as Dissenters, and Foe became an active Dissenter, fighting for religious tolerance. His bankruptcy in 1692 shaped his political and economic outlook, and he wrote numerous impassioned essays advocating new ownership laws that would do away with the traditional privileges accorded to nobility and restructure landholding in England. He offered a virtually inexhaustible stream of widely discussed suggestions to improve the economy, society, and cultural life. Foe proudly added a fictitious title of nobility to his name and began calling himself De Foe (or Defoe). There is a certain irony in the fact that Foe embellished his name with the very title whose preferential treatment he fought against so vehemently in his writings. In 1703, the Church and the government sent him to prison for a brief period on charges of "seditious libel."

He wrote his bestselling novel after meeting the sailor Alexander Selkirk in London. Selkirk's story caused quite a flurry of interest in London. In the fall of 1704, the sailor had protested conditions aboard the *Cinque Ports*, the ship on which he was traveling. The ship had been eaten away by shipworms, and Selkirk did not consider it seaworthy. The captain marooned the mutineer on the lonely island of Más a Tierra in the Juan Fernández Islands off the coast of Chile. The ship subsequently sank, and most of the crew drowned. Selkirk spent four years and four months alone on Más a Tierra, until he was rescued in February 1709 by a privateer, the crew of which included a fellow officer of the captain who had marooned him from the *Cinque Ports*. Selkirk returned to London a hero, until his changing fortune drove him out to sea once again. Meanwhile, Foe expanded Selkirk's story into a rambling tale of adventure and personal development. He left his hero in solitude for twenty-eight years, and he embellished the story with myriad remarks about religion and economic policy. One of the key themes is ownership.

Let us picture ourselves as Foe's Robinson Crusoe to figure out why ownership is so important to him. Imagine you are Robinson, spending twenty-eight years on Más a Tierra. The island is quite hilly. A deep green mountain landscape rises from the desertlike barren coast with an impenetrably lush vegetation of trees and grasses. Giant ferns as tall as trees grow along the mountain slopes. The climate is agreeable—not too cold and not too hot. And goats, left behind by unknown sailors, wander everywhere. Once you have explored the island and figured out that nothing belongs to anyone, you say: This tree fern is *my* tree fern, these goats belong to *me*, this parrot is *my* property, this house that I have built is *mine* alone. You spend days and weeks appropriating everything in sight. You can even say: This coast is *my* coast, and this sea is *my* sea. And that is precisely what Robinson does. But what good does it do him? The whole thing is a pointless exercise. As long as no one else shows up to dispute your right to these possessions, your claims to ownership don't make a bit of difference.

The notion of ownership becomes important only when other people come into play. I don't have to tell my cellphone that it belongs to me, but if someone tries to take it, I have to declare my ownership. Ownership does not occur between people and things, but is a "contract" among people, as Blackstone acknowledged when discussing the "exclusion of the right of any other individual." Blackstone's remark about the "sole and despotic dominion" over property may apply to Robinson Crusoe, but not to our society today.

I do have "sole and despotic dominion" over a bar of chocolate I buy. I can eat it right away if I feel like it, normally without consulting anyone else. But in a world that is not a deserted island, I cannot simply do what I like with my property. If Robinson had needed to dispose of used oil, he could have just poured it into the sea, but I can't; in fact, even if I dump oil into the pond in my own backyard, I could be charged with environmental pollution. Once I rent out an apartment, I'm not allowed to enter it without asking the tenants for permission or at least informing them that I'm coming, nor can I simply let my rental apartment stand vacant. I can't mistreat my dog or train it for dogfights; if I do, I can be hauled into court for cruelty to animals. That is how ownership works, even though the used oil, the backyard pond, the apartment, and the dog all belong to me.

Ownership is a complicated matter. The idea that property is the relationship between me and a thing seems wrong in at least two ways. For one thing, property is a contract between people, and for another, this "thing" is not simply a thing, but rather a complex matter entailing rights and obligations.

Robinson is not nearly as naïve as he may appear when he hunts around for property and marks his possessions. He knows perfectly well that when he declares himself the owner of all the things on his island he has grown attached to, no one is going to dispute his right to ownership. Property, he would maintain, is more about the relationship between a person and a thing than jurists would have us believe, and he is not that far off. His claims to ownership are an expression of his psychological relationship to things, and things that belong to him mean more to him than things that do not. His property matters to him, and he is indifferent to the rest.

This psychological relationship to property, a "love" of one's possessions, is one of the most underexamined chapters in the book of the human psyche, which is astonishing because yearning for and possessing objects we claim to love is of enormous significance in our society. A pioneer in research on this subject was a sociologist in Berlin, Georg Simmel, who had great insight into psychological processes. Simmel investigated a wide range of social phenomena, among them the significance of objects for human self-esteem.

In 1900, Simmel, who was then a forty-two-year-old associate professor, published *The Philosophy of Money*. Although Simmel did not mention

Defoe's protagonist by name, the key to understanding why Robinson Crusoe marked territory on his deserted island lies here. Acquiring something, even just symbolically as Robinson did, makes it your property. We might say that you absorb it into yourself and adopt it as part of your being. This absorption takes place in two directions: from the things to the "I" and the "I" to the things. In Simmel's words: "On the one hand, the whole significance of property lies in the fact that it releases certain emotions and impulses of the soul, while on the other hand the sphere of the Ego extends both over and into these 'external' objects." Possessions thus offer the opportunity to expand psychologically, or, as Simmel says, "to form an extension of the Ego."

The objects with which I surround myself are *my* objects and thus an outgrowth of myself. The clothes I wear lend my personality a visible dimension, an image that reflects on me in the eyes of others. The same goes for the car I drive, which shapes my self-image and what others think of me. The designer sofa in my living room gives shape not only to the room but also to me. The visible sign of my taste appears as part of my identity. A Porsche driver, a Rolex wearer, a kid with a Mohawk are identities in the distinctive form of character types.

Even if Robinson is not trying to define himself as a certain type of person—the kind with a flowing beard, leather pants, and a parasol—he is after what Simmel is describing, expanding and extending himself into the things he owns. Once he has built a hut, Robinson feels the pride of the homeowner, and once he has captured and bred some goats, he is filled with the pride of the farmer. In each of these proud moments, Robinson uses possessions to craft his self-image. Since there are no people to react to it, he has to play that role as well. In Simmel's words: "That self-awareness has transcended its immediate boundaries, and has become rooted in objects that only indirectly concern it, really proves to what extent property as such means nothing other than the extension of the personality into the objects and, through its domination of them, the gaining of its sphere of influence."

But why is it that to one degree or another, people find they can "realize" themselves in the possessions they acquire? And why is this acquisition more important than the possession itself, which appears rather dull by comparison? The thrill of making purchases and the accompanying emotional dynamics have yet to be the subject of sustained research. Once hunters and gatherers had weapons and tools, according to Simmel, the "extension of the personality" into objects began. Today, the acquisition of things—and the accompanying images—ranks among the primary sources of happiness in the industrialized world, perhaps because other sources of happiness—religious belief, love, and so forth—are not in very good shape in these countries. Might the increasingly brief duration of romantic relationships be a consequence of consumerism, as is often claimed, with love becoming a market of quick thrills, of acquiring things and tossing them out?

Or maybe it is just the other way around: Because love does not guarantee permanence, I look to the reliability of consumerism. Excessive consumption becomes a coping mechanism for angst or an apparent fast track to satisfaction—or both. When the emotions of other people are too complicated, I rely instead on the more dependable emotional rewards and confirmation provided by material goods. A Mercedes is still a Mercedes five years down the line, whereas a person who is dear to you now may not stay that way. This would also explain why the elderly, who are more settled in life, tend to prefer things that retain their value, while young people, who feel less need for emotional reliability, like rapid changes and embrace passing trends.

From a cultural and historical perspective, the "love of things" has skyrocketed in the industrialized nations, and we are participating in a huge social experiment. Today's economy zooms along at a breathless pace unparalleled in history, inventing new things and dispensing with the old. Few societies have called the possession of property into question. Even communism, in the form of Eastern European state socialism, had nothing against private property. The only prohibition was of private ownership of means of production used to create a "surplus value" that would distribute wealth in a capitalist manner. But never in the history of mankind has society defined itself by the *acquisition* of property to the extent that it does in today's industrialized world.

"What is property?" is more than a legal issue; it has psychological implications as well, because property offers a relatively stable opportunity to expand emotionally—albeit at the expense of alternative social opportunities for expansion. The price that the desire for ownership exacts from the owner has been a severely neglected issue in psychology, in stark contrast to the price that desire for owning things exacts from other members of society, a subject that has been discussed for centuries. At the core of this question is a philosophical problem: If it is true that property results from a contract, what principles govern this contract and a just social order?

The Rawls Game
What Is Just?

How about we play a game of dreaming up a truly just society? We have a board and a set of pieces, and we can make up rules to produce the best possible outcome for everyone. The basic setup is this: A group of people—men and women, young and old—live together in one self-contained area, namely, our board, which offers everything a person could need: plenty to eat and drink, a warm place to sleep, and lots of room to move about. To start our best possible society from scratch, we'll make the people on our board know nothing about themselves. They have no clue whether they are smart or stupid, beautiful or ugly, strong or weak, old or young, male or female. A "veil of ignorance" has been draped over their characteristics, assets, and abilities, rendering them devoid of biography.

These people have to devise rules for how to get along in order to prevent chaos and anarchy from taking over. Each of them has to attend to basic human needs—access to drinking water, food, and sleeping quarters—but the veil of ignorance prevents them from seeing themselves clearly and assessing any other requirements. So they sit down together to come up with rules that would work for them while remaining ignorant of their personal status.

What principle do you think they would agree on first? It's quite a challenge to imagine what they'd come up with, because people behind the veil do not know what they are like in real life and cannot predict what would be best for them. The veil prevents individual interests from swaying the group's decision and is designed to guarantee fairness and ensure that shared interests prevail. Since it could turn out that a given individual's initial conditions are not advantageous, people will project themselves into the role of the weakest and promote fair rules that see to the needs of the weakest among them. No one dares to suggest anything risky, because a risk might work against that individual's interests. The group draws up a list of all suggestions for distributing the important primary goods. Then the group agrees on a ranking that allows each member to get a guaranteed minimum of liberties and primary goods, with everyone obtaining a fair share. The resulting rules might look like this:

1. Each person is to have an equal right to the most extensive total system of equal basic liberties compatible with a similar system of liberty for all.

2. Social and economic inequalities are to be arranged so that they are both:

a) to the greatest benefit of the least advantaged, consistent with the just savings principle, and

b) attached to offices and positions open to all under conditions of fair equality of opportunity.

Are you persuaded, or are you at least willing to go along with this approach? If so, you are a kindred spirit of the late philosopher John Rawls, who thought up this model.

Rawls led a very eventful life before turning to philosophy. He was the second of five sons, two of whom died of diseases they had caught from him (one of diphtheria and the other of pneumonia). Rawls's parents were very active in politics, his mother in the women's rights movement and his father, an attorney, in the Democratic Party. Rawls attended the Kent School in Connecticut, then entered Princeton University in September 1939, the same month that Germany invaded Poland. By the time he graduated in 1943, the United States had entered World War II, and Rawls enlisted in the army. He served as an infantryman in the Pacific, where he toured New Guinea and the Philippines. He went to Japan just after the Americans had dropped atomic bombs on Hiroshima and Nagasaki. Rawls visited Hiroshima and observed the terrible aftermath. The army offered him the opportunity to become an officer, but he was so dismayed by his experience that he declined. He returned to Princeton for graduate school; his dissertation on moral philosophy bore the title "A Study on the Grounds of Ethical Knowledge: Considered with Reference to Judgments on the Moral Worth of Character." Rawls had a successful career as a philosopher, and in 1962 he joined the Harvard faculty as a professor of political philosophy. He was not a brilliant orator—he stuttered and was shy in front of audiences—but his colleagues, students, and friends appreciated his modesty and attentiveness. He usually spent the day in his study, sitting barefoot at the edge of his sofa with a writing pad on his knees. He liked to jot down notes while talking to people, which he would read over later and then give them a copy. He never regarded himself as a great philosopher, but rather as a man for whom philosophizing was a communal exercise in contemplation. In 1995, he suffered the first of a series of strokes that greatly impeded his work, and he died in 2002 at the age of eighty-one.

Although he wrote four major books and numerous essays, Rawls made his mark on the history of philosophy with *A Theory of Justice*, which is possibly the most illustrious book on morality to have been published in the second half of the twentieth century. Though its title is succinct, it represents a monumental attempt to craft a modern moral philosophy, with a guiding principle that is amazingly clear and simple: Fairness for everyone is the basis of justice. A society that free individuals on an equal footing would themselves devise is a fair and just society. Hence, a social order is just when everyone would have approved of it before knowing what place he or she would occupy in the society.

The first principle holds that in a just state, all citizens enjoy the same basic liberties. But because people have differing abilities and interests, social and economic inequalities are bound to emerge over the long run. One person may work harder than another, or have more business sense, or simply be luckier. The next thing you know, that person owns more than the other. Nothing can be done about that. For the state to continue being guided by fairness, Rawls introduces a second principle: Although social and economic inequalities cannot be avoided, these inequalities are acceptable only when the least advantaged still derive the greatest possible benefit.

Rawls later claimed that his book was intended only for a small circle of his friends, but its success was overwhelming. *A Theory of Justice* was translated into twenty-three languages and sold more than 200,000 copies in the United States. The enormous sensation it created forced Rawls to continue honing his theory. He spent thirty years reworking and adding to it. The underlying idea has a long history, harking back to Epicurus (see "The Distant Garden," p. 245), who envisioned a state based on a reciprocal contract. An ideal state is one that the members of a society in full possession of their mental faculties would voluntarily commit to a contract. Thomas Hobbes and John Locke took up this idea in the seventeenth century and outlined elaborate contract theories; Rousseau wrote *The Social Contract.* By the twentieth century, however, contract theories had been consigned to oblivion. Wittgenstein had attempted to banish ethics from philosophy altogether; prescriptive statements about life struck him as illogical and therefore meaningless. It was thus all the more startling that Rawls came back to the old tradition of the social contract in the late 1960s.

Rawls was unable to persuade many people of the political relevance of his work during that turbulent point in history. In 1971, people were preoccupied with the Vietnam War. There were mass demonstrations against the government, and fierce debates raged about the state and its system of property ownership, civil rights, and the freedom of the individual. Capitalism and socialism were irreconcilably opposed, and both had shown their ugly faces, in Vietnam and in Czechoslovakia. The publication of Rawls's book, which attempted a grand reconciliation, came at this unlikely moment, although Rawls had not planned his book as a response to these political tensions. But his system, which was aimed at social equalization, was too far to the left to appeal to those on the right, and those on the left regarded him as overcautious and timid. These controversial friend-or-foe lines turned the meticulously argued *Theory of Justice* into philosophical dynamite.

Conservative critics like to point out that Rawls's fictitious "original position" is not very productive. As both Rousseau and Rawls were aware, this kind of idea is a construct, and its epistemic value is debatable. In reality, critics remind us, things originated differently from the way Rawls imagined—justice and fairness are not the true driving forces of man. They argue that a need for justice, which Rawls hoped to cement by means of the original position, is much less pronounced in reality, and is trumped by the driving forces of egoism and the need for free unconstrained development, as is evident in every society. Hadn't the moral philosopher Adam Smith made a convincing case back in the eighteenth century that it is egoism—not justice—that impels a society, both economically and morally? As Smith stated, "It is not from the benevolence of the butcher, the brewer, or the baker, that we expect our dinner, but from their regard to their own interest." For the butcher to benefit, he has to sell his wares at competitive prices, or at least allow for the financial circumstances of his customers. This is how a functioning polity and a "free market" arise.

According to Adam Smith's *Theory of Moral Sentiments*, "an invisible hand" guides the pursuit of our own interests and "without intending it, without knowing it, advance[s] the interest of the society." Smith's twentieth-century admirers, first and foremost Rawls's colleague at Harvard, Robert Nozick, use this idea to defend the status quo of every society, because it is the result—for better or for worse—of the true forces driving human behavior. Inventing additional forces on the drawing board does not make sense. It is utterly misguided, Nozick explains, for Rawls to use principles of fairness to set community rules; society has no need for principles of that sort. Why shouldn't man be able simply to enjoy in peace all his natural gifts, his undeserved talents, and his fortuitous head starts in the race for the limited natural and social assets in his life? Why must his successes benefit others? Isn't it enough that they do so in the bigger picture? For Nozick, Rawls is a socialist in disguise who completely misjudges the true nature of man.

Rawls a socialist? Socialists would roar with laughter at the very idea. Here, too, the critique begins with the fictitious original position. As ignorant as those under the veil might be, Rawls stresses that they are "free persons." Making the will of a select group of individuals the basis of a theory of justice is problematic, however. As we know, not all members of a society are fully self-determined and free. What about small children and people with severe mental disabilities, who are incapable of casting a vote? If only the interests of mature adults are taken into account, these disadvantaged individuals could easily be deprived of rights—at the very least orphans and the most severely mentally disabled lacking family support. The equality of all people is thus a tricky starting point, even in a fictitious construct. Even if all people have essentially the same interests, that is not enough to make them equal.

The question of equality becomes especially thorny when Rawls's original position is applied to different countries and regions. Even if we accept that congruent interests make for a successful and good society, couldn't that same argument be used to set one society apart from others? Peter Singer (see "Beyond Sausage and Cheese," p. 138) points out that the inhabitants of wealthy countries could agree that it is in the general interest to split their surpluses among themselves instead of giving them to the inhabitants of other countries. Singer claims that the number of interests shared by people in all countries is much smaller than Rawls thinks, and he also takes issue with Rawls's stance on property. What Nozick considers leftist arguments, Rawls's leftist critics regard as too far to the right. Rawls included the right to property among the basic political liberties, arguing that property helps people maintain their independence and thus contributes to their self-respect. Only those who respect themselves are able to respect others and thus to act morally. For some leftist critics, property is given far too much weight. Rawls did not elaborate on this issue; the comprehensive and detailed index at the end of *A Theory of Justice* lists neither "property" nor "possessions."

As much as Rawls strove for a politically disinterested model and universally acceptable principles, he was unable to win everybody over, which is hardly surprising. A philosophical book that everyone can agree on has yet to be written, and if it were written, it would surely be inconsequential. Let us examine the three key points of contention in Rawls's theory, leaving aside the aforementioned political issues.

The first point is the value of a social model built on the fictional construct of the original position. Rawls's original position, unlike those in other contract theories, is not a state of nature but a state of society. The markers of the classic natural state that are found in Thomas Hobbes and elsewhere—violence, anarchy, and lawlessness—do not appear in Rawls's characterization. Rawls's original position more closely resembles a refined cooperative. And the material basis—enough goods for everyone—sounds more like Switzerland than the Sahel or Hobbes's poverty-stricken England in the seventeenth century. All rigors of nature and all deprivations are carefully kept away in order to foster and help develop man's good nature. If Rawls's original position were characterized by catastrophes and deprivations, there would be a quick end to group solidarity, even with a veil of ignorance concealing personal qualities. When threatened by a deluge, people do not debate issues of equal opportunity; they fight for a place in the boat.

The second point is whether Rawls is correct in making justice such a dominating factor. His original position, which places liberty at the top of the ranking, situates justice based on equal opportunity and on leveling the social playing field right below it, as a constraint on liberty. Effectiveness and affluence come third. The prominent position accorded to justice is laudable and makes his theory appealing. An affluent state run by a dictator—for example, Kuwait—ranks below a poor democracy. His critics accord greater importance to unrestricted freedom, stability, and efficiency than to justice: Better to have an affluent and stable, yet unjust, state, they argue, than a just but poor society. But whereas a utilitarian weighs the sum of the happiness produced by wealth (see "Aunt Bertha Shall Live," p. 118), Rawls insists that the sum of justice is what counts. The utilitarians claim that "what is good for many is just," but John Rawls insists, "What is just is good for many." This topic can be talked to death, but in the end neither side has absolute precedence over the other. Values may be more or less appealing, but it is in their nature to be subjective and not open to objective confirmation. Even a theory as ingenious as Rawls's cannot escape this problem.

The third key point of contention in Rawls's theory is the role of reason. Rawls adopts the philosophical stance of a constitutional legislator, using reason, caution, logic, and fairness to design a universally applicable organization that takes into account the needs of virtually everyone (with the regrettable exception of those with severe mental disabilities). He starts from the assumption that his principles are universally valid; but is everyone as wise, incorruptible, and rational as John Rawls? There is no explicit discussion of feelings or emotions in Rawls's book, which is surprising, since the entire theory hinges on feelings about justice. In the original position, beneath the veil of ignorance, this feeling of justice stems from self-interest. My own potential risk induces feelings of fear, so I look for general rules that would protect everyone and quell this fear. Is justice Rawls's way of channeling fear? Rawls does not say. Instead, he speaks only about a "sense of justice," and does not say much about its psychological origin.

Rawls contends that other intervening feelings, such as jealousy and envy, are highly problematic. He finds it exasperating that Sigmund Freud constructed his theory of justice on these very feelings, and he argued that only the disadvantaged clamor for justice. In Rawls, by contrast, the sense of morality seems to form part of man's nature much the way it does for

Marc Hauser (see "The Man on the Bridge," p. 112). Rawls does not devote much research to this instinct but rather uses it as a tacit premise, presumably because he—like Kant—took the old-fashioned view that it was an innate law of reason and not a feeling.

The question of whether justice or wealth should be ranked higher sets Rawls apart from utilitarians (see "Aunt Bertha Shall Live," p. 118). Jeremy Bentham and John Stuart Mill had to figure out how a free individual's pursuit of happiness could make for a just society, but Rawls had to show how a just society can lead to freedom and hence to the happiness of all. For Bentham and Mill, the state is a necessary evil; for Rawls, it is the moral legislator. This very line divides political factions even today. Is justice a matter for the state or the individual? As far as Bentham and Mill are concerned, when considering matters involving an individual's interests, if that individual's actions do not unduly restrict or impinge on other members of society, the state has no business intervening. Its role is that of a night watchman who sounds the alarm only when the building is on fire. For Rawls, by contrast, the state functions as a wise leader and dedicated teacher, in charge of reconciling interests wherever the need arises. The pluralism of individual aims—this was Rawls's last major topic before his death—ceases when it poses a serious threat to the pluralism of society as a whole. A state that is boundlessly tolerant of all political, ideological, and religious groupings can easily devastate its own foundation. Private pluralism must not be allowed to undermine political pluralism.

The theories are united in their rejection of the egalitarianism found in socialist countries. A society that aspires to nothing but equality, both argue, is at variance with human nature and inevitably stagnates or falls apart. Even Karl Marx and Friedrich Engels shared this view, commenting in *The Communist Manifesto:* "The free development of each is the condition for the free development of all."

It is intriguing to note that every theory of justice regards justice as a basis for happiness—yet justice is merely tangential to most philosophies of happiness. Rawls's straightforward, candid definition of happiness is no exception: "The main idea is that a person's good is determined by what is for him the most rational long-term plan of life given reasonably favorable circumstances. A man is happy when he is more or less successful in the way of carrying out this plan. To put it briefly, the good is the satisfaction of rational desire." The matter-of-factness with which Rawls slips in the word "happiness" when discussing the good is quite remarkable, and it seems an oddly unimaginative way of looking at human nature. From a psychological point of view, there is certainly room for improvement in *A Theory of Justice.* But if happiness does not lead to goodness, what else is needed?

Isles of the Blessed
What Is a Happy Life?

The happiest people on earth do not have paved streets or many natural resources to speak of. They have no army. Some are farmers and fishermen,
others work in restaurants and hotels. They do not understand one another
especially well—their country has the highest concentration of languages in
the world, with a population of two hundred thousand speaking more than
a hundred different tongues. Their life expectancy is rather low; most live
to be no older than sixty-three. "The people here are happy because they
are satisfied with what little they have," explains a journalist from the local
newspaper. "Life revolves around the community, the family, and doing
good deeds for others. This is a place where you don't have to worry much."
The biggest concerns are tornadoes and earthquakes.

According to the first *Happy Planet Index,* published by the New Economics Foundation in the summer of 2006, Vanuatu is the happiest nation
on earth. Vanua-what? Yes, this land really does exist. It is a relatively unknown island nation in the South Pacific, formerly known as the New Heb-
rides. The survey inquired into people's expectations in life, their overall
satisfaction, and their relationship with their environment. Evidently the
optimal setting for humans is life on a volcanic island with about seventeen
inhabitants per square kilometer; a mild climate with plenty of sun and
lush vegetation; a mix of indigenous religions and Protestants, Anglicans,
Catholics, and Adventists; modest but fair-minded working conditions

with many people self-employed; and a parliamentary democracy with a
strong prime minister, a weak president, and the British judicial system.
But the study, which included the environmental organization Friends of
the Earth, was not after these kinds of details; its purpose was to determine
the extent to which man needs to encroach on nature and inflict damage
on the environment in order to create conditions that enhance human
happiness. And the answer, with the victor here being Vanuatu, was a re-
sounding: Not much!

Compared to this volcanic island, the happiness factor in the wealthy
countries of the industrialized world—the countries of progress, high life
expectancies, and the most comprehensive array of consumer products,
leisure time, and entertainment—is pathetic. Germany is in eighty-first
place, though it is still the fourth-happiest country in Europe after Italy,
Austria, and Luxembourg. The ever-admired Scandinavian countries of
Denmark (112), Norway (115), Sweden (119), and Finland (123) are all in
the lower half. Life is much happier in China, Mongolia, and Jamaica. The
perceived quality of life in the United States, "the land of the free and the
home of the brave" (150) and in oil-rich Kuwait (159) and Qatar (166)—two
countries in which the native population is relieved from the need for gain-
ful employment by government-provided social services—is pretty miser-
able. Bringing up the rear of the 178 countries in this index are Russia,
Ukraine, the Republic of the Congo, Swaziland, and Zimbabwe.

Let us leave aside the likelihood that the days of a happy Vanuatu are
numbered; global warming and the attendant rise in sea level may wash
away this Atlantis before long. Let us ask instead what we can learn from the
happy people in the South Seas. The first lesson is simple, clear, and certainly intended by the authors of the study: Money, consumption, power,
and the prospect of living to a ripe old age are not what make people happy.
That is an interesting message, especially at a time in which the income of
broad sectors of the population is not rising, even in the wealthy countries
of the West, which is presumably the reason that savvy institutes such as the
New Economics Foundation are investigating the extent to which money
makes us happy at all and whether income and possessions are useful
gauges of the happiness and success of a society. In this regard, "happiness
economics" is a promising new branch of research, and its findings are remarkable. For example, surveys conducted by researchers in this field reveal that while the real income and the living standard in the United States

have doubled since the 1950s, the proportion of respondents who report feeling happy did not keep pace but instead remained virtually constant over the past fifty years. A detailed calculation in another study concludes that upwards of a per capita income of about $20,000, happiness no longer rises proportionally to income. A straightforward explanation for this lack of increase in happiness is that acquiring things can make you happy in the short term, but owning things cannot. (See "Robinson's Used Oil," p. 221.) Once basic demands have been met, new ones arise, and possessions are soon taken for granted. Prosperity is thus a relative matter. You are only as rich as you feel, and the point of comparison is others in your milieu. A welfare recipient in Germany is not likely to feel rich, yet the same sum of money in Calcutta might seem like a fortune.

The strange thing about these findings is that they do not have much of an influence on how we see our lives. The dream of financial independence is still predominant in the industrialized world, and achieving this dream is why we toil away for countless hours, although most of us never get to the point of being truly "free." Money and prestige are at the pinnacle of our personal value system, above even family and friends. This is all the more astonishing because the value scale of the happiness economists is exactly the reverse. According to this scale, nothing provides more happiness than relationships with other people: with one's family, spouse or partner, children, and friends. In second place is the feeling of doing something useful; this spot is often shared by health and freedom. The scale shows that most people in the wealthy West are ill advised to place so much value on money; doing so occasions systematically wrong decisions and striving for a security that few will achieve. People sacrifice their freedom and their self-determination to gain a higher income and buy things they don't need in order to impress people they don't like with money they don't have.

The problem is that our way of thinking and our entire social system are built on this material orientation, which the writer Heinrich Böll satirized back in the 1950s in his "Anecdote on the Decline of the Work Ethic." His story goes like this: In a Mediterranean harbor, a poor fisherman is dozing in the midday sun. A tourist strikes up a conversation with him and tries to convince him that he should get out and fish. "Why?" the fisherman wants to know. "To earn more money," replies the tourist, who quickly calculates how many additional catches could make the fisherman a wealthy man, with a large staff in his employ. "What for?" the fisherman again wants to know. "You'd be so rich that you could lean back and relax in the sun," the tourist explains. "But that's exactly what I'm doing now," says the fisherman, and goes back to dozing.

I remember this story because it was assigned reading in our middle school German textbook, and our young teacher had great difficulty presenting its meaning to us. Most of my fellow students, quickly persuaded by the fisherman's argument, responded by slacking off in class. In a desperate attempt to figure out why this utterly demotivating little story was part of the curriculum and supposedly pedagogically meaningful, my teacher defended the tourist and tried to convince us that more money would mean better health insurance and a secure pension fund for the fisherman. But the text was by Heinrich Böll, not Medicare. Was Böll really putting in a plug for safeguarding bourgeois values and avoiding unnecessary risk?

Happiness economists get more out of the fisherman story than the need for security that resonated with my German teacher. They regard a country's divorce and unemployment rates as a better barometer of national well-being than the gross national product, and to measure the satisfaction level of a nation and success of a government, they would find it more useful to substitute a National Life Satisfaction Index. The economist Richard Layard, at the London School of Economics, is convinced that there is more to making people happy than simply owning things. People who strive for wealth and status exhibit symptoms of addictive behavior. The quest for material goods creates a perpetual state of dissatisfaction that precludes lasting happiness.

Consequently, the growth that industrialized countries aspire to does not result in happier people. Quite the opposite—people sacrifice their happiness in the quest for growth. Even though people today have more to eat, own bigger cars, and jet off to the Maldives, their state of mind does not improve with their purchasing power, as much as we might labor under this delusion. For Layard there is only one logical consequence: Since people's fear of losses outweighs the happiness associated with acquiring things, industrialized countries need to rethink their policies. Full employment and social tranquillity, he argues, are more important than the growth rate of the gross national product. The message here is that happiness for all supersedes economic growth.

One can question the practicality of Layard's claims, but we will leave that issue aside, since the point is perfectly plain: It is not wealth and money, nor is it age, gender, appearance, intelligence, and education that determines our happiness, but rather sexuality, children, friends, food, sports, and—first and foremost—social relationships. According to the World Values Survey—the most comprehensive and wide-ranging statistical document about sociocultural, moral, religious, and political values—a divorce has about as negative an effect on well-being as losing two-thirds of one's income. Interestingly, the report shows that even the prospect of happiness contributes substantially to happiness itself. It is virtually inconceivable for someone to live without a personal vision of and longing for happiness. The dream of happiness is always there—if only as a painful reminder of all we are missing.

All these statistics notwithstanding, happiness is actually a very personal matter. The key to happiness is in your hand. The philosopher Ludwig Marcuse wrote in his *Philosophy of Happiness* (1948), "My happiness is the moment of deepest harmony with myself." But achieving this harmony is no easy matter. If it is true that there is no single entity that constitutes the self, and there are only states of the self (perhaps eight in all), what does harmony mean? Who is harmonizing with whom? And is the state of happiness somehow more "substantial" than those other states? When I am happy, am I actually closer to myself?

It is time once again to look to neuroscience and our old friends serotonin and dopamine (see "Mr. Spock in Love," p. 42, and "'A Quite Normal Improbability,'" p. 202). The idea that happiness has some connection to body chemistry will come as no surprise to anyone who has enjoyed relaxing in the sun. Sunshine lifts the spirits; in neurobiological terms, it stimulates the release of serotonin, so it is no wonder that people in Vanuatu tend to smile more than they do here. Temperature determines temperament. But neuroscientific findings about the mechanisms that generate feelings of happiness are often greatly oversimplified. We are told that positive feelings activate the left hemisphere of the brain and negative feelings the right hemisphere. That sounds a bit like the crude brain charts used in the early nineteenth century. But the interaction of feelings and consciousness, of the limbic system and the prefrontal cortex, is not quite so simple. The only simple part is that certain substances, such as caffeine, alcohol, nicotine, and cocaine, all raise the production of dopamine and sometimes of serotonin, creating a little prickle of excitement and contentment. Still, that explanation reveals little about complex and longer-lasting states of happiness. Even when we enjoy relatively simple pleasures—such as a good meal—sight, smell, and taste each has a different role, and even the atmosphere, the anticipation of the food, and other factors of that kind are important in instilling feelings of happiness.

The interplay between expectation and fulfillment is an intriguing aspect of situations that produce feelings of happiness—flirting or having sex, eating or traveling, sometimes even engaging in sports. Most neurochemical theories of happiness stop right there, before it gets interesting. Chocolate makes us happy because serotonin is released when we eat it; a mere whiff of it promotes the production of antibodies. Pleasant aromas tend to stimulate the release of serotonin. But simply increasing the amount of chocolate we eat, taking a steady stream of drugs, and surrounding ourselves with fragrant flowers will not do the trick. We have to look beyond these factors—to expectations. A jogger can experience a psychological rush because a long run releases endorphins and creates a "runner's high." But a runner can feel very different types of happiness by breaking a personal record or winning a race. That extra something doesn't stem from the natural reaction of the body while running; it comes about by way of the prefrontal cortex, which knows the runner's personal record. The success rewards the runner with happiness. An expectation has been met or exceeded.

It is no wonder that neuroscientists are now attempting to trace the elaborate intersecting pathways of feelings and consciousness. Feelings of happiness are often more than simple emotions. The fact that laughter cheers up gloomy patients, and that there are even "laughter therapists," cannot be explained by simple reflexes. Studies have shown that the mere thought of a bad experience results in a weakening of test subjects' immune systems, but if the investigator elicits pleasant memories, the subjects' moods brighten on the spot, and their resistance is enhanced.

Feelings of happiness are highly complex. They can represent extremely positive emotions (pleasure, enthusiasm, delight) and result in heightened sensitivity, hyperawareness, and receptivity. Happiness elicits an optimistic take on one's surroundings and has a constructive effect on perception and memory. When we fall in love or experience success, everything suddenly appears a little rosier. Self-satisfaction soars and our self-esteem feels dizzying. We tend to become outgoing, friendly, impulsive, spontaneous, flexible, and productive, and we feel as though we can move mountains.

But as we all know, this ecstatic harmony doesn't last—which may be a good thing. Too much serotonin leads to apathy, and an excess of dopamine can result in obsessiveness, delusions of grandeur, megalomania, and insanity. After a short time, the receptors in the brain become dulled to these chemical agents, and the magic fades. A desperate attempt to prolong what is meant to be a transitory condition can culminate in destructive cravings for drugs, sex, or success.

No one can remain in a state of absolute harmony indefinitely. Staying in the here and now, getting caught up in the moment and letting everything else, including time, fade out in a blur is a nice idea that Eastern philosophy promotes, but psychologically it can be overwhelming. From a neurochemical perspective, it transforms an exceptional state into a norm. Expansive feelings of happiness are "isles of the blessed" in the ocean of our lives, but we cannot use them as an ongoing means to a successful life.

Lasting happiness can be achieved only if our expectations are grounded in reality. If happiness and unhappiness are essentially of our own devising, they are largely a function of how we set our expectations. That is the only way to explain why people in difficult circumstances can be happier than people who lead lives of privilege. Being in deepest harmony with oneself, which is how Ludwig Marcuse defines happiness, means achieving harmony with our own expectations and the expectations of others, about which we in turn have expectations: Niklas Luhmann uses the term "expected expectations."

Of course, it doesn't do much good to be in harmony with ourselves if this inner harmony clashes with the people around us, which is one of the reasons it is so difficult to implement Eastern philosophical precepts outside the confines of a monastery.

When I was doing community service in lieu of joining the military in the mid-1980s, I met a social worker whose motto left a lasting impression on me. His goal—and his idea of the optimal goal for everyone—was to liberate himself from his expectations. Heaven forbid! Of all life expectations I have ever imagined, his was surely the grandest and least achievable, because there is no way around our own expectations. The question is not how to shed them, but how to tailor them to suit us. Another option would be to set your expectations low enough to avoid disappointment. That's not a very enticing idea, though, because low expectations generally come from a fear of life and signal a difficulty in dealing with disappointment. Wouldn't it be better just to learn to cope with disappointments more effectively? If you don't expect much, you're not likely to get anywhere.

Many great philosophers have championed the petit bourgeois morality of low expectations and have shied away from the themes of happiness and joie de vivre. In doing so, they have typically attached great importance to "contentment"—the more durable vestige of happiness. Immanuel Kant is a good example. For him, the only realistic happiness is found in fulfilling one's moral obligation, a somewhat awkward and uneasy fusion of duty and happiness. But considering the dull second half of Kant's own life, who would want to look to him for advice about happiness?

Happiness and contentment are two different things. And we should take care not to recast pleasure seeking as pain avoidance. Of course both are part of life, and everyone has his own focal points somewhere along this spectrum. It is probably fairly easy to divide our friends and acquaintances into "pleasure seekers" and "pain avoiders." Their orientations are strongly dependent on their upbringing and temperament. But giving fundamental precedence to avoiding pain over seeking pleasure, as so many religions and philosophies do, is misguided. And the much-lauded "contentment," for all its advantages, is better suited to those who are older and have already achieved a great deal in life; it would be less tempting to younger people still looking for a guiding light.

This, at any rate, is how Martin Seligman, a renowned psychologist and happiness researcher at the University of Pennsylvania, sees the matter. For him, "authentic happiness" requires a positive outlook and the pursuit of "clear goals" with "deep, effortless involvement." The result, we are told, is a gratifying life. That is all well and good, but how do I go about getting a life of that kind? Is it up to me to craft my own happiness?

The Distant Garden
Can Happiness Be Learned?

To some, he was the wisest of all philosophers; to others, he was "the Pig."
Epicurus was born in 341 B.C.E. on the island of Samos in Greece. He was a
myth during his lifetime and even more so after his death, although much
in his life remains a mystery even today because virtually everything we
know about it comes from a single source, a biography written five hundred
years later. Epicurus is said to have come to Athens at the age of eighteen. It
was the time of Alexander the Great. When the people of Athens rebelled
unsuccessfully after Alexander's death, Epicurus followed his father into
the region of Ephesus in what is today Turkey. When he was thirty-five, he
returned to Athens and acquired a garden, the famous *kepos*. This garden
soon became the center of the newly flourishing democracy in Athens, and
a meeting place for people of all social classes. A small sectlike group lived
there, communally and without private property. Women and slaves were
also welcome at the *kepos*, which annoyed many Athenians, who gossiped
about the guru and his strange customs and spread rumors about orgies and
group sex. But those who entered Epicurus' garden read the inscription
over the gate: "Stranger, here you will do well to tarry; here our highest good
is pleasure. The caretaker of that abode, a kindly host, will be ready for you;
he will welcome you with bread, and serve you water also in abundance with
these words: Have you not been well entertained? This garden does not
whet your appetite, but quenches it." Epicurus maintained his garden for

nearly thirty years, until his death in 270 B.C.E. But the *kepos* was an institu-
tion and continued to exist for almost five hundred years after his death.

Details of how Epicurus actually lived in his notorious garden and what
he taught there can be gathered indirectly from the books written by his
numerous supporters and equally numerous detractors; only a few fragments of his own writings have been preserved. Disciples and adversaries
have painted such a divergent picture that it is not easy to separate the
wheat from the chaff. His reputation was grossly distorted in later eras, especially by Christian writers.

The radical and strikingly modern aspect of Epicurus' teaching was his
uncommon insistence on relying solely on what the senses revealed about
life. Epicurus rejected anything extrasensory, paying no heed to gods or religion. And he insisted that the significance of death for our everyday lives
ought not to be overstated: "You should accustom yourself to believing that
death means nothing to us, since every good and every evil lies in sensation. . . . So long as we are existent death is not present and whenever it is
present we are nonexistent."

Epicurus' world was restricted to what could be apprehended by the
senses. Although he held logical reason in high regard, he linked all knowledge to what the senses could perceive and grasp. He did not presume to
know what lay beyond this realm of experience. Epicurus was careful not to
make sweeping statements about the nature, origins, and state of the world,
unlike so many of his predecessors in Greek philosophy. Actually, he did
not set out to provide any exhaustive explanations at all, because everywhere he looked, he discovered gaps in knowledge and flawed explanations. In lieu of crafting an all-encompassing epistemology, he devoted his
attention to the question of what constitutes a successful life within the
framework of limited human potentialities. Epicurus realized that there
was no easy answer and that he had to make allowances for the contradic-
tory nature of man.

People are programmed to seek pleasurable sensations. Pleasure is nice
and displeasure is not. The quest for pleasure is just as natural as the facts
that "fire is hot, snow is cold, and honey is sweet." Adults also aspire to
pleasurable sensations, but most pleasures—sex, food, alcohol, and so
forth—are of brief duration. The Isles of the Blessed cannot be extended to
encompass entire continents. They are of only limited use as a basis of lasting happiness; we should certainly enjoy them, but we should not expect

too much of them. Moreover, Epicurus was wary of overly large quantities. Things that are enjoyed in excess soon lose their value. Savoring a small piece of cheese slowly and thoroughly can provide more pleasure than a banquet. To enhance the joy of life in a lasting way, we should curb any childish craving for overindulgence. Regulating our needs in order to make pleasure last is possible only by employing reason to develop reliable and stable strategies that free us from dependence on quick fixes.

One such strategy is to hone the senses and to savor the many small moments in life just as fully as the big ones. Another is to reduce stress. It is not always possible to experience great pleasure, but one can try to reduce feelings of displeasure by keeping needless worrying about the future to a minimum, reining in one's ambitions, and restricting one's longings for money and possessions, all of which yield little joy and result in a harmful dependency: "Independence of external things, too, we regard as a great good. . . . For we are convinced that those who need luxury least enjoy it most. Natural pleasures are easily gained; it is the useless ones which are costly." In Epicurus' view, it is not possessions but social ties that create the most lasting happiness.

According to Epicurus' own teachings, an "Epicurean" is a well-adjusted person who draws happiness from the many small joys of life, conquers fears, and lives with others sociably and compatibly. It was only his later antagonists, above all the Christians, who distorted the image of the godless Epicurus into a guru of vice and twisted his views beyond recognition. But from a psychological point of view, Epicurus was already far ahead of the teachings of Christianity, because he recognized the inseparable interplay of body and mind, *physis* and *psyche*, and placed it squarely in the center of his philosophy. His teachings have found renewed resonance in "positive psychology," a modern line of research primarily in the United States. Positive psychologists seek criteria that have to be fulfilled for people to be happy. And they design programs to train people to become happier, because happiness, according to both Epicurus and psychologists, can and must be produced actively; it does not arise on its own. An absence of pain, stress, and troubles is not enough to make us happy. So many people without major life crises are not happy at all and are bored to tears. In other words: Happiness is lovely, but it takes work. Happiness researchers have outlined this work as a series of practical rules, which I'll now list, somewhat tongue in cheek.

The first rule is: Keep active! Our brains hunger for activity, and mental idleness puts us in a bad frame of mind. No sooner do we rest for even a day than neurons start dying off. Failing to engage your mind makes it atrophy, a process that generally goes hand in hand with feelings of lethargy and then depression. Our hormone balance suffers from a lack of dopamine. We don't need to be active around the clock, but lazing about is not going to foster happiness. Sports are wonderful, because the mind rewards itself for successful physical efforts by forming new neurons. Interests also boost the joy of life. There is something to be said for routines, but they do not make us happy in the long run. Change of pace and scenery can be sources of happiness. Wittgenstein, who was wary of the quest for happiness, swore by the opposite maxim: "I don't mind what I eat, so long as it is always the same thing." That is the surest path to unhappiness.

The second rule is: Be sociable! Epicurus did not think much of people making spectacles of themselves, either in private or in public. But he realized that there is no more lasting source of happiness than social ties. Friendship, a loving relationship, and family can create a framework in which we feel well cared for. Experiencing something together with a friend, lover, or child enhances our feeling of happiness. When men feel secure, they release oxytocin, and women release vasopressin, the "prairie vole hormones" we discussed earlier. (See " 'A Quite Normal Improbability,' " p. 202.) Living in a social network ensures that you are not alone with your cares and worries. It is no wonder, then, that a good relationship and a corresponding frequency of sex are far more important in attaining happiness than money and possessions.

The third rule is: Focus! Epicurus spent a good deal of time helping his disciples understand how to enjoy the here and now: the fragrance of flowers, the beauty of shapes, the flavor of a piece of cheese. Well-chosen and concentrated pleasures enhance the joy of life, and this is especially true of the pleasure we find in other people. The more deeply we become involved with another person, the more intense are our feelings and empathy. From a neuroscience perspective this means: Savor your states of mind, at least those that lift your spirits. And when you engage in an activity, give it your all. People who think about getting fat while eating a good meal or who keep looking at their watches while having a nice conversation are depriving themselves of their experience. Giving an occasional thought to the future might be a good idea, but thinking about the future all the time robs you of the moment. As John Lennon put it, "Life is what happens to you while you're busy making other plans."

The fourth rule is: Have realistic expectations! Happiness is a question of what you expect. People often make things too hard on themselves—or too easy. Either way, the result is discontent. Push yourself too hard and you suffer avoidable stress, but set the bar too low and you suffer a lack of dopamine, with listlessness and indifference sure to follow. And the ensuing lethargy may in turn lead you to shy away from challenges, which only perpetuates the problem.

The fifth rule is: Think good thoughts! This may be the most important rule of all. Epicurus and positive psychology agree that happiness does not come about by chance but grows from the "right" thoughts and feelings, namely, those that produce pleasure and avoid pain. A favorite psychological nugget is: "Act as though you're happy, and you will be!" Easier said than done. If things aren't going well for me, I am not likely to summon the strength to feign a good mood. The Russian writer Fyodor Dostoyevsky, who had keen insights into the human psyche, once remarked on the subject of thinking good thoughts: "Everything's good. . . . Everything. Man is unhappy because he doesn't know he's happy. It's only that. That's all, that's all! If anyone finds out, he'll become happy at once, that minute."

The key point is that it is more or less up to me to judge the events in my life. Of course people may disagree as to how far this freedom can take me. When I pore over the book of my life, do I linger over the uplifting passages or the sad and boring ones? Some people are able to focus on the bright side of life, while others see nothing but gloom and doom. A possible route of access to the book of my life is to recognize the role of my mind in judging my feelings. Why do I dwell on the negative and become obsessed with it? I may not have much say over whether I perceive things in a negative or a positive light, but I surely have some degree of freedom in how I assess my feelings. This freedom can be trained. Sorting out and gaining perspective on one's feelings while or just after experiencing them is a major challenge, but it can be done. (See "Do Be Do Be Do," p. 212.)

People often recommend jotting down negative feelings as they occur, thus allowing them to be examined by the cortex without delay and alleviated to some degree. Writing down a few counterarguments can't hurt as well. Positive psychologists encourage us to keep a diary of happiness to learn how better to recall the good times. Another precept of happiness psychology is the saying: "Don't take yourself too seriously; laugh at yourself." This, too, is easier said than done; first you have to know how. When I consider this maxim, I can't help thinking about my friend Lutz, who told me about a training course for managers in which the teacher encouraged the group to show more spontaneity, whereupon a Swiss participant whipped out his pen and noted carefully in his lined notebook: "Become more spontaneous!" Learning to laugh at yourself is a worthy but challenging task, which goes along with high self-expectations. It is easier to learn to avoid sources of displeasure, such as comparisons, which invariably culminate in feelings of inferiority and make us think thoughts like these: *I don't look like that model in the magazine* (of course, neither does the model); *I earn less than some of my classmates; I'm not as witty as that other guy; I'm not as happy as my brothers and sisters.* As long as you cling to beliefs like these, you won't be happy.

A sixth point is not to take the quest for happiness too far. There is an art to taking unhappiness in stride. In most, if not all, cases, there is a silver lining in the cloud of unhappiness. Some people who suffer debilitating ailments report that they have been living life more fully since they became ill. Crises, struggles, and even tragedies can be constructive, leading to new beginnings; we often don't realize the good that can come from them. Wrestling with what we cannot change is a common pursuit, although we are warned against doing so by psychologists promoting happiness.

The seventh and last point is to recognize the pleasure that work affords. It is closely linked to the first one, activity. Work is something that forces us to be active, and most people need this pressure to stay active enough. Work is the best therapy, and unemployment robs people of that therapy, which can result in a deficiency of dopamine and serotonin and a feeling of ineptitude and sluggishness. Sigmund Freud contended that happiness results from the ability to love and to work.

And there you have the seven rules. We can certainly quibble about some of the specifics, and about the feasibility of applying them in our everyday life. These rules are not all that simple to adhere to, and rattling off a list of them is not the solution. The most intriguing question—and the most neglected by popular psychologists—is this: To what extent is it in my power to shape my actions? Positive psychology makes the most out of every neuroscientific finding that comes along, but the basic debate on the issue of "Can I will what I will?" is generally skirted. What good are the cleverest maxims if I cannot implement them? Addressing this question could yield exciting results.

Does this clarify the issue of happiness? Philosophically, perhaps, but psychologically there is still quite a lot to discover. Why do some people seem to have their life routines down pat? Why do some of us always know exactly what to do? And why do most of us manage to muddle through? It's probably not a matter of some of us understanding happiness better than others, because people who appear to sail through life are not always happier. So is happiness overrated? Are a happy and a successful life perhaps not ultimately the same thing at all? Is there something more important than happiness?

The Matrix Machine
Does Life Have Meaning?

Let me tell you why you're here. You're here because you know something. What you know you can't explain, but you feel it. You've felt it your entire life. That there's something wrong with the world, you don't know what it is, but it's there. Like a splinter in your mind, driving you mad. It is this feeling that has brought you to me.

———

Something is wrong with the world, but don't bother looking for these words in a history of philosophy, because you won't find them. They were spoken by Morpheus, a character in the film *The Matrix*, written and directed by two brothers, Andy and Larry Wachowski. The movie was a big box office and critical success at the turn of the twenty-first century—and rightly so. Rarely has there been such a philosophical film about the nature of existence.

The film tells the story of Neo, a computer hacker who learns from Morpheus that the world in which he and all other people think they live is not the real world; it is a virtual world, created by networked computers. It is the Matrix. After mankind made the planet Earth uninhabitable, computers took over and created the Matrix, exploiting people as a source of energy by placing them in pods filled with liquid nutrients and deluding them with a simulated reality. Offered the chance to learn the truth by Morpheus, Neo frees himself from the Matrix in a long and difficult struggle. In the end, he evolves into a kind of Christ figure, a redeemer of mankind.

The movie draws on a whole series of models, in particular on two novels, *Star Diaries* and *Golem XIV*, by the Polish science fiction writer Stanislaw Lem. The motif of life in a virtual, nonreal world is also found in Daniel Galouye's novel *Simulacron Three*, which was made into two movies. *The Matrix* also draws on the philosophy of Jean Baudrillard and incorporates Gnostic motifs. But the copyright for the idea that all existence on earth is merely illusory goes neither to the Wachowski brothers nor to Galouye, Lem, or Baudrillard, but to the Greek philosopher Plato.

In his famous "allegory of the cave," in book 7 of his *Republic* (ca. 370 B.C.E.), Plato describes a strange scenario: A group of people have lived in an underground cave since early childhood. Shackled to a wall of rock, these people can move neither their heads nor their bodies; they can only gaze at the cave wall facing them. Their only source of light is a fire burning behind them. Between the fire and their backs, images and objects being carried past them cast shadows on the wall. The prisoners see only the shadows of these objects as well as their own shadows and those of their fellow prisoners. Even when the bearers of the objects speak, it sounds as though the shadows themselves are speaking. Without any knowledge of what is really going on beyond what they can perceive, the cave dwellers regard the shadows as the sole true world. And there is no emerging from this existence. A prisoner who managed to see the light of day would eventually figure out what was going on in the cave, but he would not be able to enlighten the others because his explanations would lie beyond what they could picture, and he would be ridiculed: "Would it not be said of him that he had returned from his journey aloft with his eyes ruined?"

Naturally Plato was not scripting a screenplay for a science fiction film or thriller when he wrote this allegory. He simply wanted to show that the philosophical mind needs to detach and free itself from the sensory domain step by step in order to advance to the true nature of things. Plato had far less regard for knowledge gained through the senses than for abstract reasoning. Even so, his allegory of the cave made him the father of all Matrix visions. Let us return to *The Matrix* for a moment. Neo breaks out of his simulated life although he does not appear to be faring at all badly in it. But why? We could actually picture life in the Matrix as a veritable paradise. Let us imagine that as long as people are attached to the Matrix, they can choose whatever kind of life they would like. They can live it up as George Clooney or Scarlett Johansson, shoot fantastic goals as Ronaldinho or Kaká, or spend every night with a dream lover. But in contrast to the situation in the film, they are well aware that these are projections of their own desires and that this world is not real, although it feels perfectly real. Would anybody want to live that way for very long?

At first they might find it exhilarating to play out a second life of their own devising, but would the feeling last? What kind of life would it be to enjoy nonstop success, with everything that guarantees happiness at your fingertips? A terrible life!

Clearly there is something more important than happiness, because a guaranteed happiness would bore us to death. Everything in life attains its value by means of contrast. It is fine to wish for an abundance of happiness, but not for everlasting happiness. In the words of that clever philosopher George Bernard Shaw, "A lifetime of happiness! No man alive could bear it: it would be hell on earth!" But it is not just the specter of monotonous happiness that makes life in the Matrix so daunting. Worse still is the idea that one cannot make decisions about one's own life. Self-determination is such an important asset that happiness determined from outside ourselves is not an enticing prospect for most people. People need to craft their happiness through their own efforts; happiness handed to you on a silver platter loses its value. What significance would winning have if losing were not an option? As Leo Tolstoy insisted, happiness consists not in doing what you want, but in wanting what you do.

I don't know whether that convinces you, but I think Tolstoy's comment touches on what people like to call the "meaning of life," an issue that many philosophers are loath to tackle these days, since they associate it with populist self-help books or fuzzy New Age thinking. The question of the meaning of life, once considered lofty and important, is now considered hokey. More than 2,400 years ago, when the Greeks laid the foundations for what we now call Western philosophy, they tried to address this very question—although there is no direct ancient Greek counterpart to the phrase "meaning of life." But the question—What truly matters?—was essentially the same.

In this book, we have encountered many philosophers who tackled this question, directly or indirectly. Let us shine the spotlight on our philosophers one last time as they take their final bows.

Prior to the modern era, philosophers did not engage with the question of the meaning of the world, believing that this was not an issue for man, since God had already provided the answer. People in the Middle Ages, the Renaissance, and the Baroque era thus had no need to delve into it. The Church told them what God's ideas and objectives for man were, and that was that. But the turning point that shifted our consciousness into the center of the world in lieu of the world order laid down by God led directly to the question of the meaning of life, to which serious attention was devoted beginning in the late eighteenth and the early nineteenth centuries.

For Immanuel Kant, the purpose of life was to fulfill one's moral obligation, which is, as we have seen, a rather dreary aim. For Jean-Jacques Rousseau, it was to live according to one's own nature and never do what goes against the grain. For Jeremy Bentham, it meant ensuring the greatest possible pleasure for oneself and others. William Paley saw the meaning of human life in generating the greatest number of "useful works."

The question experienced a real boom in the mid-nineteenth century. The philosophical heirs of Kant, Fichte, and Hegel were somewhat at a loss when contemplating the monumental works of their forebears. Philosophy had been a shining beacon and had declared itself the crown jewel of the arts and sciences, able to shed light on all of life's questions, yet it was unable to designate the ingredients of a successful life. Its gigantic structures of thought were built on a very narrow foundation of practical insight.

Arthur Schopenhauer, Søren Kierkegaard, Ludwig Feuerbach, and, indirectly, Karl Marx all sought to provide a new answer to the question. Schopenhauer adamantly denied that we exist "in order to be happy." Since man is the slave of his will, he argued, little latitude remains for a free and higher meaning. Only the arts—in particular, music—offer man a higher pleasure. Friedrich Nietzsche and Sigmund Freud also built on this idea. For them, the very question of the meaning of life was an expression of physical or mental weakness. A healthy person does not need a higher meaning in life; happiness comes from music (Nietzsche) or love and work (Freud). For Ernst Mach, the question of the meaning of life dissolved along with the "ego." If the butterfly no longer has the same ego as the caterpillar, and a child's differs from a man's, there is no need to impose a universal meaning on all of life. The sense of what truly matters—which Mach called the "economy of thought"—steers clear of the "meaning of life."

The major figures of twentieth-century philosophy made a point of rejecting clear-cut answers and not engaging with that issue. A telling example is Ludwig Wittgenstein. For him, the question of the meaning of life was one of those "nonsensical questions," by its very nature incapable of being answered. "The solution of the problem of life is seen in the vanishing of the problem. (Is not this the reason why those who have found after a long period of doubt that the sense of life became clear to them have then been unable to say what constituted this sense?)" For Sartre, by contrast, life takes on meaning when I realize myself through action. Since the world as a whole has no meaning, I am free to supply my own, which remains a work in progress that comes and goes along with the individual. For Peter Singer, Sartre's approach lacks a social dimension. His book *How Are We to Live?* discusses the merits and demerits of pushing the Sisyphean stone up the hill in the quest to "make the world a better place."

There are also explanations of the meaning of life based in evolutionary biology, but they are best left out of the discussion. For the biophilosopher Daniel Dennett, the two evolutionary principles of adaptation and mutation also apply to all questions of human culture: What makes sense for nature makes sense for humans. For a sociologist like Niklas Luhmann, that is nonsense, because "meaning" originates in communication and constitutes a sophisticated evolutionary achievement specific to man. Symbolic communication by means of language cannot be derived from genes' striving for "fitness" throughout the ages. If man were just nature, it would be inconceivable for people to employ technology that destroys the foundations of their own lives, as this destruction clearly contradicts the biological theory of adaptation as a universal principle of life.

Neuroscience is no better equipped to answer the question of the meaning of life. "Meaning" is neither a scientific unit of measurement nor an object nor an electrophysiological process. Meaning is invisible to itself; a scale has no idea what it weighs.

The only way to address the question of the meaning of life today is subjectively, to ask what meaning I see in *my* life. The reason is simple: Meaning is not a characteristic of the world or of nature, but a quintessentially human construction. "Meaning" is a need and an idea cooked up in our vertebrate brains. The point is not to find meaning in the world; instead, we have to *furnish* meaning to ourselves. The question of meaning is thus a human question. Even questions of objective meaning in nature invariably adhere to human ideas, which are dependent upon our consciousness, that is, human logic and human language.

Possibly the primary reason underlying our need for meaning is the knowledge that we have to die someday. The brain does not enjoy contemplating day by day, hour by hour, and second by second the certainty that it is approaching its extinction. Some paleoanthropologists use this awareness to draw the line between animals and people.

The question of meaning in life is thus shaped by uniquely human concerns. And, like all human knowledge, it is an outgrowth of our personal experiences, which is why the best we can hope for is to find our *own* meaning in life. But why are we so bent on exploring *the* meaning of life? And why should life have this *one* meaning? The need to zero in on a single meaning is very human. We seem to devote far more thought to the question of the meaning of life than to why and by what criteria we are actually seeking it. In other words, we examine everything except the quest itself. Writers have enjoyed poking fun at this. "If there's no meaning in it, that saves a world of trouble, as we needn't try to find any," the King of Hearts says in Lewis Carroll's *Alice's Adventures in Wonderland.* And the worldly-wise British aphorist Ashleigh Brilliant went one step further when he wrote: "Life may have no meaning. Or even worse, it may have a meaning of which I disapprove."

The idea that life has a particular meaning might not be so appealing after all. Typically, the quest to find meaning in life evolves as we age. In our younger years, we search for an objective meaning and a goal in life, but later in life, we start to wonder: Did *my* life have meaning? In other words: Did I live it well? The question of meaning loses a great deal of its epistemic aspect, and philosophical reflection yields to psychological stock taking and self-justification. Here it is less a question of "meaning" than of fulfillment: Have I made something of my life that has given me lasting pleasure?

Many biologists would surely agree that the goal of life is to live it. That is how nature obviously thought of it—assuming nature is capable of thought. But of all the characteristics that can be found in proteins and amino acids, meaning is not one of them. Quite possibly the most elegant scientific response is offered in the novel *The Hitchhiker's Guide to the Galaxy* by the British science fiction writer Douglas Adams. Aliens invent a supercomputer, Deep Thought, for the sole purpose of answering "the Ultimate Question of Life, the Universe, and Everything." Deep Thought

takes a full seven and a half million years to calculate the result, then an-
nounces that they will not like it. After a bit of stalling, the computer spits
out the Ultimate Answer: "Forty-two!" The aliens are taken aback by this
seemingly senseless statistic, but Deep Thought, sounding every bit like
Wittgenstein, defends this numerical answer by declaring that the question
it was fed made no sense. Anyone who would pose such an imprecise question, the computer declares, is not in a position to make head or tail of the
answer. To mollify them, Deep Thought offers to design and build an even
bigger computer to formulate a proper question. The computer—which
Deep Thought dubs "Earth"—is built, and it begins to search for the question. But Earth never gets past the quest for the Question to the Ultimate
Answer. Just before the program runs out, Earth is demolished—to clear the
way for a hyperspace bypass.

Perhaps writers and aphorists are the only ones to glean the truth. "I
believe that in the end, man is such a free being that his right to be what he
thinks he is cannot be disputed," the physicist and author Georg Christoph
Lichtenberg wrote. And that holds for the question of the meaning of life as
well. When I was a child, my favorite book was Lloyd Alexander's *Chronicles
of Prydain*. The aged enchanter Dallben explains to his foster son, Taran,
who is out to find some answers: "In some cases we learn more by looking
for the answer to a question and not finding it than we do from learning the
answer itself." Like Taran, I was somewhat put off by this answer back then;
it struck me as a cop-out, and just an excuse, even coming from a wise old
enchanter. Today I think Dallben was right—at least when it comes to a
major question like the meaning of life. The only ones ever to have truly
grasped the meaning of life are the cast of Monty Python, who reveal the
mystery to us at the close of their film *The Meaning of Life:*

> Now, here's the meaning of life. . . . Well, it's nothing very special,
> really. Uh, try and be nice to people, avoid eating fat, read a good
> book every now and then, get some walking in, and try and live to-
> gether in peace and harmony with people of all creeds and nations.

And if you ask me: Keep your sense of curiosity alive, make your good
ideas a reality, and fill your days with life—not your life with days.

Notes

Introduction

xviii **who sought to become the "poet" of his own life** Rüdiger Safranski, *Nietzsche: A Philosophical Biography*, trans. Shelley Frisch (New York: Norton, 2003), p. 27.

Clever Animals in the Universe

3 **Once upon a time** Safranski, *Nietzsche*, p. 85.

5 **"All we need . . . is a *chemistry*"** Friedrich Nietzsche, *Human, All Too Human*, trans. Marion Faber, with Stephen Lehmann (Lincoln: University of Nebraska Press, 1996), p. 14.

6 **"We are unknown to ourselves"** Friedrich Nietzsche, *On the Genealogy of Morals and Ecce Homo*, trans. Walter Kaufmann (New York: Vintage, 1967), p. 15.

7 **"I know my destiny"** Safranski, *Nietzsche*, p. 28.

7 **"We are simply temporal"** Arthur Schopenhauer, *Parerga and Paralipomena*, vol. 2, trans. E.F.J. Payne (Oxford: Clarendon Press, 1974), p. 88.

Lucy in the Sky

10 **Now on to the second story** Donald C. Johanson and Maitland A. Edey, *Lucy: The Beginnings of Mankind* (New York: Simon & Schuster, 1981).

12 **"We've got it"** Ibid., pp. 17–18.

13 **"A geological episode of unimaginable proportions"** Richard Leakey, *Origins Reconsidered: In Search of What Makes Us Human* (New York: Anchor, 1993), p. 9. See also Leakey, *The Origin of Humankind* (New York: Basic Books, 1994).

13 **In the western region of the Great Rift** Gerhard Roth, *Das Gehirn und seine Wirklichkeit* (Frankfurt: Suhrkamp, 2000).

13 **The brains of the australopithecines** Ernst Pöppel, *Grenzen des Bewusstseins* (Frankfurt: Insel, 2000). See also Dorothy Cheney and Robert Seyfarth, *How Monkeys See the World: Inside the Mind of Another Species* (Chicago: University of Chicago Press, 1992).

14 **The notion of "right" and "left"** Paul Watzlawick, *How Real Is Real? Confusion, Disinformation, Communication* (New York: Vintage, 1977), and his *Invented Reality* (New York: Norton, 1980).

The Cosmos of the Mind

18 **What is the most complex thing in the world?** Santiago Ramón y Cajal, *Texture of the Nervous System of Man and the Vertebrates*, 3 vols., trans. Pedro Pasik (New York: Springer, 1999f.). Ramón y Cajal's autobiography has been translated into English as *Recollections of My Life*, trans. E. Horne Craigie and Juan Cano (Cambridge, MA: MIT Press, 1989). For studies of the history of neuroscience, see M. R. Bennett and P.M.S. Hacker, *History of Cognitive Neuroscience* (Malden, MA: Wiley-Blackwell, 2008), and Stanley Finger, *Origins of Neuroscience: A History of Explorations into Brain Function* (New York: Oxford University Press, 2001). Among the numerous overviews of the brain and the field of neuroscience are V. S. Ramachandran, *A Brief Tour of Human Consciousness: From Impostor Poodles to Purple Numbers* (New York: Pi Press, 2004), and William H. Calvin, *How Brains Think: Evolving Intelligence, Then and Now* (New York: Basic Books, 1996).

23 **"There can be no doubt"** Immanuel Kant, *Critique of Pure Reason*, trans. Norman Kemp Smith (New York: Palgrave Macmillan, 2003), p. 41.

24 **"the Janitor's Dream"** Calvin, *How Brains Think*, p. 36.

A Winter's Eve in the Thirty Years' War

26 **"At this time I was in Germany"** René Descartes, *The Philosophical Writings of Descartes*, vol. 1, trans. John Cottingham, Robert Stoothoff, and Dugald Murdoch (New York: Cambridge University Press, 1985), p. 116.

29 **"the grandfather of the Revolution"** Friedrich Nietzsche, *Beyond Good and Evil*, trans. Marion Faber (New York: Oxford University Press, 2009), sect. 191, p. 80.

31 **"I knew I was a substance"** Descartes, *Philosophical Writings of Descartes*, p. 127. For a biography of Descartes, see A. C. Grayling, *Descartes: The Life of René Descartes and Its Place in His Times* (New York: Free Press, 2005). For an overview of Descartes' impact on modern philosophy, see Russell Shorto, *Descartes' Bones* (New York: Doubleday, 2008). For a neuroscientific perspective on Descartes, see Antonio R. Damasio, *Descartes' Error: Emotion, Reason, and the Human Brain* (New York: Putnam, 1994).

Mach's Momentous Experience

34 **"On a bright summer day"** Ernst Mach, *Contributions to the Analysis of the Sensations*, trans. Cora May Williams (Chicago: Open Court Publishing Company, 1897), p. 23, fn. 1.

35 **"The ego," he asserted** Mach, *Contributions to the Analysis of the Sensations*, p. 20.

36 **Mach quipped that a sensation** Ernst Mach, *Knowledge and Error: Sketches on the*

Psychology of Enquiry, trans. Thomas McCormack and Paul Foulkes (Dordrecht, Holland: D. Reidel, 1976), p. 359.

36 **"The ego is unsavable"** Mach, *Contributions to the Analysis of the Sensations,* p. 20. On Mach's life and works, see *Ernst Mach: Physicist and Philosopher,* ed. R. S. Cohen and Raymond J. Seeger (New York: Springer, 1975).

36 **"succession of perceptions"** David Hume, *A Treatise of Human Nature,* vol. 1, ed. David Fate Norton and Mary Norton (New York: Oxford University Press, 2007), p. 47.

38 **"object of inner sense"** Immanuel Kant, *Critique of Pure Reason,* trans. Norman Kemp Smith (New York: Palgrave Macmillan, 2003), p. 329.

38 **"travelers to unimaginable lands"** Oliver Sacks, *The Man Who Mistook His Wife for a Hat* (New York: Touchstone, 1998), p. ix.

39 **Many neuroscientists tend to the view** Gerhard Roth, *Fühlen, Denken, Handeln* (Frankfurt: Suhrkamp, 2003), pp. 378–411. On the question of the self in philosophy today, see Werner Siefer and Christiane Weber, *Ich—Wie wir uns selbst erfinden* (Frankfurt: Campus, 2006), and Thomas Metzinger, *Being No One: The Self-Model Theory of Subjectivity* (Cambridge, MA: MIT Press, 2003).

41 **"Man is an individual"** Niklas Luhmann, *Die Soziologie und der Mensch,* vol. 6 of *Soziologische Aufklärung* (Wiesbaden: Verlag, 2008), p. 130.

Mr. Spock in Love

42 **The year is 2267** The *Star Trek* episode "This Side of Paradise" can be found at www.memory-alpha.org.

45 **neuroscience has taken it up instead** Roth, *Fühlen, Denken, Handeln,* pp. 285–373.

46 **Wilhelm Wundt identified three central contrastive pairs** Wilhelm Max Wundt, *Outlines of Psychology,* trans. Charles Hubbard Judd (Leipzig: W. Engelmann, 1907).

46 **More recently, Paul Ekman** Paul Ekman and Wallace V. Friesen, *Unmasking the Face* (Englewood Cliffs, NJ: Prentice Hall, 1975), and Paul Ekman, *Emotions Revealed* (New York: Henry Holt, 2003).

46 **a list of fifteen** His list of fifteen "basic emotions" is on page 55 of Paul Ekman, "Basic Emotions," in *Handbook of Cognition and Emotion,* ed. Tim Dalgleish and Mick Power (Sussex, UK: Wiley, 1999), pp. 45–60.

Ruling the Roost

50 **He was a difficult man** The authoritative edition of Freud's works is Sigmund Freud, *The Complete Psychological Works of Sigmund Freud: The Standard Edition,* 24 vols. (London: Hogarth, 1973). The classic biography of Freud is Ernest Jones, *The Life and Work of Sigmund Freud,* 3 vols. (New York: Basic Books, 1957). An outstanding recent biography is Peter Gay's *Freud: A Life for Our Time* (New York: Norton, 2006).

54 **"be such as to overthrow"** Sigmund Freud, *Beyond the Pleasure Principle*, trans.
    C.J.M. Hubback (London: International Psycho-Analytical Press, 1922), p. 78.

55 **One well-known example** Daniel J. Simons and Christopher Chabris, "Gorillas
    in Our Midst: Sustained Inattentional Blindness for Dynamic Events," *Perception*
    28 (1999), pp. 1059–74.

56 **A large part of our unconscious** For analyses of the unconscious, see Roth,
    Fühlen, Denken, Handeln, pp. 225–41; Timothy D. Wilson, *Strangers to Ourselves:*
    Discovering the Adaptive Unconscious (Cambridge, MA: Harvard University Press,
    2002); and Antonio R. Damasio, *Looking for Spinoza: Joy, Sorrow, and the Feeling*
    Brain (New York: Harcourt, 2003).

57 **Brain researchers today dream** A new synthesis of neuroscience and psycho-
    analysis is offered in Eric R. Kandel, *Psychiatry, Psychoanalysis, and the New*
    Biology of Mind (Washington, DC: American Psychiatric Publishing, 2005); the
    essay under discussion is on pp. 5–26. See also François Ansermet and Pierre
    Magistretti, *Biology of Freedom*, trans. Susan Fairfield (New York: Other Press,
    2007).

Now What Was That?

59 **Eric Richard Kandel's story begins** Eric R. Kandel, *In Search of Memory: The*
    Emergence of a New Science of Mind (New York: Norton, 2007). See also Larry R.
    Squire and Eric R. Kandel, *Memory: From Mind to Molecules* (Greenwood Village,
    CO: Roberts and Company, 2009).

60 **The terrain onto which Kandel had ventured** For a study of memory research,
    see Douwe Draaisma, *Why Life Speeds Up as You Get Older: How Memory Shapes Our*
    Past, trans. Arnold Pomerans and Erica Pomerans (New York: Cambridge Uni-
    versity Press, 2006); Daniel L. Schacter, *Searching for Memory: The Brain, the Mind,*
    and the Past (New York: Basic Books, 1997); Hans Markowitsch, *Dem Gedächtnis*
    auf der Spur: Vom Erinnern und Vergessen (Tübingen: Wissenschaftliche Buchge-
    sellschaft, 2009).

62 **the story of Kim Peek** The life of the savant Kim Peek is described in Fran Peek,
    The Real Rain Man: Kim Peek (Salt Lake City: Harkness, 1997).

The Fly in the Bottle

66 **In the fall of 1914** The story of Wittgenstein's study of the traffic accident in Paris
    and the quotation about the proposition can be found in Ludwig Wittgenstein,
    Notebooks, 1914–1916, vol. 1, trans. G.E.M. Anscombe (Oxford: Blackwell, 1998),
    p. 7 (September 29, 1914) and p. 80 (August 2, 1916), respectively. For a biography
    of Wittgenstein, see Ray Monk, *Ludwig Wittgenstein: The Duty of Genius* (New York:
    Free Press, 1990). For his family background, see Alexander Waugh, *The House*
    of Wittgenstein: A Family at War (New York: Doubleday, 2008). For information on
    Wittgenstein and the Vienna Circle, see Ludwig Wittgenstein et al., *The Voices of*
    Wittgenstein: The Vienna Circle, ed. Gordon Baker (New York: Routledge), 2003.

67 **"My ferocious German"** Bertrand Russell, *Logical and Philosophical Papers, 1909–13*, vol. 6, ed. John Slater and Bernd Frohmann (New York: Routledge, 1992), p. xxv.

67 **He encouraged Wittgenstein to criticize** The groundbreaking work by Russell that Wittgenstein dissects is Bertrand Russell's *Principles of Mathematics*; this 1903 classic was reprinted in 2009 by Routledge, New York.

68 **"a 'critique of language'"** Ludwig Wittgenstein, *Tractatus Logico-Philosophicus*, trans. David F. Pears and Brian F. McGuinness (New York: Routledge, 2001), sect. 4.0031, p. 23.

69 **"What we cannot speak about"** Ibid., sect. 7, p. 89.

70 **"Joseph saw, distinguished, categorized"** Oliver Sacks, *Seeing Voices: A Journey into the Land of the Deaf* (Berkeley: University of California Press, 1989), pp. 40, 44.

71 **Chomsky provided a credible explanation** Chomsky's pioneering work on the nature and acquisition of grammar is found in Noam Chomsky, *Language and Mind* (New York: Harcourt, Brace, Jovanovich, 1972).

72 **"hermit, ascetic, guru"** Gilbert Ryle, "The Work of an Influential but Little-Known Philosopher of Science: Ludwig Wittgenstein," in *Ludwig Wittgenstein: Critical Assessments*, vol. 3, ed. Stuart Shanker (London: Croom Helm, 1986), p. 139.

73 **"Our language can be seen as an ancient city"** Ludwig Wittgenstein, *Philosophical Investigations*, trans. G.E.M. Anscombe (Oxford: Blackwell, 1998), p. 7e.

73 **"the meaning of a word"** Ibid., p. 20e.

73 **"a main source of our failure to understand"** Ibid., p. 49e.

73 **"What is your aim in philosophy?"** Ibid., p. 103e.

73 **The new discipline of analytical philosophy** For an introduction to analytical philosophy, see Hans-Johann Glock, *What Is Analytic Philosophy?* (New York: Cambridge University Press, 2008).

74 **John Langshaw Austin . . . John Rogers Searle** J. L. Austin's major work is *How to Do Things with Words* (New York: Oxford University Press, 1976). John R. Searle's major work is *Speech Acts: An Essay in the Philosophy of Language* (New York: Cambridge University Press, 1970).

74 **"If a lion could talk"** Wittgenstein, *Philosophical Investigations*, p. 223e.

Rousseau's Error

79 **Rousseau was a true eccentric** On Rousseau's life, see Leo Damrosch, *Jean-Jacques Rousseau: Restless Genius* (New York: Mariner Books, 2007).

80 **"I fell across the question"** Jean-Jacques Rousseau, *The Confessions and Correspondence, Including the Letters to Malesherbes*, vol. 5 of *The Collected Writings of Rousseau*, trans. Christopher Kelly (Hanover, NH: University Press of New England, 1990), p. 575.

81 **"Men are wicked"** This quote comes from Rousseau's *Discourse on Inequality*, in Jean-Jacques Rousseau, *The Discourse and Other Early Political Writings*, trans. Victor Gourevitch (New York: Cambridge University Press, 1997), pp. 197–98.

82 **Its founder was Robert Weiss** Robert Weiss published the results of his loneliness research in the modern classic *Loneliness: The Experience of Emotional and Social Isolation* (Cambridge, MA: MIT Press, 1975).

The Sword of the Dragon Slayer

84 **Three adults lunged** The story of Fawn is told by Frans de Waal in *Good Natured: The Origins of Right and Wrong in Humans and Other Animals* (Cambridge, MA: Harvard University Press, 1996), pp. 45ff. See also de Waal's *Chimpanzee Politics*, 25th anniv. ed. (Baltimore: Johns Hopkins University Press, 2007).

85 **revealed the astonishing extent** On the social behavior of primates, see also Frans de Waal, *Peacemaking Among Primates* (Cambridge, MA: Harvard University Press, 1990).

85 **Darwin's mid-nineteenth-century proof** A purely Darwinist view of evolution is offered by Robert Wright, *The Moral Animal: The New Science of Evolutionary Psychology* (New York: Pantheon Books, 1994).

86 **"The ethical progress of society"** Thomas Henry Huxley, *Evolution and Ethics* (Princeton, NJ: Princeton University Press, 1989), p. 141.

86 **"sword forged by *Homo sapiens*"** De Waal, *Good Natured*, p. 2.

The Law Within Me

89 **"Two things . . . fill the mind"** Immanuel Kant, *Critique of Practical Reason*, trans. Lewis White Beck (New York: Macmillan, 1993), p. 169.

91 **"The understanding . . . does not draw"** Immanuel Kant, *Prolegomena to Any Future Metaphysics*, trans. Gary Hatfield (New York: Cambridge University Press, 1997), pp. 73–74.

92 **the Italian philosopher Giovanni Pico della Mirandola** Giovanni Pico della Mirandola, *On the Dignity of Man*, trans. Paul J. W. Miller et al. (Indianapolis: Hackett, 1998).

93 **"schematism of our understanding"** Immanuel Kant, *Critique of Pure Reason*, trans. Norman Kemp Smith (New York: Palgrave Macmillan, 2003), p. 183. For background information about Kant, see Manfred Kuehn, *Kant: A Biography* (New York: Cambridge University Press, 2002).

The Libet Experiment

95 **Arthur Schopenhauer** On Schopenhauer's life, see Rüdiger Safranski, *Schopenhauer and the Wild Years of Philosophy*, trans. Ewald Osers (Cambridge, MA: Harvard University Press, 1991).

97 **"What opposes the heart"** Arthur Schopenhauer, *The World as Will and Representation*, trans. E.F.J. Payne (New York: Dover, 1966), p. 218.

98 **"thousands of years of philosophizing"** Ibid., p. 199.

98 **"fundamental error of all philosophers"** Ibid., p. 206.

99 **he experimented on several patients** Libet's experiments are described and in-
terpreted in Benjamin Libet, *Mind Time: The Temporal Factor in Consciousness*
(Cambridge, MA: Harvard University Press, 2005). On the recent debate about
the freedom of the will, see Christian Geyer, ed., *Hirnforschung und Willsfreiheit:
Zur Deutung der neuesten Experimente* (Frankfurt: Suhrkamp, 2005); Helmut Fink,
ed., *Freier Wille—frommer Wunsch?* (Paderborn: Mentis-Verlag, 2006); and
Michael Pauen, *Illusion Freiheit? Mögliche und unmögliche Konsequenzen der Hirnforschung* (Frankfurt: S. Fischer, 2006). The two most influential German neuroscientists on the subject of the freedom of the will are Gerhard Roth (coauthor,
with Klaus-Jürgen Grün), *Das Gehirn und seine Freiheit* (Göttingen: Vandenhoek &
Ruprecht, 2006), and Wolf Singer, *Ein neues Menschenbild? Gespräche über Hirnforschung* (Frankfurt: Suhrkamp, 2003), esp. pp. 24–34.

The Case of Gage

103 **September 13, 1848** For a detailed account of the life of Phineas Gage, see Mal-
colm MacMillan, *An Odd Kind of Fame: Stories of Phineas Gage* (Cambridge, MA:
MIT Press, 2000). See also John Fleischman, *Phineas Gage: A Gruesome but True
Story About Brain Science* (Boston: Houghton Mifflin, 2002).

104 **neuroscientists Hanna and Antonio Damasio** The Damasios' research and
conclusions are found in Antonio R. Damasio, *Descartes' Error: Emotion, Reason,
and the Human Brain* (New York: Putnam, 1994), and Hanna Damasio et al., "The
Return of Phineas Gage: Clues About the Brain from the Skull of a Famous Patient," *Science* 264, no. 5102 (May 20, 1994), pp. 1102–5.

105 **"it is as if the moral compass"** De Waal, *Good Natured*, p. 217.

105 **"a machine that tells you"** Tove Jansson, *Finn Family Moomintroll*, trans. Eliza-
beth Portch (New York: Farrar, Straus & Giroux, 1958), p. 167.

I Feel What You Feel

108 **Rizzolatti has been examining the function of neurons** See Giacomo Rizzolatti
and Corrado Sinigaglia, *Mirrors in the Brain: How Our Minds Share Actions, Emotion,
and Experience*, trans. Frances Anderson (New York: Oxford University Press,
2008). An earlier book on this subject is Maksim I. Stamenov and Vittorio
Gallese, *Mirror Neurons and the Evolution of Brain and Language* (Philadelphia:
John Benjamins, 2002).

The Man on the Bridge

112 **Harvard psychologist Marc Hauser** Marc D. Hauser, *Moral Minds: How Nature
Designed Our Universal Sense of Right and Wrong* (New York: HarperCollins, 2006).

113 **the origin of our morality** The development of moral feelings is also explained

in Frans de Waal, *Primates and Philosophers: How Morality Evolved* (Princeton, NJ: Princeton University Press, 2006), and in his *Our Inner Ape: A Leading Primatologist Explains Why We Are Who We Are* (New York: Riverhead, 2006).

116 **"Moral progress is a matter of wider and wider sympathy"** Richard Rorty, *Philosophy and Social Hope* (New York: Penguin, 2000), pp. 82–83.

Aunt Bertha Shall Live

118 **Jeremy Bentham was born in 1748** The classic biography of Bentham, written in 1905, is Charles Milner Atkinson, *Jeremy Bentham: His Life and Work* (Charleston, SC: BiblioBazaar, 2009). A more recent collection of Bentham's writings, with an introduction by Ross Harrison, is *Selected Writings on Utilitarianism* (Ware, UK: Wordsworth, 2001). John Bowring edited Bentham's complete works in eleven volumes: *The Works of Jeremy Bentham* (Edinburgh: W. Tait, 1843).

The Birth of Dignity

123 **Imagine the following situation** The example with the violinist originated in Judith Jarvis Thomson, "A Defense of Abortion," *Philosophy and Public Affairs* 1, no. 1 (Fall 1971), pp. 47–66. My example draws on the variant by Peter Singer in his *Practical Ethics*, 2nd ed. (New York: Cambridge University Press, 1999), pp. 146–47.

125 **Kant writes that the embryo is a being** Kant's ideas about the freedom of children conceived in wedlock can be found in paragraph 28 ("On the Right of Domestic Society, Title 2, Parental Rights") of part 1 of the "Doctrine of Right" of his *Metaphysics of Morals*, trans. Mary Gregor (New York: Cambridge University Press, 1996), p. 64. His ideas about infanticide are in the same text, in part 2, near the conclusion of section E ("On the Right to Punish and to Grant Clemency"), p. 109.

126 **"Better to be Socrates dissatisfied"** John Stuart Mill, *Utilitarianism and Other Essays* (New York: Penguin, 1987), p. 281. On the historical background, see Robert Jütte, *Geschichte der Abtreibung: Von der Antike bis zur Gegenwart* (Munich: Beck, 1993). For an overview of utilitarian arguments, see also Norbert Hoerster, *Ethik und Interesse* (Stuttgart: Reclam, 2003).

End of Life

132 **"Warnemünde is a cheerful place"** Beate Lakotta recounts the story of Alexander Nicht in *Der Spiegel*, no. 46 (November 13, 2006).

133 **The major argument** On the euthanasia discussion from the perspective of an advocate, see Norbert Hoerster, *Sterbehilfe im säkularen Staat* (Frankfurt: Suhrkamp, 1998), and Singer, *Practical Ethics*, pp. 127–57. Günter Altner presents an opposing view in *Leben in der Hand des Menschen: Die Brisanz des biotechnischen Fortschritts* (Zurich: Primus, 1998), esp. pp. 225–78.

Beyond Sausage and Cheese

138 **In the fall of 1970** Peter Singer, *Animal Liberation* (New York: Harper, 2001). See also Peter Singer, ed., *In Defense of Animals* (New York: Harper Perennial Modern Classics, 2009).

139 **"The day *may* come"** Jeremy Bentham, *An Introduction to the Principles of Morals and Legislation*, ed. J. H. Burns and H.L.A. Hart (New York: Oxford University Press, 1996), p. 283.

140 **Singer's book on liberating animals** The second important father of animal rights philosophy is Tom Regan, *The Case for Animal Rights* (Berkeley: University of California Press, 1983). On the question of eating meat, see Michael Pollan, *The Omnivore's Dilemma* (New York: Penguin, 2007), and Jonathan Safran Foer, *Eating Animals* (New York: Little, Brown, 2009). See also Richard David Precht, *Noahs Erbe: Vom Recht der Tiere und den Grenzen des Menschen* (Hamburg: Rowohlt, 2000). Issues of consciousness and animal ethics are examined by David DeGrazia, *Taking Animals Seriously: Mental Life and Moral Status* (New York: Cambridge University Press, 1996).

141 **a now classic essay** The essay by Thomas Nagel, "What Is It Like to Be a Bat?" was first published in *Philosophical Review* 83, no. 4 (October 1974), pp. 435–50, and can also be read online at evans-experientialism.freewebspace.com/nagel.htm.

142 **"We don't know"** Giacomo Rizzolatti's comment about barking is taken from www.infonautik.de/rizzolatti.htm.

Great Apes in the Cultural Arena

145 **"Jerom died on February 13"** Steven Wise, *Rattling the Cage* (New York: Perseus Publishing, 2001), p. 1.

145 **a movement initiated by Peter Singer** Peter Singer and Paola Cavalieri, eds., *The Great Ape Project: Equality Beyond Humanity* (New York: St. Martin's Griffin, 1994). For an opposing view, see Claudia Heinzelmann, *Der Gleichheitsdiskurs in der Tierrechtsdebatte: Eine kritische Analyse von Peter Singers Forderung nach Menschenrechten für Grosse Menschenaffen* (Stuttgart: Ibidem, 1999).

146 **he was not entirely wrong** On the close relationship between primates and humans, see Jared Diamond, *The Third Chimpanzee: The Evolution and Future of the Human Animal* (New York: Harper, 2006); the quotation about "future taxonomists" is on p. 23.

147 **Japanese ethologists** For animal and ape intelligence, see Donald R. Griffin, *Animal Thinking* (Cambridge, MA: Harvard University Press, 1985).

147 **"Now we must redefine tool"** This telegram is quoted at www.janegoodall.org/janes-story.

148 **a bonobo named Kanzi** On feats of intelligence demonstrated by Kanzi and other primates, see Sue Savage-Rumbaugh and Roger Lewin, *Kanzi: The Ape at the Brink of the Human Mind* (Hoboken, NJ: John Wiley, 1996).

148 **Koko, a female gorilla** Francine Patterson's experiments with Koko are recorded on Koko's website, www.koko.org, and described in detail in Francine Patterson and Eugene Linden, *The Education of Koko* (New York: Holt, Rinehart and Winston, 1981); the examples cited here are on pp. 185, 151, and 191.

151 **"Chimpanzees are charming"** Richard Wrangham et al., *Chimpanzee Cultures* (Cambridge, MA: Harvard University Press, 1996), p. 392.

The Wail of the Whale

153 **But since 1973** Statistics on the destruction of global habitats are found in Edward O. Wilson, *The Diversity of Life* (New York: Norton, 1999).

154 **James Lovelock** Lovelock's philosophy is set forth in James Lovelock, *The Revenge of Gaia* (New York: Basic Books, 2007).

154 **Beauty in nature cannot be equated** On ecology and morality, see Klaus Michael Meyer-Abich, *Praktische Naturphilosophie: Erinnerungen an einen vergessenen Traum* (Munich: C. H. Beck, 1997); Hans Jonas, *Das Prinzip Verantwortung: Versuch einer Ethik für die technologische Zivilisation* (Frankfurt: Suhrkamp, 1984); Konrad Ott, *Ökologie und Ethik: Ein Versuch praktischer Philosophie* (Tübingen: Attempto, 1994); and Julian Nida-Rümelin and Dietmar von der Pfordten, eds., *Ökologische Ethik und Rechtstheorie* (Baden-Baden: Nomos, 1997).

Tears of a Clone

159 **What is the Raelian cult up to** New directions in genetic engineering are outlined in William J. Thieman and Michael A. Palladino, *Introduction to Biotechnology* (Upper Saddle River, NJ: Benjamin Cummings, 2008). For a critical perspective on genetic engineering, see Alexander Kissler, *Der geklonte Mensch: Das Spiel mit Technik, Träumen und Geld* (Freiburg: Herder, 2006). Roland Graf weighs theological arguments in *Klonen: Prüfstein für die ethischen Prinzipien zum Schutz der Menschenwürde* (St. Ottilien: Eos, 2003). For a discussion of the debate about embryonic stem cells, see Thomas Heinemann and Jens Kersten, *Stammzellforschung: Naturwissenschaftliche, ethische und rechtliche Aspekte* (Freiburg: Alber, 2007); Gisela Badura-Lotter, *Forschung an embryonalen Stammzellen: Zwischen biomedizinischer Ambition und ethischer Reflexion* (Frankfurt: Campus, 2005); and Karsten Klopfer, *Verfassungsrechtliche Probleme der Forschung an humanen pluripotenten embryonalen Stammzellen und ihr Würdigung im Stammzellgesetz* (Berlin: Duncker & Humblot, 2006).

Ready-made Children

Practical advice about diagnostic issues is found in Michael Ludwig, *Kinderwunschsprechstunde* (Berlin: Springer, 2007). The ethical chaos of reproductive medicine is discussed in Martin Spiewak, *Wie weit gehen wir für ein Kind? Im Labyrinth der Fortpflanzungsmedizin* (Frankfurt: Eichborn, 2005), and in Petra Gehring, *Was ist*

Biomacht? Vom zweifelhaften Mehrwert des Lebens (Frankfurt: Campus, 2006). Lee M. Silver explores scientific advances in reproductive medicine in *Remaking Eden: How Genetic Engineering and Cloning Will Transform the American Family* (New York: Harper Perennial, 2007). See also Theresia M. de Jong, *Babys aus dem Labor: Segen oder Fluch?* (Weinheim: Beltz, 2002).

"Bridge into the Spirit World"

175 **Robert White, a neurosurgeon from Cleveland** For an overview of developments in neurobionics in the late 1990s, see Hans-Werner Bothe and Michael Engel, *Neurobionik: Zukunftsmedizin mit mikroelektronischen Implantaten* (Neustadt: Umschau, 1998). The *Journal of Neural Engineering* (www.iop.org/EJ/journal/JNE) provides the latest information on developments in this field.

180 **The philosopher Thomas Metzinger** Thomas Metzinger's essays on the dangers posed by recent advances in neuroscience can be found at www.philosophie.uni-mainz.de/metzinger. See also Metzinger's *Neural Correlates of Consciousness* (Cambridge, MA: MIT Press, 2000), esp. pp. 6–7. Metzinger's latest book, *The Ego Tunnel* (New York: Basic Books, 2009), provides a nontechnical overview.

The Greatest Conceivable Being

185 **Anselm of Canterbury** On Anselm's life, see Richard W. Southern, *Saint Anselm: A Portrait in a Landscape* (New York: Cambridge University Press, 1992).

188 **Thomas Aquinas was Italian** The classic study of Thomas Aquinas is G. K. Chesterton, *Saint Thomas Aquinas* (New York: Sheed & Ward, 1933).

189 **new proofs of God have been emerging** On proofs of the existence of God, see J. L. Mackie, *Miracle of Theism: Arguments For and Against the Existence of God* (New York: Oxford University Press, 1982).

190 **neurologist named Michael Persinger** Michael Persinger, *Neuropsychological Bases of God Beliefs* (Santa Barbara, CA: Praeger, 1987).

190 **His younger colleague . . . Andrew Newberg** Rhawn Joseph, Andrew Newberg, et al., *NeuroTheology: Brain, Science, Spirituality, Religious Experience* (San Jose, CA: University Press, 2003); Andrew Newberg et al., *Why God Won't Go Away: Brain Science and the Biology of Belief* (New York: Ballantine, 2002); Martin Urban, *Warum der Mensch glaubt: Von der Suche nach dem Sinn* (Frankfurt: Eichborn, 2005).

192 **"Anyone who supposes"** Rudolf Bultmann: *Interpreting Faith for the Modern Era* (Minneapolis: Augsburg Fortress Press, 1991), p. 80.

The Archdeacon's Watch

193 **after Darwin arrived at Cambridge** The information about Darwin's studies at Cambridge is from Adrian Desmond and James Moore, *Darwin: The Life of a Tormented Evolutionist* (New York: Norton, 1994).

194 **William Paley, born in July 1743** Edmund Paley, ed., *The Works of William Paley*. vol. 1. (London: Longman and Co., 1838).

196 **"that the watch must have had a maker"** William Paley, *Natural Theology* (Whitefish, MT: Kessinger Publishing, 2009), pp. 6, 13.

197 **"Make a change in any part of the human body"** Ibid., p. cci.

198 **"We can no longer argue that"** *The Autobiography of Charles Darwin*, ed. Francis Darwin (New York: Dover, 1958), p. 63.

198 **"Natural selection, the blind, unconscious"** Richard Dawkins, *The Blind Watchmaker* (New York: Norton, 1996), p. 5.

198 **"Natural selection will never produce"** Charles Darwin, *On the Origin of Species by Means of Natural Selection* (New York: Modern Library, 1993), p. 256.

198 **Darwin's contemporary Jean Pierre Marie Flourens** Flourens's critique of Darwin is found in *Examen du livre de M. Darwin sur l'origine des espèces* (Paris: Garnier, 1864).

198 **Lord Kelvin, led the opposition to Darwin's theory** Lord Kelvin's *On the Origin of Life* can be read at www.zapatopi.net.

199 **intelligent design theory** The Discovery Institute's William Dembski lays out the case for "intelligent design" in *Intelligent Design: The Bridge Between Science and Theology* (Downers Grove, IL: InterVarsity Press, 2007). An introduction to the world of theoretical biology is found in Claus Emmeche, *Das lebende Spiel: Wie die Natur Formen erzeugt* (Hamburg: Rowohlt, 1994).

200 **"We are in the position of a little child"** Denis Brian, *Einstein: A Life* (Hoboken, NJ: Wiley, 1997), p. 186.

"A Quite Normal Improbability"

203 **He was born in 1927 in Lüneburg** For an account of Luhmann's life, see Dirk Baecker et al., *Theorie als Passion* (Frankfurt: Suhrkamp, 1987).

203 **the famous American social systems theorist** Talcott Parsons's major works are *Structure of Social Action*, 2 vols. (New York: Free Press, 1967) and *The System of Modern Societies* (Upper Saddle River, NJ: Prentice Hall, 1971).

204 **the Chilean neuroscientist Humberto Maturana** Maturana's philosophy is summarized in Humberto Maturana and Francisco Varela, *The Tree of Knowledge: The Biological Roots of Human Understanding* (Boston: New Science Library, 1987); see p. 40 for the statement about how living beings "produce themselves and specify their own limits."

206 **"own happiness in the other's happiness"** Niklas Luhmann, *Love as Passion*, trans. Jeremy Gaines and Doris L. Jones (Palo Alto, CA: Stanford University Press, 1998), p. 137.

207 **"External supports are dismantled"** Ibid., p. 156.

207 **For Gerhard Roth . . . it is incomprehensible** Roth's critique of Luhmann is in Gerhard Roth, *Fühlen, Denken, Handeln* (Frankfurt: Suhrkamp, 2003), p. 557; a discussion of the neurobiology of love is on pp. 365–73. For additional commentary about love from a systems theory perspective, see Karl Lenz, *Soziologie der Zweier-*

beziehung, 2nd ed. (Opladen: Westdeutscher Verlag, 2003), and Christian Schuldt, *Der Code des Herzens: Liebe und Sex in den Zeiten maximaler Möglichkeiten* (Frankfurt: Eichborn, 2005). Recent anthologies on the philosophy of love include Peter Kemper and Ulrich Sonnenschein, eds., *Das Abenteuer Liebe: Bestandsaufnahme eines unordentlichen Gefühls* (Frankfurt: Suhrkamp, 2004), and Kai Buchholz, ed., *Liebe: Ein philosophisches Lesebuch* (Munich: Goldmann, 2007). A modern classic with a psychological perspective is Peter Lauster, *Die Liebe: Psychologie eines Phänomens,* 35th ed. (Hamburg: Rowohlt, 2004). The current state of intimacy across cultures is explored in Anthony Giddens, *The Transformation of Intimacy: Sexuality, Love and Eroticism in Modern Societies* (Palo Alto, CA: Stanford University Press, 1993).

208 **It is hard to say whether animals experience feelings of love** On love in the animal kingdom, see Jeffrey M. Masson and Susan McCarthy, *When Elephants Weep: The Emotional Lives of Animals* (New York: Delta, 1996), pp. 64–90.

209 **studies of prairie voles** The significance of oxytocin for prairie voles is examined in Larry Young, Roger Nilsen, Katrina G. Waymire, Grant R. MacGregor, and Thomas R. Insel, "Increased Affiliative Response to Vasopressin in Mice Expressing the V1a Receptor from a Monogamous Vole," *Nature* 400, no. 19 (1999), pp. 766–76.

Do Be Do Be Do

213 **Simone de Beauvoir's *The Mandarins*** The American edition of Simone de Beauvoir's *The Mandarins,* translated by Leonard M. Friedman, was published by Norton in 1999.

213 **"In life, a man commits himself"** Jean-Paul Sartre, *Existentialism Is a Humanism,* trans. Carol Macomber (New Haven, CT: Yale University Press, 2007), p. 37.

214 **"The influence of therapists on morals"** Luhmann, *Love as Passion,* p. 166.

214 **"condemned to be free"** Jean-Paul Sartre, *Being and Nothingness: A Phenomenological Essay on Ontology,* trans. Hazel E. Barnes (New York: Washington Square Press, 1966), p. 653.

216 **"Man is nothing other than his own project"** Sartre, *Existentialism Is a Humanism,* p. 37.

217 **"What we usually understand by 'will' "** Ibid., p. 23.

217 **Sartre's life** On Sartre's life, see Bernard-Henri Lévy, *Sartre: The Philosopher of the Twentieth Century,* trans. Andrew Brown (Cambridge, UK: Polity, 2003).

218 **not only a "sense of reality"** Robert Musil discusses the "sense of reality" and "sense of possibility" in the fourth chapter of his novel *The Man Without Qualities,* vol. 1, trans. Eithne Wilkins and Ernst Kaiser (New York: Capricorn Books, 1965), pp. 11–14.

218 **Gerhard Roth tells us** Roth's reflections about freedom of the will are in Gerhard Roth, *Fühlen, Denken, Handeln* (Frankfurt: Suhrkamp, 2003), pp. 494–545.

218 **"Our intellect can be regarded"** Gerhard Roth, "Gehirn, Willensfreiheit und Verhaltensautonomie," in *Gehirn-Geschichte-Gesellschaft,* ed. Andreas Ziegler (Bremen: Lurija Gesellschaft, 2002), p. 28.

219 **feelings can be learned** On the ability to learn feelings, see Bruce Lipton, *The Biology of Belief* (Santa Rosa, CA: Mountain of Love / Elite Books, 2005).

Robinson's Used Oil

221 **"There is nothing which so generally strikes the imagination"** Blackstone's definition of property is found in William Blackstone, *Blackstone's Commentaries on the Laws of England* (Clark, NJ: Lawbook Exchange, 2003), book 2, chap. 1, para. 2.

222 **an unsuccessful merchant named Daniel Foe** On Foe's life, see Paula R. Backscheider, *Daniel Defoe: His Life* (Baltimore: Johns Hopkins University Press, 1992).

223 **Let us picture ourselves as Foe's Robinson Crusoe** A good overview of the question of property is found in an essay collection edited by Andreas Eckl and Bernd Ludwig, *Was ist Eigentum? Philosophische Positionen von Platon bis Habermas* (Munich: Beck, 2005).

224 **Georg Simmel** Simmel's views about the psychology of property ownership are in Georg Simmel, *The Philosophy of Money*, trans. Tom Bottomore and David Frisby (New York: Routledge, 2004), esp. chap. 4, "Individual Freedom."

225 **"On the one hand"** Ibid., pp. 322–24.

The Rawls Game

229 **John Rawls, who thought up this model** John Rawls, *A Theory of Justice* (Cambridge, MA: Harvard University Press, 1999); the rules appear in various forms throughout the book, and are given their "final statement" on p. 266. See also John Rawls, *The Law of Peoples* (Cambridge, MA: Harvard University Press, 2001). A good introduction to Rawls's philosophy is offered in Wolfgang Kersting, *John Rawls: Zur Einführung* (Hamburg: Junius, 2001).

231 **a state based on a reciprocal contract** For an overview of the contract theory, see Michael von Grundherr, *Moral aus Interesse: Metaethik der Vertragstheorie* (Berlin: Gruyter, 2007) and Hans Christoph Timm, *Solidarität unter Egoisten? Die Legitimation sozialer Gerechtigkeit im liberalen Staat* (Hamburg: Kovac, 2004).

232 **"It is not from the benevolence of the butcher"** Adam Smith, *Wealth of Nations* (New York: Oxford University Press, 2008), book 1, chap. 2, 1.2.2., p. 22.

232 **"an invisible hand"** Adam Smith, *Theory of Moral Sentiments* (Whitefish, MT: Kessinger Publishing, 2004).

232 **Rawls's colleague at Harvard, Robert Nozick** Robert Nozick spells out his objections to Rawls in his *Anarchy, State, and Utopia* (New York: Basic Books, 1974).

233 **Peter Singer . . . points out that the inhabitants of wealthy countries** Peter Singer's critique of Rawls is contained in his *Practical Ethics*, 2nd ed. (New York: Cambridge University Press, 1999).

235 **"The free development of each"** Karl Marx and Friedrich Engels, *The Communist Manifesto* (New York: Oxford University Press, 2008), p. 26.

235 **"The main idea is that a person's good"** Rawls, *Theory of Justice*, pp. 79–80.

Isles of the Blessed

237 **According to the first *Happy Planet Index*** The *Happy Planet Index* is found at www.happyplanetindex.org, and the website of the New Economics Foundation is www.neweconomics.org.

239 **the writer Heinrich Böll satirized** Heinrich Böll's story is in his volume *Erzählungen* (Cologne: Kiepenheuer & Witsch, 2006).

240 **The economist Richard Layard** Richard Layard lays out his arguments in *Happiness: Lessons for a New Science* (New York: Penguin, 2005). On happiness economics, see also Bruno S. Frey and Alois Stutzer, *Happiness and Economics: How the Economy and Institutions Affect Human Well-Being* (Princeton, NJ: Princeton University Press, 2002), and Harald Willenbrock, *Das Dagobert-Dilemma: Wie die Jagd nach Geld unser Leben bestimmt* (Munich: Heyne, 2006).

241 **According to the World Values Survey** The World Values Survey can be found at www.worldvaluesurvey.org.

241 **"My happiness is the moment of deepest harmony with myself"** Ludwig Marcuse, *Philosophie des Glücks, von Hiob bis Freud* (Zurich: Diogenes, 1972).

241 **neuroscientific findings about the mechanisms** On the neurobiology of happiness, see Roth, *Fühlen, Denken, Handeln*, pp. 356–64.

244 **Martin Seligman** For Seligman's prescriptions for attaining happiness, see Martin Seligman, *Authentic Happiness: Using the New Positive Psychology to Realize Your Potential for Lasting Fulfillment* (New York: Free Press, 2002), esp. p. 116.

The Distant Garden

245 **To some, he was the wisest** Two studies of the philosophy and influence of Epicurus are Howard Jones, *The Epicurean Tradition* (New York: Routledge, 1989), and Bernard Frischer, *The Sculpted Word: Epicureanism and Philosophical Recruitment in Ancient Greece* (Berkeley: University of California Press, 1982). On the life of Epicurus, see Malte Hossenfelder, *Epikur* (Munich: Beck, 2006).

245 **"Stranger, here you will do well to tarry"** The inscription over Epicurus' garden gate is found in Seneca, *Moral Epistles*, vol. 1, trans. Richard M. Gummere (Loeb Classical Library, Cambridge, MA: Harvard University Press, 1917–25), epistle 21.

246 **"You should accustom yourself to believing"** George K. Strodach, ed. and trans., *The Philosophy of Epicurus* (Evanston, IL: Northwestern University Press, 1963), pp. 179–80.

247 **"Independence of external things"** Kenneth Atchity and Rosemary McKenna, eds., *The Classical Greek Reader* (New York: Oxford University Press, 1998), p. 240.

247 **"positive psychology"** On the state of positive psychology, see Ann E. Auhagen,

Positive Psychologie: Anleitung zum "besseren" Leben (Weinheim: Beltz, 2004). See also Mihaly Csikszentmihalyi, *Flow: The Psychology of Optimal Experience* (New York: Harper & Row, 1990), and his *Finding Flow: The Psychology of Engagement with Everyday Life* (New York: Basic Books, 1998), as well as Michael Argyle, *The Psychology of Happiness* (New York: Routledge, 2002); Daniel Gilbert, *Stumbling on Happiness* (New York: Vintage, 2007); and Daniel Kahneman, Ed Diener, and Norbert Schwarz, *Well-Being: The Foundations of Hedonic Psychology* (New York: Russell Sage, 2004).

249   **"Everything's good"**   Fyodor Dostoyevsky, *The Possessed*, trans. Constance Garnett (New York: Modern Library, 1936), p. 239.

The Matrix Machine

252   **"Let me tell you why you're here"**   www.whatisthematrix.warnerbros.com.

253   **"Would it not be said of him"**   Plato's question is from part 7, 517a, of *The Republic*, trans. Paul Shorey, in Plato, *Collected Dialogues*, ed. Edith Hamilton and Huntington Cairns (Princeton, NJ: Princeton University Press, 1961), p. 749.

254   **Clearly there is something more important than happiness**   Robert Nozick advances the idea of the Matrix machine as evidence of the dubious nature of happiness in his book *The Examined Life* (New York: Simon & Schuster, 1990).

256   **"The solution of the problem of life"**   Wittgenstein, *Tractatus Logico-Philosophicus*, sect. 6.521, pp. 88–89.

256   **For Peter Singer, Sartre's approach lacks**   Peter Singer's remarks about the meaning of life can be found in his book *How Are We to Live? Ethics in an Age of Self-Interest* (Amherst, NY: Prometheus Books, 1995); the quotation about making the world a better place is on p. 231.

256   **For the biophilosopher Daniel Dennett**   Dennett lays out his biophilosophical explanation in his *Darwin's Dangerous Idea: Evolution and the Meanings of Life* (New York: Simon & Schuster, 1995).

257   **"If there's no meaning in it"**   Lewis Carroll, *The Annotated Alice*, ed. Martin Gardner (New York: Norton, 1999), p. 123.

257   **"Life may have no meaning"**   Ashleigh Brilliant's brilliant ideas and sayings can be found at www.ashleighbrilliant.com.

257   **"the Ultimate Question of Life"**   Deep Thought calculates "the Ultimate Question of Life" in Douglas Adams, *The Ultimate Hitchhiker's Guide to the Galaxy* (New York: Del Rey, 2002), p. 121.

258   **"In some cases we learn more"**   Lloyd Alexander, *The Book of Three*, in *The Chronicles of Prydain* (New York: Henry Holt, 1999), p. 9.

Index

About the Author

RICHARD DAVID PRECHT is a German writer and journalist. He studied philosophy, art history, and literature at the University of Cologne and has worked for various newspapers and TV programs. He lives in Luxembourg.

About the Translator

SHELLEY FRISCH, who holds a doctorate in German literature from Princeton University, is author of *The Lure of the Linguistic* and translator of numerous books from German, including biographies of Nietzsche, Einstein, and Kafka, for which she was awarded the 2007 Modern Language Association Translation Prize for a Scholarly Study of Literature. She lives in Princeton, New Jersey.